Yesterday's Monsters

Yesterday's Monsters

THE MANSON FAMILY CASES
AND THE ILLUSION OF PAROLE

Hadar Aviram

UNIVERSITY OF CALIFORNIA PRESS

University of California Press, one of the most distinguished university presses in the United States, enriches lives around the world by advancing scholarship in the humanities, social sciences, and natural sciences. Its activities are supported by the UC Press Foundation and by philanthropic contributions from individuals and institutions. For more information, visit www.ucpress.edu.

University of California Press
Oakland, California

Cataloging-in-Publication Data is on file at the Library of Congress.

ISBN 978-0-520-29154-6 (cloth : alk. paper)
ISBN 978-0-520-29155-3 (pbk. : alk. paper)
ISBN 978-0-520-96528-7 (ebook)

Manufactured in the United States of America

28 27 26 25 24 23 22 21 20
10 9 8 7 6 5 4 3 2 1

To my son, Río,
may you grow up in a world of nonviolence,
compassion, and forgiveness

CONTENTS

ILLUSTRATIONS

FIGURES

PHOTOS

TABLE

PREFACE AND ACKNOWLEDGMENTS

I did not expect to write a book about the Manson Family murders. My previous work focused not on the sensational and unique but rather on the mundane and obscure aspects of the criminal process in an effort to educate about realities experienced by many but understood by few. But by 2014, I became intrigued by parole.

While writing my first book, *Cheap on Crime: Recession-Era Politics and the Transformation of American Punishment,* and afterward, I met many people—scholars, policy makers, reformers, politicians, formerly and currently incarcerated people—who were frustrated about the unfulfilled promise of criminal justice reform in the aftermath of the 2008 recession. The focus was on the low-hanging fruit of nonviolent crime because compassion for seemingly nonthreatening people was more politically expedient and attitudes toward violent offenders seemed entrenched. I found myself wondering about those incarcerated for offenses that were difficult to forgive. Do we regard violent criminals as irredeemable? Who decides, and how? I decided to examine the parole process, which has received very little scholarly attention, and to investigate how our correctional apparatus handled people who had spent decades behind bars. I immediately thought of the people who would curry as little political favor as possible and decided to learn how their stories were understood by the Board of Parole Hearings ("the Board") of the California Department of Corrections and Rehabilitation (CDCR). To my pleasant surprise, CDCR was very helpful in sending me, for a reasonable fee, the transcripts of all relevant parole hearings, and I immersed myself in the world of seven people whose ages ranged from the mid-sixties to the eighties, who had spent the vast majority of their adult lives behind bars, repeatedly revisiting their past, planning for their future, and expressing their evolving understanding of themselves to the gatekeepers at the prison exit door.

Along the way I was helped by many people who know plenty about the opaque and complicated world of parole hearings. Joan Petersilia expressed enthusiasm about my project, shared her immense experience with CDCR, and directed me to useful literature. Kimberly Richman graciously shared helpful comparisons to parole cases in which she had helped and participated, and she also connected me to the Peer Reentry Navigation Network (PRNN). The men and women at PRNN inspired me in their optimistic and pragmatic efforts to rebuild their lives after decades in prison, and their parole officers and therapists offered a hindsight perspective of the process. Kathryne Young kindly shared insights from her interviews with parole commissioners. Keith Wattley of Uncommon Law shared his vast knowledge of the lifer parole process, both in personal conversation and at his well-attended "lifer schools" in Berkeley. The late Karlene Faith spoke to me at length in her Vancouver home about the early days of Patricia Krenwinkel's, Susan Atkins's, and Leslie van Houten's incarceration. Jason Campbell talked to me about representing Bobby Beausoleil and insightfully compared his experiences as a parole attorney and a public defender. Bobby Beausoleil generously and candidly talked to me about his experiences of incarceration and parole.

Several colleagues helped improve the book. David Ball, Cassia Hessick, and John Chin organized a workshop in which I got valuable feedback on the cultural and historical framework of the book. David Ball, Alessandro Corda, Paul Kaplan, Daniel LaChance, and Kim Richman read chapters and offered helpful feedback. Dan Berger offered sage advice about period documents and permissions. Participants at the Western Society of Criminology Annual Meeting, as well as at the Law and Society Annual Meeting, both held in 2016, asked excellent questions. Journalists at *Fortune* magazine, the Marshall Project, and the History Channel offered opportunities to clarify my perspective for public readership.

At Hastings, special thanks go to Kate Bloch, Binyamin Blum, Veena Dubal, Jared Ellias, Eumi Lee, Aaron Rappaport, David Takacs, and particularly Reuel Schiller, whose perspective as a legal historian of the 1960s and 1970s was priceless. Dean David Faigman, Academic Dean Morris Ratner, and Research Dean Scott Dodson awarded me the Miller Professorship, which provided necessary resources for my work. My students, particularly the members of the Criminal Law Society and the *Hastings Race and Poverty*

Law Journal, inspired me to engage a generation that did not experience the Manson Family murders as a cultural phenomenon.

The book would never have come to life without the excellent work of my team of fact-checkers and research assistants. Rachel Aronowitz, An Dang, Rachel Lieberstein-Ross, and Philip Dodgen were on this journey from the project's inception and helped with the qualitative analysis. Chelsea Lewis meticulously helped bring the manuscript up to submission standards. Chuck Marcus provided outstanding and knowledgeable library assistance, especially with fascinating archival materials. Barbara Armentrout carefully and thoroughly edited the manuscript. Brian Craig prepared the meticulous and helpful index.

The process of working on the book was pleasant, collaborative and enriching thanks to the professionalism and patience of everyone at the University of California Press, particularly Maura Roessner, Sabrina Robleh, Madison Wetzell, Dore Brown, and Chris Sosa-Loomis.

Any mistakes, omissions and inaccuracies are, of course, my own.

Empathy is a human superpower; it enables us to break the barriers between "me" and "the other" and understand the ember of emotion at the core of the human experience. My grandmother Aviva Katvan reminded me of the challenges of struggling with aging and infirmity. My parents, Yael and Haim Aviram, are of the generation of the Manson Family inmates, and their thoughtful lives of public service offered an interesting parallel to those lived behind bars. My mentors Rick Geggie, June Nason, Donald Rothberg, Shahara Godfrey, Eve Decker, and Robin Gayle taught me about suffering and compassion. Similarly supportive were my music and fitness communities, as well as my friends Russ Bain, Eric Chase, Heather Eloph, Inbal Etgar, Rosie Etis, Yael Finberg-Liebi, Shachar Fuman, Samantha Godwin, Francisco Hulse, Amit Landau, Schachar Levin, Anat Levtov, Ruti Levtov, Katie Morrison, Tal Niv, Jacqueline Omotalade, Annick Persinger, Scott Roberts, Jonelle Rodericks, Robert Rubin, Jonathan Swerdloff, Jonathan Trunnell, and Raeeka Shehabi-Yaghmai.

I am infinitely grateful to my life partner, Chad Goerzen, who brought his curiosity and patience to the project, and to our cats, Gulu and Inti, who provided much-needed levity. In the summer of 2017 our lives changed when we adopted our son Río, who flooded our lives with love, tenderness, and laughter.

This book takes no position on the question of release for the inmates, and I invite you, gentle reader, to draw your own conclusions. I will, however, say that immersing myself in these lives, as reflected in the hearing transcripts, has deepened my comprehension that there is no "other." The pain of victims and their grieving family members, of inmates, and of correctional employees flows through the same river of life. Writing this book awakened me to the core of the Buddha's spiritual legacy: "Hatred does not cease by hatred, but only by love; this is the eternal rule." May we all live by this wisdom and strive to end suffering for all beings.

Introduction

On the night when Tex Watson, Patricia Krenwinkel, Susan Atkins, and Linda Kasabian, members of Charles Manson's "family," dressed in dark clothes and armed with knives, "creepy-crawled" into 10050 Cielo Drive, I hadn't been born yet. But as a child, the heinous murders frightened and disquieted me. I remember visiting the Shalom Tower wax museum in Tel Aviv,[1] mostly devoted to the history of Israel and the Jewish people, which included a large-scale tableau of the murder of Sharon Tate and her friends. The diabolical, jeering expressions of the murderers haunted my childhood nightmares. That a California murder could be deemed so exceptional, cruel, and unspeakable as to terrorize an Israeli child is a testament to its legacy.

The murders' profound resonance in public consciousness cannot be understated. Commentators have famously identified them as a watershed moment that ushered in the end of an age of innocence, peace, and nonviolence. In her oft-quoted memoir *The White Album,* in an essay titled "On the Morning After the Sixties," Joan Didion writes:

> This mystical flirtation with the idea of "sin"—this sense that it was possible to go "too far," and that many people were doing it—was very much with us in Los Angeles in 1968 and 1969. . . . The jitters were setting in. I recall a time when the dogs barked every night and the moon was always full. On August 9, 1969, I was sitting in the shallow end of my sister-in-law's swimming pool in Beverly Hills when she received a telephone call from a friend who had just heard about the murders at Sharon Tate Polanski's house on Cielo Drive. The phone rang many times during the next hour. These early reports were garbled and contradictory. One caller would say hoods, the next would say chains. There were twenty dead, no, twelve, ten, eighteen. Black masses were imagined, and bad trips blamed. I remembered all of the day's misinformation very

clearly, and I also remember this, and wish I did not: I remember that no one was surprised.[2]

Charles Manson and his followers became the personification of the flaws and monstrosity beneath the surface of American society. David Williams remarks,

> "I am the man in the mirror," says Charles Manson. And in that at least he may be right. "Anything you see in me is in you. . . . I am you. . . . And when you can admit that you will be free. I am just a mirror." Nor is that the least that he is right about. . . . We found in him an icon upon which to project our own latent fears. No one was surprised because everyone knew the potential was there, in each and all of us. So Manson became a living metaphor of Abaddon, the God of the bottomless pit. We, as a collective culture, looked into Manson's eyes and saw in those dark caves what we most feared within ourselves, the paranoia of what might happen if you go too far. He was the monster in the wilderness, the shadow in the night forest, the beast said to lurk in the Terra Incognita beyond the edges of the map. By projecting our monsters onto Manson, and then locking him up for life, we imagined we had put the beast back in its cage.[3]

WHY VIOLENT CRIME?

Sensational and heinous crimes such as the Manson Family murders—in criminological parlance, "redball crimes"—have fueled not only public imagination, but also public policy. Many accounts of the emergence of mass incarceration point to the immense sway of heinous crimes as an important factor in the American punitive turn. In *Making Crime Pay,* Katherine Beckett shows how Nixon's election propaganda and later Reagan's war on drugs played on public fears of the "worst of the worst."[4] Punitive new laws against violent and sex offenders in the 1980s and 1990s—the "decade of the victim"—bore the names of victims of such crimes: Megan's Law,[5] the Adam Walsh Act,[6] the Jacob Wetterling Act,[7] the Matthew Shepard and James Byrd Jr. Hate Crime Act,[8] Jessica's Law,[9] Marsy's Law.[10]

The high valence of these crimes meant that, until 2008, it would have been nearly impossible for any politician, Republican or Democrat, to appear "soft on crime." Indeed, as Jonathan Simon powerfully explains in *Governing through Crime,* the resulting culture reshaped the master status of the American citizen as a potential crime victim and led to a profound transformation of public and private life into spaces of prevention, oppression, and social control.[11] Recently, however, as an effect of the Great Recession of 2008 and other developments,[12] political and economic changes have enabled lawmakers, policy makers, and advocates across the political spectrum to espouse a retreat from the carceral project. Several states have abolished the death penalty or placed moratoria upon its use,[13] legalized recreational marijuana,[14] and introduced sentencing and incarceration reforms.

Efforts to combat mass incarceration are generally more palatable when they address nonviolent offenders.[15] It is easier to obtain support for downgrading simple possession offenses or for trying nonviolent offenses as misdemeanors rather than felonies.[16] However, such reforms alone are insufficient for transforming incarceration patterns because most state inmates are incarcerated for violent felonies.[17] In some states, indeed, the Obama-era bipartisan retreat from incarceration made headway in addressing punishments that are usually reserved for the "worst of the worst": the death penalty, life without parole, and solitary confinement.[18] Despite California's leadership in prison decrowding, reform for violent offenders has had mixed results. The effort to abolish the death penalty failed in 2012 and again in 2016,[19] reflecting California voters' enduring appetite for capital punishment.[20] The struggle against long-term solitary confinement produced a settlement that emptied segregation units but left some enforcement issues unaddressed.[21] The efforts to ameliorate severe sentences for juveniles have been tempered by court discretion.[22] Indeed, California's contribution to the decline in incarceration mostly involved nonviolent offenders: the Schwarzenegger administration "downgraded" nonviolent felonies to misdemeanors; the Public Safety Realignment Act of 2011, which considerably reduced California's prison population and was described by Joan Petersilia and Jessica Snyder as "the biggest penal experiment in modern history,"[23] targeted only nonserious, nonsexual, nonviolent offenders, colloquially known as the "non-non-nons"; Proposition 36, which successfully amended the Violent Crime Control and Law Enforcement Act of 1994, improved the lot only of felons whose third "strike" was nonviolent;[24] and Proposition 47, which led to the release of a considerable number of inmates, targeted only nonviolent offenses and left violent offenses intact.[25]

The reluctance of California, a blue, progressive state with a Democratic legislature, to extend its recession-era policies to violent criminals, might be attributed to its political culture. In *The Politics of Imprisonment,* Vanessa Barker argues that the extent to which public involvement produces harsh justice depends on the patterns of civic engagement and trust in government.[26] California features a combination of extreme political polarization and neopopulism. The impasse in California's legislature, which is limited in its ability to change budgetary and constitutional provisions, has created a political environment in which reforms are often pursued via referendum. Consequently, complicated proposals have to be oversimplified into yes/no questions, and voters are bombarded with propaganda that often obscures the real motives and consequences of the proposed reform.[27] To attract voters, proponents of punitive policies—primarily California's victims' movement, supported and funded by its influential prison guards' union[28]—craft arguments that bring an emotive, passionate quality to crime control, making the victims' pain central to the justification and legitimacy of punishment. The legislative apparatus appears weak and unresponsive by comparison. As a result, penal policies, targeting particularly violent crime perpetrators, have spiraled out of control and, more importantly, cemented the legitimacy of harsh punitive policies with arguments of victims' rights and public safety. As Jonathan Simon argues in *Mass Incarceration on Trial,* this led to a regime of "total incapacitation," regardless of offense or dangerousness, characterized by abysmal prison conditions and unacceptable health care standards rife with iatrogenic disease and death, which were justified because the recipients of this so-called health care were violent, monstrous inmates.[29] The reliance on long-term solitary confinement, widely recognized as torture by psychologists and international officials,[30] was also justified by targeting the "worst of the worst."[31] These trends have effectively retrenched public opinion regarding violent offenders, regardless of their deeds, personal conditions, age, or health, as a monolithic category of irredeemable individuals who must be subjected to incapacitating control—a trend noticeable for sex offenders as well.[32]

Is there redemption for violent offenders? The decisions regarding their fate are made by the Board of Parole Hearings behind closed doors. I set out to examine the parole process, inspired by Joan Petersilia's scholarship[33] and Nancy Mullane's and John Irwin's books on lifers, which contain interviews with parolees and information on the parole process.[33] Apart from those, and from Frederic Reamer's monograph on his experiences as a parole board commissioner,[34] very little scholarship has examined parole hearings. The few scholars who analyzed parole hearing transcripts—such as Laqueur and Copus, "Synthetic Crowdsourcing"; Liberton, Silverman, and Blount, "Predicting Parole Success for the First-Time Offender"; Weisberg, Mukamal, and Segall, *Life in Limbo;* Vîlcică, "Revisiting Parole Decision Making"; and Young, Mukamal, and Favre-Bulle, "Predicting Parole Grants"[35]—used them mostly quantitatively, to predict parole suitability. I therefore focused my effort on a qualitative understanding of the process.

WHY THE MANSON FAMILY CASES?

This book examines the Manson Family from an uncommon perspective: their later lives as prison inmates filtered through the prism of their parole hearings. The shocking facts are familiar: Manson, a long-time convict and aspiring musician, acquired a considerable number of followers, many of them young women, in San Francisco's Haight-Ashbury district, who traveled with him to Southern California.[36] In 1969, Manson and his followers committed several heinous murders: the killing of musician Gary Hinman; the murders of actress Sharon Tate, eight months pregnant at the time, and her house guests Jay Sebring, Abigail Folger, Wojciech Frykowski, and Steven Parent; the murders of Leno and Rosemary LaBianca; and the murder of ranch hand Donald "Shorty" Shea.[37] In 1971, after a lengthy police investigation and a dramatic trial in Los Angeles County, Manson and the other perpetrators were sentenced to death, but they benefited from an unexpected legal occurrence: on April 24, 1972, the California Supreme Court ruled in *People v. Anderson*[38] that the death penalty statute was unconstitutional. Consequently, 107 California death sentences were commuted to life imprisonment, and they so remained even after the state's capital punishment scheme was "fixed" by Proposition 17.[39] Therefore, the Manson Family defendants became eligible for parole as early as 1978 and have been attending parole hearings for almost forty years. With the exception of Steve "Clem" Grogan, who was released in 1985, seven of them have remained in California prisons: Bruce Davis, Charles "Tex" Watson, Susan Atkins (who died in 2010), Patricia Krenwinkel, Leslie Van Houten, Robert "Bobby" Beausoleil, and Manson himself (who died in 2017). Three of the inmates (Davis, Van Houten, and Beausoleil) have been recommended for parole, but as of 2019 the governor has reversed all Board decisions to release them.

In choosing these cases I hoped that their high profile would encourage the public to learn more about an opaque process that is subject to minimal judicial review. The media has invariably covered each of the Manson Family parole hearings, yielding predictable public commentary about the deservedness of continued incarceration for the inmates, which I felt could yield public interest in parole in general. The cases are also important because of their emotional valence: the victims' families pioneered the rise of the victim movement in California and provided a very public face to the pain and devastation wreaked by homicide. At the same time, the passage of decades since the crimes and the maturation and transformation of the offenders from teenagers and adolescents to people in their 60s, 70s, and 80s provides an interesting dimension not often covered by the public accounts of the crimes and trials.

The Manson Family cases are obviously atypical. For one thing, all inmates in this study are white, whereas California's lifer population is plagued by an overrepresentation of inmates of color. In addition, the high profile of the cases suggests unique political dimensions. Despite these limitations, these case studies have unique strengths. First, these cases are historically interesting in their own right, not only because of the original crimes but because of their unique contribution to the formation of extreme punishment in California; the Manson cases shaped the state's parole process and were shaped by it in return. Second, the extensive timeline and abundant materials enabled me to examine longitudinal changes during the entire era of California parole hearings since the decline of parole board power in the late 1970s. Third, and perhaps most important, while the parole board does, of course, recommend inmates for release, it is also helpful to see what it *can do* when it is unmotivated to recommend release and how it can subvert judicial review to interpret facts and reactions in an environment of almost unfettered discretion. Some of my findings are specific to these particular defendants (especially regarding the effects of the crimes' notoriety) but, according to the attorneys I interviewed, other findings reflect common occurrences in parole hearings of their other clients—an observation validated by the few existing qualitative studies of parole hearings.

METHODS

The hearing transcripts, spanning the years 1978–2019, were provided by California Department of Correction and Rehabilitation's Executive Analysis Unit in accordance with the Public Records Act. Because of the project's time span, many transcripts were made before there were computers and digitalization, and the pdf files are photocopies of typewritten records. I conducted a three-phased analysis of the records.

The first phase was done with the help of four research assistants, who were at the time law students at University of California, Hastings College of the Law: Rachel Aronowitz, An Dang, Philip Dodgen, and Rachel Lieberson. After familiarizing ourselves with the legal landscape of parole, each of us listed themes we expected to find in the hearings, and we built our initial codebook from a long brainstorming session in which all of us contributed themes and nodes. There was considerable overlap in the themes we expected to find. I then introduced the students to the concept of grounded theory analysis,[40] in which the themes and nodes emerge from the source material itself. The choice to generate our own initial list of codes proved helpful to the subsequent enrichment of the codebook with additional themes and nodes,[41] which we created communally on a shared online platform to ensure consistency. Initially, each of us was responsible for analyzing all the parole hearings pertaining to one or two inmates, which enabled each student to become familiar with individual incarceration journeys. I monitored coding consistency by analyzing random hearings for each inmate and comparing my own coding to those of the students, and I was encouraged to see overwhelming overlap in our collective coding choices.

Following the first phase, we attended a "lifer school" offered by UnCommon Law, a nonprofit dedicated to representation of lifers on parole and litigation on their behalf; we watched Olivia Klaus's documentary *Life After Manson* about Patricia Krenwinkel[42]; and each student wrote a short reflection paper. All the students reported a deep sense of meaning and satisfaction with the project, a profound understanding of the complexities of the parole process, and a deepened ability to empathize with the inmates, regardless of their opinion about their parole suitability.

I pursued the second and third phases of the analysis on my own in order to become more personally engaged with the book's subjects. Using the same codebook, I conducted a second content analysis of the entire corpus, this time by year. Starting with the 1978 hearings, I analyzed all hearings pertaining to all inmates that occurred that year, then moved to each subsequent year, until I reached the present. I took this new tack not only for internal validation but also to identify longitudinal developments and changes in emphasis, vocabulary, and process and to examine whether the penological changes in California were reflected in the transcripts. The second phase yielded more factors and identifiers for the codebook, which focused on longitudinal developments in California: notably, the rise of the victim movement in the late 1980s and early 1990s and the rediscovery of age (particularly adolescence) as a mitigating factor in the mid-2000s.

In the third phase, I analyzed the transcripts by their own structure, reading first the sections about the inmates' past, then those about their prison experiences, and finally those addressing their postrelease plans. This phase enriched the codebook with themes pertaining to the stranglehold of the "past" phase of the hearing on the "present" and "future" phases, thus adding an important dimension to my understanding of the locus of "insight."

I triangulated my findings from the transcripts with other archival materials, including the California Senate hearings on cults and newspaper coverage of the hearings. Also, people interested in the Manson Family approached me to raise various issues, such as the availability of life without parole in Leslie Van Houten's third trial and Tex Watson's alleged taped confessions. These issues were largely irrelevant to my inquiry, but I pursued them to the extent that they clarified themes from the parole hearings.

To complement the archival research, I conducted interviews with several attorneys that represented the inmates in parole hearings, most notably Keith Wattley, founder of UnCommon Law and Patricia Krenwinkel's attorney, and Jason Campbell, Bobby Beausoleil's attorney. The interviews with the lawyers were journalistic in nature and therefore did not require Institutional Review Board approval, but I did create a consent form that emphasized that the publication of this book while its subjects are still imprisoned and at the mercy of the parole board would require caution.

This caution was at the forefront of my concerns when reaching out to the inmates themselves. It arose from my interview with Karlene Faith, who had tutored the Manson Family girls in the early period of their incarceration. Faith's friendship with Leslie Van Houten yielded a rich correspondence, much of which was reproduced, with Van Houten's permission, in Faith's book *The Long Prison Journey of Leslie Van Houten*.[43] After the book's publication, to Faith's dismay, the parole board referred to it at Van Houten's 2003 hearing to the latter's detriment, deducing "lack of insight" from the letter snippets in the book. I wanted to avoid a similar scenario in which my own work could become a negative factor in my subjects' parole hearings. I therefore carefully cautioned all the inmates in my introductory letters to them that their collaboration with me could yield legal consequences and that I would do everything in my power to ensure that my critique of the parole process not be attributed to them. Most of the inmates did not respond to my invitation to be interviewed and, for the reasons explained above, I did not push them to do so. One inmate—Bobby Beausoleil—graciously agreed to participate and we spoke several times on the telephone; at no point did he ever express criticism of the Board or the parole process.

To emphasize: this book's critical analysis of the parole board and its processes is *mine alone* and should in no way be attributed to any of the people I interviewed or to the people whose stories are depicted in it. I have taken special care not to attribute my own critiques to my interlocutors, and to the extent that the book reflects participants' hopelessness or frustration, I hope the Board will take these as natural human reactions rather than interpret them negatively.

Despite my critique of California's parole system, *Yesterday's Monsters* takes no stance on these inmates' parole suitability. I leave it to my readers to form their own judgment. This position also enabled me, in good faith, to approach the Tate family with genuine compassion for their plight and invite them to contribute their perspectives. They did not respond to my inquiry.

I also wanted to distinguish my project from the opportunistic exploitation of the Manson Family members in popular culture. It was an easy decision to donate all book royalties to UnCommon Law. This was not only a moral choice but a way to assure my interviewees that I had no intention of commercially benefiting from their cases; rather, my intention was to encourage open debate about the parole process in California.

PAROLE AS A PERFORMATIVE SPACE

The unique source material for this book offers not only an account of the Manson Family's parole hearings but also general findings about parole. My point of departure is that the hearing is a performative space in which inmates are expected to conform to a meticulously choreographed set of expectations. *Performativity,* a term coined by John Austin, is the capacity of speech and communication to act or to consummate an action (in contrast to simply conveying information).[44] In *The Presentation of Self in Everyday Life* Erving Goffman treated interpersonal interactions as theatrical performances, in which communicating with others is an effort to shape others' opinion of one's self by structuring one's appearance, mannerisms, and overall impression in a particular way.[45] Paramount to playing the role of the "self" is the agreed-upon definition of the situation—in other words, the social context for a given interaction—which provides a framework for the performative interaction. Performativity was particularly useful to Goffman in his work on total institutions, where he identified the rites of passage, social expectations, and rigid hierarchies that characterize the all-encompassing experience of the inmates' lives.[46]

Like other total-institution experiences, the parole hearing features a ritualized interaction between the board members, the inmate, and the other participants, according to clearly delineated rules that are closely related to the inmate's incarceration. The inmate/performer is constantly guided—by the board and by his or her attorney—to behave in particular ways and to display and verbalize specific emotions and considerations using a particular verbal and nonverbal vocabulary. The board expects the parole candidate not only to pursue a particular course of action (namely, disciplinary obedience and participation in rehabilitative programming) but also to weave his or her past crime, present perceptions, and future prospects into an all-encompassing, coherent, and convincing presentation of self, referred to as *insight*. The meaning of *insight*, as the transcripts demonstrate, is elusive and ever-changing, but it can generally be understood as a narrative that demonstrates profound understanding of, and accountability for, the crime, the lifestyle that led to it, and the personal growth since then, as well as efforts to change one's life course.

Reframing one's criminal history in retrospective is not limited to the parole hearing. In *Making Good,* Shadd Maruna argues that people who desist from crime have constructed powerful narratives of their past, in which they demonstrate deep understanding of the causes of their behavior.[47] These narratives allow them to feel in control of their future and to take practical steps toward it. Similar narratives can be found in books in which lifers tell their personal histories to a sympathetic listener, such as journalist Nancy Mullane or criminologist John Irwin, and in works in which formerly incarcerated people discuss their feelings regarding reentry, citizenship, and identity, such as Jeff Manza and Christopher Uggen's *Locked Out.*[48] Storytelling and autobiographies that frame the storyteller's criminal behavior have been regarded an illuminating resource for researchers, from Clifford Shaw and Henry McKay's interviews with Chicago juvenile delinquents all the way to today's use of narrative criminology.[49] But autobiographical storytelling has as much to do with the listener as with the speaker. In *Showing Remorse,* Richard Weisman discusses the acceptable expressions of remorse in the courtroom and on parole, highlighting the popular understanding that inability to show remorse in a way that is readable to the authorities is perceived as a serious human flaw.[50]

In the context of the California parole hearings, what is deemed an acceptable performance of insight is malleable. As inmates and their lawyers construct what they deem to be a potentially successful insight performance, the Board continuously moves the goal posts. What counts as acceptable remorse, truthful account of the facts of the crime, a knowledgeable presentation of self, and a sensible rehabilitation plan is in constant flux, conforming to shifting legal requirements and political fashions. Consequently, the inmates must walk a tightrope between consistency and truthfulness in their retelling of the facts, between mitigation and accountability in their insight narrative, between authenticity and innovation in consecutive parole hearings, and between the optimal, the practical, and the acceptable paths to rehabilitation in prisons that offer meager, and declining, rehabilitative opportunities. Despite these contradictory and confusing requirements for acceptable performance, the Board preserves sufficient legitimacy to engender hope in the hearts of its subjects, generating a series of repeat performances, changing tactics, and periodic reinterpretations of the self, in the hopes of redeeming their spoiled identity and convincing the Board of their sincerity.

PLAN OF THE BOOK

Chapter 1 lays out the structure of parole in California. It explains the basic setting of the California Board of Parole Hearings, its role in the context of a determinate sentencing system, and its processes. Relying on Title 15 of the California Code of Regulations, I explain the considerations for a suitability determination, emphasizing the considerable discretion entrusted to the Board and the governor's veto power. I then walk the reader through the structure of a typical hearing and explain the trajectory of a typical lifer case through a series of successive parole hearings. This chapter also explains the delicate interplay between the California Supreme Court and the correctional authorities, with particular attention to the renewed hope for parole prompted by the court's decision in *In re Lawrence* and its progeny.

In chapter 2 I explain the contribution of the Manson Family cases to the construction of California parole and, more generally, to the development of the "extreme punishment trifecta": the oft-imposed but seldom-executed death penalty; the latecomer sentence, life without parole; and the gradual politicization of life with parole from a sentence of approximately twelve years with a realistic chance of release to a de facto version of life without parole. As I show through primary archival sources, at every junction, the California legal process, heavily shaped by the nascent victims' rights movement and the legislative initiative process, shifted away from a logic of professional, clinical assessment of rehabilitation toward a deeply politicized process largely reliant on the manipulation of public emotions and fears. Proponents of these shifts often invoked the Manson Family cases as a cautionary tale, eventually prevailing in merging the three most serious criminal sentences into one virtually indistinguishable regime of interminable incarceration.

Chapter 3 explains how the Manson cases came to occupy central stage in the California penal rhetoric. Relying on narrative theory, I show how one account of the murders—the "Helter Skelter" narrative, which attributes the murders to Manson's theory of an apocalyptic race war and his plan for world domination—came to shape the public discourse around the Family's crimes and crystallize their symbolic importance, muting two subversive, mitigating stories: the "cult" narrative, which perceives the Family through the lens of brainwashing and coercion and constructs Manson's followers, particularly the women, as sympathetic victims, and the "common criminals" narrative, which explains the murders in the context of a drug deal gone awry and ordinary (albeit heinous) wrongdoing.

Understanding the rhetorical power of the Helter Skelter narrative is crucial for comprehending the Board hearings themselves, to which I turn in chapter 4. This chapter takes on the construction of the inmates' past, particularly how their crime of commitment is framed. I find that, around the mid-1980s, the court record becomes calcified as the definitive account of the crime, any deviation from which is perceived as "minimizing." I also identify the birth of "insight," discussing how the carefully scripted atmosphere at the hearings renders impossible the authentic expression of remorse. I also show the longitudinal changes in the role of the prosecutor, whose input at the hearings shifts from a mere "legal helper" to the "moral memory" of the Board, commenting on the inmates' present and future with the same comfort as on their past. Finally, I show how the expansion of victims' voices in the hearings through Marsy's Law created an opportunity for the Tate family to galvanize and organize the performance of victimization before the Board in a way that silenced alternative experiences of victimization and frustrated real opportunities for apology and forgiveness.

The manifestation and display of insight are further examined in chapter 5, which turns its attention to the inmates' incarceration experience. I start by examining the Board's discussion of the inmates' disciplinary write-ups, showing the frustrating aspects of correcting inaccuracies and misunderstandings in the inmates' central files, as well as the need to frame grievances as personal failings in order to effectively demonstrate insight. I then turn to the imperative to participate in "programming," framed not as an occupation or avocation, but as a karmic undoing of the personal flaws that led to the crime by reshaping and repairing the self. The Board's expectations ignore the paucity of rehabilitative offerings, as well as the inaccessibility of programming for inmates housed in heightened security conditions. The transcripts evince a clear preference for self-help drug programming, with a curious emphasis on technocratic memorization of the Twelve Steps and deep suspicion about any unofficial or individualistic paths for personal growth, especially academic and artistic. I also discuss the special case of religious programming: relying on the transcripts of three born-again Christian inmates, I show the Board's oscillation between suspicion of the converts' sincerity and rebuke of their overzealousness. This chapter ends with an analysis of the way the inmates perform and express their present selves, and more specifically with their attendance and willingness to answer questions. The Board's bafflement in hearings that the inmate does not attend shows cracks in the performative façade and demonstrates the Board's efforts to maintain ownership of the narrative as the commissioners address an absent actor.

Chapter 6 turns to the Board's construction of the inmates' future prospects, and specifically how these are eclipsed by the inmates' pasts. I begin by examining the Board's treatment of risk assessment evaluations. These turn out to be a panacea of diverse, and often conflicting, materials, offering the Board flexibility to find and cite evidence that confirms their intuitive sense of risk within the parameters allowed by judicial review. The chapter also discusses the Board's suspicion of unrealistic or ambitious parole plans. While skepticism about postrelease plans is definitely warranted in many cases, the focus on individual responsibility obscures the lack of a functional reentry continuum and blames the inmates themselves for their incomplete preparation for postrelease. I then discuss the role of letters of support and opposition. The discussion of support letters awards the inmate the opportunity to portray a harmonious family life, which is sometimes disrupted by objections from the prosecutor and sometimes generates fodder for victims' families' arguments about the equivalence between the inmates' future hopes and the dashed hopes of the victims. The treatment of opposition letters is a good example of the politicization of the parole process, because the shift away from petitions filed by people directly impacted by the crime and toward petitions filed by strangers awards the public a form of moral participation at the hearing, orchestrated by the victims' families. Finally, even after *Lawrence,* I show how the inmates' past overshadows the physical reality of aging, disease, and dying, as well as the obvious decline in criminal risk with age.

Finally, chapter 7 attempts to predict the possibility that the Manson Family inmates will ever be granted parole. It examines sociolegal developments, such as the emergent understanding of youth as a mitigating factor and the increased understanding of cults, and institutional developments, such as changes in the Board's makeup. It also examines the enduring symbolism of the Manson crimes and other factors that might hinder release. I end with recommendations for reform in parole hearings: a reorientation of the process from past to future; a focus on external, measurable indicia of rehabilitation, rather than on surmises of insight and sincerity; a serious investment in evidence-based educational and vocational opportunities, as well as a state-mandated reentry pipeline, to offer inmates realistic avenues for seeking (and demonstrating) rehabilitation; a healthier role for victims in the parole process that allows for diverse narratives of victimization, memory, and compassion; and a healthy dash of humility about human ability to judge goodness, reform, and transformation.

This book strives not only to add to the academic conversation but also to provoke thought and discussion among policy makers. The Manson Family cases, albeit atypical in important ways, offer an opportunity to examine the contradictions that underlie parole hearings. Currently, the artificial nature of the hearings places an emphasis on performance, rather than authenticity, and risks producing both false positives and false negatives. It is important to offer lifers a prospect of hope, rehabilitation, and a law-abiding postrelease life. I invite you to honestly reexamine the parole ritual and the ways in which it frames, guides, and sometimes derails the inmates' process of rehabilitation and personal growth.

ONE

The California Parole Process

> O nobly-born (so and so by name), the time hath now come for thee to seek the Path [in reality]. Thy breathing is about to cease. Thy guru hath set thee face to face before with the Clear Light; and now thou art about to experience it in its Reality in the Bardo state, wherein all things are like the void and cloudless sky, and the naked, spotless intellect is like unto a transparent vacuum without circumference or centre. At this moment, know thou thyself; and abide in that state.
>
> *The Tibetan Book of the Dead*

At the entrance to the Division of Parole building in Sacramento, the meeting agenda is posted on a board. I follow the signs to the second floor, where a long corridor leads to a metal detector. Passing through the checkpoint, I enter a large hall. The other attendees seem to know each other; most are wearing suits and lanyards indicating some official function. A few attendees wear T-shirts that identify them as members of reentry organizations and volunteer groups. On the stage, a long table bears name tags for twelve people. In a minute, the executive board of the California Board of Parole Hearings will convene. The twelve commissioners will walk on stage and discuss the processes by which almost two thousand lifers hope to petition for their freedom this year.

We are called to order as the commissioners enter the room. Their roll call reveals a diverse group in terms of race and gender, but their professional backgrounds are almost uniformly from the law enforcement field. On their agenda this afternoon is an update to the software by which the Board runs its operations: the IT representative assures them that the glitches will be fixed soon. The commissioners are encouraged to follow the new procedures for reporting their decisions using the software.

The meeting then proceeds to a closed session, and the outsiders are asked to leave. On my way out, I glance again at the agenda; it contains a list of upcoming court cases, which suggests that Board plans to discuss their strategies in anticipation of judicial review of their decisions to deny parole.

THE CONCEPT OF PAROLE

The term *parole,* from the French word meaning "word [of honor]," refers to an inmate's promise to behave appropriately and abide by certain rules in exchange for release from prison.[1] In her account of parole history, Joan Petersilia notes that the modern concept of parole is attributed to prison innovator Alexander Maconochie, warden of the Norfolk Island penal colony, who introduced a "mark system" by which inmates, through good behavior and hard work, earned increasing privileges and responsibilities until they were deemed fit to regain freedom.[2] While Maconochie's policies were regarded as too lenient and led to his dismissal,[3] the idea of redeemability through prison programming resonated with nineteenth-century criminological positivism, particularly in Ireland. From there, as Petersilia notes, parole was imported to the United States, where it was first implemented in the Elmira Reformatory in New York. Elmira inmates were gradually promoted, through good behavior, to conditioned and supervised release. Initially, supervision was conducted by volunteers, who submitted written reports to the institute; this position was later professionalized, becoming the modern parole officer.[4] Conditioning release on good behavior and rehabilitation prospects became the norm for all offenders by the 1950s, a perfect complement to indeterminate sentencing and what was at least the ostensible goal of incarceration: reforming the offender. It also legitimized the existence of parole boards, whose members were touted as experts in behavioral change and in determining, on the basis of clinical findings and the inmates' records, whether they constituted a danger to society.[5] But this account obscures a grimmer reality of capricious decision-making and procedural flaws. Petersilia writes:

> Parole boards, usually political appointees, were given broad discretion to determine when an offender was ready for release—a decision limited only by the constraints of the maximum sentence imposed by the judge. . . . In the early years, there were few standards governing the decision to grant or deny parole, and decision-making rules were not made public. One of the longstanding criticisms of paroling authorities is that their members are too often selected based on party loyalty and political patronage, rather than profes-

sional qualifications and experience.... In his book, *Conscience and Convenience,* David Rothman ... reported that in the early 20th century, parole boards considered primarily the seriousness of the crime in determining whether to release an inmate on parole. However, there was no consensus on what constituted a serious crime. "Instead," Rothman wrote, "each member made his own decisions. The judgements were personal and therefore not subject to debate or reconsideration." ... These personal preferences often resulted in unwarranted sentencing disparities or racial and gender bias.... As has been observed, "no other part of the criminal justice system concentrates such power in the hands of so few."[6]

The capriciousness of parole decisions is masterfully displayed in a series of classic scenes in Frank Darabont's *The Shawshank Redemption,*[7] in which one of the protagonists, Red, faces the parole board. The first scene, set in 1947, sees Red enter the hearing room, remove his cap, and wait by a chair facing the parole board.

> MAN #1: Sit.
>
> *Red sits, tries not to slouch. The chair is uncomfortable.*
>
> MAN #2: We see by your file you've served twenty years of a life sentence.
>
> MAN #3: You feel you've been rehabilitated?
>
> RED: Yes, sir. Absolutely. I've learned my lesson. I can honestly say I'm a changed man. I'm no longer a danger to society. That's the God's honest truth. No doubt about it.
>
> *The men just stare at him. One stifles a yawn.*
>
> CLOSE-UP—PAROLE FORM
>
> *A big rubber stamp slams down: "REJECTED" in red ink.*[8]

The same scene repeats itself in 1957:

> MAN #1: It says here you've served thirty years of a life sentence.
>
> MAN #2: You feel you've been rehabilitated?
>
> RED: Yes sir, without a doubt. I can say I'm a changed man. No danger to society, that's the God's honest truth. Absolutely rehabilitated.
>
> CLOSE-UP—PAROLE FORM
>
> *A big rubber stamp slams down: "REJECTED."*[9]

These scenes portray the parole hearing as a ritualized, inauthentic performance. First, they show the rigidity and lack of nuance displayed by the parole board. Second, they show that both the board and the inmate conform to an unchanging script: the board uses the term *rehabilitation,* and the inmate, in return, recites what he thinks the board expects to hear. Third, the script reveals the expected performance of rehabilitation, which consists of three elements: displaying lack of risk, professing an internal transformation, and exuding sincerity. And lastly, they set the stage for the third and last hearing, in 1967, in which Red deviates from the script:

MAN #1: Your file says you've served forty years of a life sentence. You feel you've been rehabilitated?

Red doesn't answer. Just stares off. Seconds tick by. The parole board exchanges glances. Somebody clears his throat.

MAN #1: Shall I repeat the question?

RED: I heard you. Rehabilitated. Let's see now. You know, come to think of it, I have no idea what that means.

MAN #2: Well, it means you're ready to rejoin society as a—

RED: I know what you think it means. Me, I think it's a made-up word, a politician's word. A word so young fellas like you can wear a suit and tie and have a job. What do you really want to know? Am I sorry for what I did?

MAN #2: Well . . . are you?

RED: Not a day goes by I don't feel regret, and not because I'm in here or because you think I should. I look back on myself the way I was . . . stupid kid who did that terrible crime . . . wish I could talk sense to him. Tell him how things are. But I can't. That kid's long gone, this old man is all that's left, and I have to live with that.

(beat)

Rehabilitated? That's a bullshit word, so you just go on ahead and stamp that form there, sonny, and stop wasting my damn time. Truth is, I don't give a shit.

The parole board just stares. Red sits drumming his fingers.

CLOSE-UP—PAROLE FORM

A big rubber stamp SLAMS down—and lifts away to reveal the word "APPROVED" in red ink.[10]

Red's off-script authenticity and his heretical disillusionment with the term *rehabilitation* eventually lead to his release. But more importantly, it contrasts with his previous display of *performed* sincerity ("that's the God's honest truth"). Red may well have been convinced, in his heart of hearts, that even in 1947 he was no longer dangerous to society (he refers to himself, calmly, in conversation with his friend Andy, as "the only guilty man in Shawshank"), but if so, he chooses to express his conviction in a way that he believes will conform to the parole board's expectations.

These scenes say at least as much about the period in which they were written as about the period they depict. Darabont adapted *The Shawshank Redemption* from a short 1982 novella by Stephen King,[11] just as American jurisdictions shifted from indeterminate to determinate sentencing schemes. Prior to the shift, a judge would typically sentence a felon to a broad range, measured in years, and the parole board's responsibility extended within this range, allowing it to grant parole whenever the inmate was deemed to have been rehabilitated. The universality of this sentencing system meant that the parole board's prerogative to decide on early releases—or, otherwise stated, releases at the shortest end of the sentencing range—extended to all felony sentences, leading conservatives to object to significant shortening of sentences that "coddled" offenders,[12] and leading some progressives to express concerns that parole was arbitrarily granted and created racial and class disparities.[13] Combined with research that cast doubt on the entire enterprise of prison rehabilitation,[14] the penal conversation shifted from rehabilitation to retribution.[15] California was one of the first states to enact determinate sentencing,[16] which was at least partly a response to perceived problems of indeterminate sentencing.[17]

DETERMINATE SENTENCING:
THE DIMINISHING SCOPE OF PAROLE

Had Red stayed in prison until his next parole hearing in 1977, he would have been among a gradually decreasing group of parole-eligible inmates. Gradually, all states and the federal government shifted to determinate sentencing,[18] though not all eliminated discretion in release.[19] In some states, the sentence is a function of offense severity and criminal history and is calculated using a grid created by a professional sentencing commission.[20] The rigidity of the grid and the judicial discretion to depart from it varies across states.[21] A consequence of sentencing rigidity was a diminishing need for discretion regarding release; according to Petersilia, by the end of 1998, fourteen states had abolished parole hearings for all offenders.[22]

California's determinate sentencing scheme is unique in several respects. First, efforts to create a sentencing commission in California have repeatedly failed,[23] so the state's sentencing structure therefore consists of a patchwork of legislation created by the legislature and public referenda. In general, felonies are punished by a choice among a "triad" of sentences. For example, a simple second-degree robbery with no aggravating circumstances can be punished by two, three, or five years in state prison.[24] Subsequent laws, created by the legislature or passed by voter initiatives, create "enhancements" to the basic triad linked to aggravating factors, such as the involvement of a weapon[25] or gang-related circumstances.[26] Before the mid-2000s, the middle sentence in each triad was the presumptive sentence, and judges would impose the high or low sentence only if they found aggravating or mitigating circumstances, respectively. Following a series of landmark Supreme Court cases on sentencing and the right to a jury,[27] this arrangement was deemed unconstitutional: in *Cunningham v. California* the Supreme Court found that, under the "triad" system, aggravating circumstances shifting the sentence from the middle to the high number on the triad should be found by a jury, not by a judge.[28] In response to the *Cunningham* decision, the California legislature canceled the presumptiveness of the middle sentence, allowing California judges absolute discretion in picking any of the three sentences that they deem appropriate.[29]

Still, once a sentence from the triad has been imposed, there is very little flexibility regarding the inmate's release date. A limited amount of "good time credits," translatable to days deducted from one's sentence, is "earned" at the moment of intake and can be taken away for disciplinary reasons,[30] but in general, inmates can expect to serve the vast majority of the term to which they were sentenced. The ideology behind this rigidity was a companion to the ideology that yielded determinate sentencing: in order for inmates to serve comparable incarceration periods for comparable crimes, there has to be "truth in sentencing"—namely, a guarantee that the sentence imposed by the judge will indeed be served.[31]

Any inmate released in California is subject to postconviction supervision. Before 2011, all felons released from prison were placed under the supervising auspices of the California Division of Adult Parole Operations. Following the 2011 Criminal Justice Realignment,[32] inmates convicted of felonies statutorily defined as nonviolent, nonserious, and non–sex-related are presumptively punished by incarceration in county jail and, after release, supervised by the county probation department.[33] The California Department of Corrections and Rehabilitation (CDCR) and the Board have no jurisdiction over these individuals, but the local and state authorities follow the same procedural rules for granting parole, supervising parolees, and revoking parole.[34] Moreover, even after realignment, the Board retains its supervisory jurisdiction where the commitment offense involves a serious felony, a violent felony, a third-strike sentence, any crime where the person is deemed a high-risk sex offender, or any crime for which a person is required to undergo mental health treatment.[35] For all parolees, in accordance to reports by their assigned parole officer, the Board may extend the period of parole, revoke parole, or discharge parole, though the ability to return parolees to prison for trivial and technical violations was significantly curtailed by the Schwarzenegger administration.[36]

Most of these felons will have served most of their determinate sentences before release. The shift to determinate sentencing in 1977 left only a minority of inmates subject to a regime of indeterminate sentencing, including those serving life sentences[37]—an "island" of indeterminate sentencing within the overall determinate sentencing scheme.[38] These sentences can be identified in the California Penal Code as carrying a range, typically a number of years to life. This category of sentences includes homicide offenses; people convicted of first-degree murder without aggravating circumstances (which could yield a death sentence or life without parole) are sentenced to twenty-five years to life.[39] The same sentence applies to second-degree murderers of police officers; other second-degree murders carry a sentence of twenty years to life.[40] Some nonhomicide offenses, such as aggravated kidnapping, also carry a sentence of life with parole.[41] California therefore did not fully abolish parole hearings; it merely decreased their applicability to a minority of cases.[42] For lifers, as well as for people who are eligible for youth offender parole or elderly parole,[43] the Board not only supervises after release,[44] but it determines the length of the inmates' sentences and recommends their release.[45]

PAROLE GRANTING RATES

Since the idea of parole emerged in an era characterized by belief in rehabilitation and redeemability, it reflected the notion that the board would be a compassionate exit door, a mechanism of release. Indeed, there is some experimental support for the notion that human decision-makers may be more compassionate and lenient than statistical, computerized risk assessment mechanisms. In 1980, Yael Hassin sampled cases heard by Israeli parole boards, coding the variables that were available to the board, then fed the same variables to a computer program. She found that the committee failed to accurately predict recidivism in 75.4 percent of its decisions, while the computer was wrong in only 30.3 percent of the cases.[46] But Hassin's research design could detect situations in which the board erred only on the side of leniency, not those in which offenders that were not set free would have desisted had they been released. Other work on human decision-making in parole has pointed out its arbitrariness—Shai Danziger, Jonathan Levav, and Liora Avnaim-Pesso found that after taking "food breaks," judges lean more favorably toward release.[47] While the methodology of statistical risk prediction has become far more sophisticated since Hassin's study, and today's parole boards receive actuarial risk assessment reports based on standardized algorithms,[48] the final determination still rests with human decision-makers: the California Board's recommendation, which, since 1988, can be vetoed by the governor.[49]

But the notion of parole as a compassionate exit door would be transformed by the punitive animus of the determinate sentencing era, in which boards and governors would become sensitized to the concern about terrifying crime committed by hastily released parolees. Much of this outcry was based on factually inaccurate premises. Petersilia notes, relying on Peggy Burke's critique, the infamous parolees whose crimes prompted punitive legislation—Polly Klaas's murderer, Richard Allen Davis, and Megan Kanka's murderer, Jesse Timmendequas—were both released automatically at the end of their prison period, rather than by parole board decision.[50] Despite these facts, the fear of wrongly releasing dangerous perpetrators who would subsequently commit heinous crimes has led to serious concerns about parole board functions, weakening their authority, and introducing statistical risk prediction software to help guide their decisions.

Indeed, the odds of success before the California Board are fairly slim. In 2012, only 670 out of 4,760 hearings resulted in a favorable decision.[51] In previous years, the chance of a parole grant was even grimmer. The number of suitability hearings grew exponentially with the number of inmates serving long terms in prison, but, as figure 1 shows, the number of parole grants did not change proportionally to the number of hearings.

Figure 2, which excludes the years 1978–1980, in which only a few hearings were held, reveals the more complex longitudinal changes in parole grants, showing the lowest percentage of success during the 1990s—the "decade of the victim"—and increasing since the Great Recession of 2008. From 1988 onward, these numbers reflect not only Board decisions but also gubernatorial vetoes.

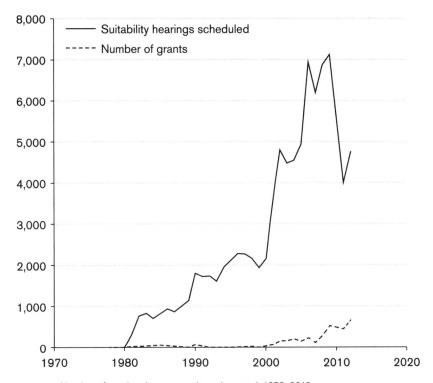

FIGURE 1. Number of parole releases sought and granted, 1978–2012.

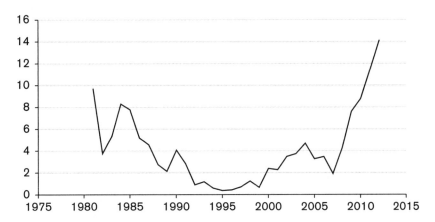

FIGURE 2. Percentage of parole grants out of all suitability hearings, 1981–2012.

Figures 1 and 2 suggest that, in the case of parole, political considerations not only affect gubernatorial releases but also trickle down into the parole board's decision-making process. Indeed, legislative and political battles over the years have transformed the frequency of parole hearings, the initial date of parole eligibility, and the even the acceptable criteria for release. Until the late 2000s, most of these changes made parole grants less likely. In its 2008 decision *In re Lawrence*,[52] the California Supreme Court forbade the Board to deny parole merely on the basis of the seriousness of the crime, and some commentators have credited *Lawrence* with the recent increase in releases.[53]

PAROLE COMMISSIONERS

CDCR oversees the largest concentration of prisoners serving life sentences of any state prison system in the country. The California lifer population, which is sentenced for indeterminate sentences of life with parole, almost tripled to an unprecedented 34,164 inmates between 1992 and 2009.[54] According to a report by the Sentencing Project, in 2017, 34,607 inmates were serving a sentence of life with parole, 5,090 were serving life without parole, and 994 were serving "virtual life"—sentences of fifty years or more.[55] The aggregate of these populations is a third of the overall California prison population. With a few minor exceptions, only members of the first category—life with parole, which applies to more than a quarter of the population—are eligible for a parole hearing. Over 1,800 of them appear before the Board every year, and approximately 75 percent are denied parole.[56]

The Board consists of twelve commissioners appointed by the governor and subject to Senate confirmation, dozens of vice-commissioners who are civil servants, and administrative and legal staff.[57] Board members are independent of other governing bodies as an administrative unit of the government.[58] The biographies of parole commissioners reveal that, until the recent appointment of two former defense attorneys, the Board was invariably composed of people from law enforcement backgrounds—former police officers, sheriffs, and correctional officers. Not a single commissioner has a clinical background in therapy, psychology, or social work.[59] This is not a California anomaly: Dirk van Zyl Smit and Alessandro Corda note that the parole board "in most states [is] made up of political appointees with no particular qualifications. [In most states] members of the paroling authority are appointed by the governor. Moreover, for the most part no particular expertise in the field of criminal justice, still less in specifics of implementation, is required."[60] Until recently, commissioners received no further training beyond their professional backgrounds. In the last few years, under Jennifer Shaffer's leadership as chief commissioner, the Board has introduced continuing education for its commissioners on topics such as substance abuse and mental illness.[61]

The Board of Parole Hearings' executive board holds a monthly two-day executive meeting in Sacramento. The meeting is open not only to state officials but also to representatives of victims' and offenders' families, members of other state agencies that interface with the Board, and representatives of rehabilitation and reentry organizations. The agenda for the meeting is published online in advance so that interested members of the public can participate.[62] At the open session, the Board discusses various administrative issues.[63] The closed session addresses strategies in cases subject to litigation.

Parole hearings are typically conducted by three commissioners or vice-commissioners, who are assigned to a particular prison for a week at a time on a rotational basis. Given the size of the state and the remoteness of many of its high-security prisons, where lifers are typically housed, rotations require a considerable amount of travel. This also means that inmates are not guaranteed a particular composition at their hearing. An inmate may be assigned, by pure chance, commissioners he or she has never seen before, or ones he or she has already met in prior hearings.[64]

SCHEDULING PAROLE HEARINGS: ELIGIBILITY FOR PAROLE AND MARSY'S LAW

In California, inmates sentenced to life with parole become eligible for parole consideration within a year of their Minimum Eligible Parole Date (MEPD).[65] From that date forward, lifers receive a parole hearing every year while incarcerated, unless the Board extends the period between hearings based on evidence that the inmate has not progressed toward the next step in rehabilitation, or unless the inmate waives the right to a hearing in a particular year.[66]

Prisoners who committed life crimes prior to November 8, 1978, have an MEPD of seven years. However, for offenders who were convicted of first- or second-degree murder for crimes committed on or after this date, the MEPD is twenty-five and fifteen years, respectively.[67] Moreover, the CDCR website explicitly states that "these inmates are sentenced to the possibility of parole, not the assurance of it, recognizing that their maximum potential sentence is life."[68]

The periods before hearings and between hearings have occasionally been a source of public concern. In 2008, California voters approved Proposition 9, or Marsy's Law, ostensibly a victims' rights bill, which significantly affected the scheduling of parole hearings.[69] The proposition created a new standard under which lifers who are denied parole must presumptively wait fifteen years for another opportunity to plead their case unless "the [Board] finds by clear and convincing evidence that the criteria relevant to the setting of parole release dates . . . are such that consideration of the public and victim's safety" does not warrant such an extended deferral period. If parole is denied by the Board, the prisoner has a right to a written opinion that provides the reasons for denial.[70] If the fifteen-year presumption is rebutted, the Board may extend denial lengths of three, five, seven, or ten years.[71] In addition, inmates who know their records do not demonstrate improvement since the last hearing and who fear an adverse parole decision and damning language on their record if they perform poorly at a hearing might strategically decide to defer their hearing in the hopes of appearing with a stronger record at a future date.[72]

THE PAROLE HEARING

The nuts and bolts of the parole hearing are provided in the California Code of Regulations, Title 15. Under the code, the Board panel "shall set a release date unless it determines that the gravity of the current convicted offense or offenses, or the timing and gravity of current or past convicted offense or offenses, is such that consideration of the public safety requires a lengthier period of incarceration."[73] For this purpose, "all relevant, reliable information available to the panel shall be considered in determining suitability for parole."[74] Under the code, this information might pertain to

> [c]ircumstances of the prisoner's social history; past and present mental state; past criminal history, including involvement in other criminal misconduct which is reliably documented; the base and other commitment offenses, including behavior before, during, and after the crime; past and present attitude toward the crime; any conditions of treatment or control, including the use of special conditions under which the prisoner may safely be released to the community; and any other information which bears on the prisoner's suitability for release.[75]

Within this fairly rudimentary statutory framework, the Board is vested with very broad discretion in considering these factors and their relative weight.[76] Ultimately, the California Supreme Court has stated that the Board's role is to determine whether the inmate represents a current danger to society.[77]

Title 15 establishes a list of circumstances "tending" to show unsuitability.[78] The first one pertains to the commitment offense, if the prisoner committed the crime in an especially "heinous, atrocious or cruel" manner. Examples include multiple victims, dispassionate and calculated manner, abuse or defilement of the victim, callousness in carrying out the crime, or an inexplicable or trivial motive. Other factors for unsuitability include a previous record of violence, an unstable social history, sadistic sexual offenses, psychological problems, and misbehavior while at the institution.[79] To date, the most common suitability factor relied upon in governors' reversals of Board decisions is the commitment offense itself.[80] This is not unique to California; research conducted nationally consistently finds the nature and seriousness of the crime ranking high in the importance of the factors most often considered by parole boards.[81]

The hearing differs considerably from a criminal trial, both procedurally and evidentiarily. The burden of proof at a parole hearing is preponderance of the evidence;[82] coerced and involuntary statements made by the parolee may be considered by the Board of Parole Hearings;[83] and relaxation of evidence rules allows for the admissibility of many hearsay documents.[84]

The hearings are semipublic and are attended by the inmate and his or her attorney, media representatives,[85] observers for education and informational purposes,[86] victims or victims' representatives,[87] and representatives of the district attorney's office responsible for prosecuting the committal offense.[88] Other interested parties may submit statements for the record.[89] Of the parties mentioned above, only the inmate, his or her attorney, victims or victims' representatives, and representatives of the district attorney's office responsible for committal offense have a right to be notified of the time and location of the hearing.[90]

The inmates' rights in the parole process differ considerably from the rights "package" guaranteed to criminal defendants. The California Supreme Court has recognized the inmates' liberty interest embedded in their expectation for release, but it has stated that interest is trumped by the overriding statutory concern for public safety.[91] Within the process, inmates have the right to be notified a month in advance of the week in which the hearing will occur;[92] to view materials contained in their file, such as probation reports, psychological evaluations, and documents submitted by interested parties (victims and representatives of the district attorney's office);[93] and to ask and answer questions at the parole hearings and submit documents in response to any materials considered by the Board.[94] At the conclusion of the hearing, the inmate has a right to a copy of the transcript, as well as a copy of the decision specifying the information considered and the reasons for the decisions.[95]

Following the Board's recommendation to grant parole, the file is sent to the governor for approval, modification, or reversal, within 120 days.[96] The governor can only exercise this authority "on the basis of the same factors which the parole authority is required to consider"; in the pre-*Lawrence* era, governors consistently relied on the solitary statutory factor of the commitment offense and whether the offense qualified as "especially heinous, atrocious or cruel manner."[97]

PAROLE REPRESENTATION AND PANEL ATTORNEYS

The constitutional right to counsel under *Gideon v. Wainwright* covers only criminal trials and mandatory appeals and does not extend to parole hearings.[98] Nonetheless, California law provides indigents representation in some situations, such as appeals and habeas proceedings for death row inmates.[99] Similarly, Title 15 requires that inmates facing parole hearings receive representation if they cannot afford a private attorney.[100] The Board maintains the Panel Attorney Appointment Program, which is a list of attorneys willing to represent inmates in parole hearings. The process for being listed was revised in 2013, when eligible attorneys entered a one-time public lottery for selection and a total of fifty-nine active attorneys were placed on the list, classified by regional proximity. Priority was given to attorneys experienced in parole hearing representation. CDCR's guide to the program requires that panel attorneys comply with some health requirements, such as a tuberculin test, to enable them to enter correctional institutions.[101]

Compensation for parole representation is fairly modest. Panel attorneys submit a reimbursement form, under which they can claim $25 per appointment, $50 for parole packet review, $75 for central file review, $100 for each meeting with the client, and $175 for a personal appearance at the hearing (en banc meetings may also be reimbursed.) Some private attorneys do parole work to supplement their legal practice, while others specialize in parole cases. A unique participant in the parole "market" is Uncommon Law, a nonprofit dedicated to lifer cases and spearheaded by experienced parole attorney Keith Wattley. Wattley also runs an annual "lifer school"—a one-day workshop for attorneys about parole representation—and offers lifer clinics in several law schools.

The nature of legal representation for parole hearings considerably differs from ordinary trial work. Attorneys do not speak much at the hearing; Wattley often explains that "it is bad news if you have to do the talking."[102] Most of the attorney's work consists of preparing the client for the hearing and assembling supportive evidence on the client's behalf—more of a "director" than an "actor" role. An effective attorney is attuned to the Board's expectations and coaches, or advises, the client to conform to them. Because of the informality of the process, the flexibility in evidence admission standards, and the conventions that have developed over time, personal relationships and experience can become very important to the quality of representation.

The attorney-client relationship at the hearing can also be fairly amorphous. Inmates can, and occasionally do, choose to appear before the Board pro se. Attorneys sometimes encounter difficulties in cooperation from inmates or their families, and they sometimes state to the Board that they were unable to meet with the inmate prior to the hearing. Some attorneys ask to withdraw from representation under these circumstances, while others will nonetheless make arguments on behalf of the client they have not met. Beyond the regular ethical obligations imposed by the California bar, there are no specific ethical guidelines or requirements for attorneys representing clients in parole hearings.

GRANTING PAROLE

If parole is granted, the parolee is subject to general statutory conditions,[103] which require reporting to an agent of record within twenty-four hours of release, reporting a change of address within seventy-two hours, receiving approval before traveling fifty miles from the parolee's residence, refraining from criminal contacts, reporting any arrest to the agent of record, and refraining from owning, using, or having access to weapons.[104] In addition to these, the Board may impose more specific conditions,[105] some of which have been categorized by statute. For instance, a parolee that has been convicted of a crime requiring sex offender registration may not reside within two thousand feet of a park or K–12 school.[106] While the Board has the power to decide what, if any, special conditions a parolee must abide by, these conditions will be deemed invalid if they are unrelated to the parolee's criminal conviction, curtail conduct that is not criminal in nature, or forbid conduct unrelated to future criminality.[107] Also, parole conditions that restrict the exercise of certain fundamental rights must be reasonably related to a compelling state interest,[108] be reasonable,[109] and not contravene public policy.[110]

The period of parole supervision varies depending on the commitment offense. Nearly all inmates determinately sentenced can serve up to three years on parole,[111] but in some cases the period is greatly extended. For instance, prisoners convicted of continued sexual abuse of a child are subject to twenty years and six months of parole.[112] In some cases, such as a first-degree murder conviction, the parole period may be in place for life.[113] In practice, however, most first-degree murderers serve either three or seven years on parole, depending on the timing of their conviction. Second-degree murderers typically serve five years on parole.[114] The Board can reduce or extend the period of parole. In practice, an extension of the period of parole usually occurs through parole revocation and reinstatement.[115] Typically, parole period terminates after the parolee has served the entire term of the parole. Termination can also occur if the Board discharges the parole for good cause or by operation of law.[116] There exists a presumptive discharge date for parolees who serve continuous parole without any violations. The parole is administratively discharged if the Board does not retain it within thirty days of the presumptive discharge date.[117] Retention of a parolee past the presumptive discharge date requires a finding of good cause by the Board.[118] The parolee has no right to be present during the decision process of retention but does have a right to receive notification of retention, which includes the reasons for retention.[119] The parolee is permitted to appeal the decision and present evidence that tends to show a mistake of fact in the decision.[120] An associate chief deputy commissioner reviews the case and makes a final decision (which requires the signature of a second commissioner) to retain or discharge the parole.[121]

The Board can revoke the parole of any parolee under its jurisdiction for good cause. Some good cause bases for revocation include violations of general or special parole conditions, absconding, failing to sign an agreement regarding sex offender registration, failure to be tested for tuberculosis when required, or failure to pay restitution.[122] The Board can also revoke parole in order to administer psychiatric treatment of a parolee.[123] Following the

Criminal Justice Realignment, parolees who suffer a parole revocation can serve up to 180 days in custody instead of the traditional twelve months in custody.[124] The time spent in custody does not count toward parole credits; it merely extends the period of parole by the number of days spent in custody.[125] For parolees who are subject to life parole, revocation may result in a return to custody to serve their life sentence with the annual parole consideration hearings.[126] Parolees do not have the full range of constitutional protections during parole hearings. For instance, for parolees subject to superior court jurisdiction, the court is not required to state a reason for suspension and can issue arrest warrants for parolees at its discretion.[127]

JUDICIAL REVIEW OF PAROLE HEARINGS: THE *LAWRENCE* REVOLUTION

Recent years have seen more vigorous judicial review of processes before the parole boards than ever before, often resulting in favorable decisions for inmates and sometimes producing precedents that were helpful to entire categories of parolees. The Second District Court of Appeals' 2000 decision *In re Rosenkrantz* marked the first judicial decision in which the court ordered relief for a lifer, voiding the parole board's decision not to release, and eventually resulting in a parole grant for the petitioner.[128] But Rosenkrantz's victory was short-lived: the governor reversed his parole grant and he had to resort to the courts again. In the resulting decision, the California Supreme Court upheld the governor's denial of parole, holding that the severity of the crime in itself could be grounds for denial of parole, as long as the Board identifies specific aspects of the act that evince "especially heinous, atrocious or cruel" crime, which under parole regulations is grounds for denial.[129] This decision was subsequently affirmed *In re Dannenberg,* in which a petitioner who was convicted of murdering his wife but claimed to have no memory of the events was denied parole on the basis of the heinousness of his crime.[130]

Rosenkrantz and *Dannenberg* had a mixed effect on parole hearings. On one hand, the court's willingness to critically examine and even reverse the Board's recommendation signaled encouragement to inmates that they could prevail on judicial review and prompted more legal challenges of parole denials. On the other hand, the bottom line was that, as long as the Board and the governor acted to protect public safety, they could rely on the seriousness of the crime as a basis for denial. Lower courts differed in their interpretation of the decisions: some courts accepted any finding regarding the severity of the crime at face value and deferred to the board or governor's finding of risk, whereas other courts pointed out that the *Rosenkrantz-Dannenberg* rule essentially gave the authorities carte blanche to deny parole based on the original crime, regardless of the time that had passed or of any evidence presented by the inmate as to rehabilitation efforts and insight. Since the parole hearing process inherently encompasses only those convicted of very serious crimes, it is easy to point to cruel and heinous elements. Indeed, later court decisions found that the parole board pointed to "cruel and heinous" crime-related factors in 100 percent of the cases in which it denied parole.[131]

This unfettered discretion of parole commissioners and the governor was further muddled in 2008 with two Supreme Court decisions announced on the same day: *In re Lawrence* and *In re Shaputis*.[132]

Lawrence had served more than two decades in prison without incident for murdering her lover's wife in 1971 and became eligible for parole in 1990.[133] In August 2005, the Board recommended Lawrence for parole for the fourth time, concluding that she was "unlikely to commit additional crimes because of her maturation, advancing age, and the absence [of] history of significant violent crime."[134] However, in January 2006, the governor reversed the Board's decision, determining that "the gravity alone of this murder" sufficed for parole denial because "the underlying crime was a cold, premeditated murder carried out in an especially cruel manner and committed for an incredibly petty reason."[135]

After the fourth reversal by the governor, Lawrence petitioned for habeas corpus and, in May 2007, prevailed.[136] The California Supreme Court affirmed, holding that "when a court reviews a parole decision of the Board or the Governor, the relevant inquiry is whether some evidence supports the decision ... regarding whether the inmate constitutes a current threat to public safety, and not merely whether some evidence confirms certain factual findings regarding dangerousness." In addition, the court held that the "immutable and unchangeable circumstances of parole applicant's murder offense,"[137] which formerly constituted sufficient evidence for denial,[138] would now need to be supplemented by a finding of "current dangerousness"[139]—actual evidence that the inmate still poses a threat to public safety[140]—and inmates whose prison record was overall positive should be released even if the circumstances of their crime were "cruel and heinous."

In *Life after Murder* Nancy Mullane portrays *Lawrence* as a revolutionary decision that ushered new hope for release.[141] Mullane accompanies the journey of five lifers as they undergo parole hearings shortly after *Lawrence*. She meets the men in prison as they prepare for the hearing, during the wait for the governor's approval, and later as they exit prison and resume postrelease life. Mullane's interlocutors speak thoughtfully and reflectively about their original crimes, attributing them to a combination of youth, substance dependency, and sheer misfortune. Eventually, all five men receive parole, an outcome that suggests that *Lawrence* signified a real turn in parole grants.

But the impact of *Lawrence* was somewhat moderated by its companion case, *Shaputis*. There, the Supreme Court reiterated that, while the heinousness of the crime in itself was not *sufficient* evidence of risk, it was still a permissible factor to consider in addition to other factors. *Shaputis* even offered the Board a blueprint for bypassing *Lawrence:* it would be permissible to deny parole to inmates who, in addition to the "cruel and heinous" nature of their crime, do not show sufficient "insight" into why they committed the crime in the first place.[142] Rather than constraining the Board's decision on its merits, *Shaputis* can therefore be read as requiring a shift in rhetoric: where the Board could previously rely on the definition of the crime as "heinous and cruel" to deny parole, it could now reach the same conclusion if it found that the inmate lacked "insight."

The shift was not insignificant. While "heinousness and cruelty" could be subject to interpretation, Title 15, as mentioned above ("The Parole Hearing"), did offer a list of factors to consider, which enable not only determining "heinousness and cruelty" in a particular case but also in a comparison across cases. By contrast, the statute offers no definition of "insight," rendering it a highly subjective determination. The term *insight* might encompass several components, whose interconnections could be unclear and vary dramatically from case to case: a coherent explanation of the circumstances of the crime, a genuine expression of remorse, and a presentation of a new and transformed self that seeks to distance itself from the crime. Moreover, establishing whether genuine insight exists is a delicately interpretive task, in which the Board might rely on the inmate's words, deeds, or nonverbal demeanor, without having to provide falsifiable evidence as to this determination. In addition, since expressions of insight are highly individualized, the Board could plausibly deny parole to an inmate it deems as lacking insight while granting it to another inmate whose similar verbiage (perhaps with different affect) it sees as evidence of insight. This last factor is compounded by the cultural variations in expressing sentiments of regret and remorse. As Alison Renteln shows in *The Cultural Defense,* legal actors sometimes harshly judge defendants whose apparently numb or irresponsive affect reflects their cultural background.[143] As an example, parole attorney Keith Wattley told me that when representing African American men before the Board, he has sometimes seen Board members observe that the inmates appear "angry" and has had to intervene and explain the cultural stereotypes that muddled the interpretation.[144]

An additional complication is California's aforementioned two-tiered parole process, under which the governor may continue to overturn Board decisions by "connecting evidence of statutory factors to the inmate's current dangerousness." However, the governor's decision, just like the Board's decision, is subject to judicial review, and courts must determine if "the governor or Board articulated this rational nexus between the factual evidence and current dangerousness."[145] Accordingly, the *Lawrence* ruling shifts the way the parole board and the governor treat lifer parole decisions "by focusing on the nexus and not just the existence of evidence."[146]

Because of the two-tiered process, it is difficult to tell whether the increase in parole releases reflects the legal changes following *Lawrence* or the political winds blowing in the governor's mansion. Between 1990 and 2013, the number of California inmates released from prison after serving sentences of life with parole increased by more than 1,000 percent.[147] Furthermore, while not equal to the number of inmates actually paroled, the number of suitability hearings with a grant result increased by nearly 10 percent from 2008 to 2012.[148] In addition, more than 2,200 inmates who had been serving life sentences in California have been paroled over the past five years, which is more than three times the number of lifers paroled in each of the previous nineteen years combined.[149] Virtually all of these releases are the work of Jerry Brown, whose reversal rate for murder cases never exceeded 20 percent.[150] This policy stood in stark contrast to his predecessors, Governors Gray Davis and Arnold Schwarzenegger, who had blocked 95 percent of murder parole decisions and 70 percent of murder cases, respectively;[151] between 1999 and 2003, for example, Davis reviewed 371 parole decisions and approved only nine.[152]

The delicate dance between the Board and the governor was occasionally addressed by the courts even before Brown's tenure. In *In re Loresch*, the court explicitly addressed Governor Schwarzenegger (who had reversed the Board's recommendation on pure speculation that the inmate in question could relapse into drug abuse and become violent), urging him to reconsider his approach to the parole process in order to restore confidence in the Board's determinations and to stop second-guessing their findings.[153] Later, in *In re Calderon,* the court stated that the governor's decisions were clearly made not by the governor but by his legal staff (stopping just short of accusing the staff of political considerations in vetoing parole grants).[154] The court urged the decision-makers to understand the "magnitude of the problem" of unfounded reversals of Board decisions. However, when evidence is present, courts tend to be more flexible. In *In re Ross,* the court reviewed the governor's decision in a case that had been sent back to him after the petitioner's earlier habeas victory.[155] The court held that, when the case comes back to the governor, he can consider new evidence not previously addressed as long as it relates to public safety. *Ross* echoes the general principle of flexible and malleable evidence rules in parole hearing, as well as the general premise that the parole hearing is not a criminal trial.

The flexibility of parole hearings and gubernatorial decisions also raise important questions about inmates' access to judicial review. The question of standard of review, and appealability in general, of prospective parolees' petitions to review parole denials that had arguably violated *Lawrence* had occupied the Ninth Circuit for years with no resolution, until the court decided *Hayward v. Marshall.*[156] In *Hayward,* the court held that, like state courts, federal courts must consider whether the Board or governor followed *Lawrence* by denying parole only where current evidence showed that a prisoner would endanger public safety.

The effect of *Hayward* on judicial review is mixed. On one hand, the Ninth Circuit was willing to accept that a finding of "low to moderate" risk (as opposed to "no risk" or simply "low risk") in a psychological evaluation *could* support denial of parole in some cases. On the other hand, a subsequent case left the door open to federal challenges of parole denials. In *Pearson v. Muntz,* the Ninth Circuit chided the California attorney general's effort to argue that, under *Hayward,* California lifers had no right to judicial review of their parole hearing.[157] The court used strong language to characterize the attorney general's position as a "fundamental misunderstandings of *Hayward*" and restated that the *Lawrence* holding applies to all judicial reviews of parole hearings.

CONCLUSION

It would be a mistake to assume that the California Penal Code, the California Code of Regulations, and a compendium of federal court decisions veritably capture the content and meaning of the parole hearing. The statutes and case law provide merely skeletal scaffolding for the Board's and the governor's vast discretion. While courts are willing to intervene and hear appeals, it is fairly difficult to challenge a parole decision via judicial review. Over time, the Board has developed a unique procedural and linguistic libretto for its hearings, complete with expectations to which parolee hopefuls are expected to conform. These expectations are, to some extent, conveyed and mediated via the attorneys who represent parolees at the hearings, though their ability to prevail on legal arguments is limited.

With this legal framework in mind, we now turn to examine the sociopolitical context in which parole became scarce and unattainable. As the next chapter shows, the Manson Family murders played a pivotal role in shaping parole in particular and the extreme punishment landscape in California in general and were then shaped, in turn, by the resulting process.

_____

TWO

The Manson Family Cases
and the Birth of the
"Extreme-Punishment Trifecta"

O nobly-born, that which is called death hath now come. Thou art departing from this world, but thou art not the only one; [death] cometh to all. Do not cling, in fondness and weakness, to this life. Even though thou clingest out of weakness, thou hast not the power to remain here.

The Tibetan Book of the Dead

In late November 2017, after forty-six years of incarceration, Charles Manson died in prison of natural causes at the age of eighty-three. His death sparked several retrospectives. The History Channel asked why he hadn't been executed since he had been sentenced to death, and *Fortune* magazine calculated that keeping him in prison for all those years had cost taxpayers over $1 million.[1] The premise underlying both articles was that Manson's incarceration was an aberration, a diversion from the natural and expected consequence of his trial: the death penalty. Indeed, along with his followers who participated in the murders—Susan Atkins, Patricia Krenwinkel, Leslie Van Houten, Bruce Davis, Charles "Tex" Watson, and Robert "Bobby" Beausoleil— Manson was sentenced to death in 1971.[2] However, in 1972 all death sentences, including those of Manson and the "family," were commuted to life with parole. Under these circumstances, one might regard their lengthy incarceration periods as fair: these are, after all, people who were "supposed" to be put to death in the 1970s, and their continuous incarceration is, in a way, a manifestation of that original intent. But such a conclusion misses important historical dimensions.

As I explain in this chapter, the Manson Family murders and the fate of their perpetrators figured prominently in the public debate about punishment in California. Far from being an outlying response to a legal "accident," these cases became the cautionary tales that begat the return of the death penalty in 1978, the birth of life without parole in the same year, and the idea that life with parole—which implied, until 1978, a considerable but not extreme prison sentence—could extend for decades of incarceration. Moreover, these three developments were not unrelated; the idea that Californians could feel comfortable with interminable prison sentences has, in effect and in rhetoric, blurred the differences between California's three variations of extreme punishment for heinous crimes: death ("life under the unlikely threat of execution"), life without parole ("the other death penalty" or "slow death"), and life with parole ("life de facto"). While Manson and his followers received the latter punishment, theirs was not an already-existing draconian version of life with parole; their cases played an important role in a shift toward extreme incarceration, where the three punishment options blended into an indistinguishable regime in which aging and dying behind bars became normalized through parole denials and gubernatorial reversals.[3]

THE TRIFECTA OF EXTREME PUNISHMENT

Before explaining the emergence of the trifecta of extreme punishment, it is important to point out the functional equivalence of the death penalty, life without parole, and life with parole. Since its reinstatement in California, the death penalty has been oft imposed, but rarely carried out; only thirteen inmates have been executed and approximately 750 remain behind bars. Similarly situated are California's 4,594 lifers-without-parole (4,500 men and 94 women—3.5 percent of the prison population).[4] Members of both groups can expect to be incarcerated for the rest of their lives, and the prospect of an execution for the former is almost as impossible as for the latter.

The blurred line between the death penalty and life without parole has generated a lively debate among reform advocates about death penalty abolition. Activist groups, with considerable justification, refer to life without parole as "the other death penalty," arguing that supporting death penalty abolition merely reinforces "a false hierarchy between forms of state-sanctioned death."[5] Some academics express concerns that death penalty abolition would merely "normalize LWOP [life without parole] as a supposedly humane alternative to the death penalty";[6] others point out that innocent men fighting for exoneration face additional difficulties as lifers, because they do not receive the free representation awarded to death row inmates.[7] Others, including me, advocate for death penalty abolition for pragmatic reasons, recognizing that penal reform is unavoidably incremental and that the road to reforming life without parole passes through capital punishment abolition.[8]

My support for incremental reform does not stem from a disagreement with the basic premise that the death penalty (without an execution) and life without parole are analogous. If anything, the argument against incremental reform does not go far enough.[9] For in addition to fewer than 5,000 lifers without parole, California prisons house more than four times that number of lifers with parole—more than 26,000, or about a fifth of the total prison population—with very few releases before the 2010s. These numbers are a direct consequence of the politicization of the parole process. As Matt Levin explains, Jerry Brown's predecessors faced enormous political disincentives to approve parole, because "no governor wanted to stand accused of letting a convicted murderer roam the streets." As a consequence, "for most of the past two decades, the odds that a lifer would ever set foot outside prison walls were slim. In 2010, a parole-eligible offender who had committed murder stood a 6 percent chance of leaving prison through the conventional parole process." Indeed, so marked was the improvement in chances of release under the second Brown administration that in its first two years, "more lifers were released from prison (1,205) than during the previous three administrations combined (1,168)."[10]

The large number of lifers with parole serving the effective equivalent of life without parole is a direct product of the changes in the late 1970s and 1980s. In 1980, the median length of time served on a California life sentence for first-degree murder was less than twelve years.[11] By 2012, the equivalent figure was more than twenty-eight years, and a person convicted of first-degree murder today would not be even considered for parole before serving twenty-five years.[12] Even these figures are deceptive; they represent only the sentences of people who were actually released on parole, and as Michael Brodheim notes, they "take no account of the (much longer) time served by the increasing number of lifers who have yet to be released—and, depending on the political winds, may never be released." Brodheim found that "from 2000 to 2011, despite a law that commanded the parole board to 'normally' find them suitable for parole, life-sentenced prisoners were dying at a rate that exceeded their rate of release from prison."[13] Brodheim, a formerly incarcerated man paroled after thirty-four years in prison (twenty years after he became eligible for parole), lists 3,956 men and women who, as of December 31, 2016, had been incarcerated for more than a quarter century.

How did life with parole evolve into "life de facto," barely distinguishable from its extreme-punishment siblings: the death penalty and life without parole? What role did the Manson Family cases play in normalizing such extreme sentences? A good place to start is the political turmoil resulting from death penalty abolition in the early 1970s—a decision perceived as elitist and unpopular—and the consequent punitive countertrend.

FURMAN V. GEORGIA, PEOPLE V. ANDERSON, AND THE "CLASS OF '72"

The Manson Family trial for the Tate-LaBianca murders was characterized by scandal, outrageous behavior, and a media frenzy. Manson and his codefendants (Atkins, Krenwinkel, and Van Houten) engaged in antics and outbursts during the trial, shaving their heads, scarring their foreheads, and even physically lunging toward the judge, leading to Manson's frequent removals from the trial room. Manson's attorney, Irving Kanarek, was legendary for his numerous objections and obstructionist tactics: his behavior at the trial landed him twice in jail for contempt. In addition, there was the unusual intervention by President Nixon: during the trial, Nixon famously declared Manson guilty, giving rise to objections and arguments about partiality. Even with a strong case against universally reviled defendants, the prosecutors felt that achieving a conviction, as well as a death sentence, was a struggle, and they were very invested in the outcome.[14]

Following their conviction, Manson, Atkins, Krenwinkel, and Van Houten were sentenced to death on April 19, 1971, but their tenure on death row would be short-lived. On February 18, 1972, the California Supreme Court decided *People v. Anderson,* in which it found the death penalty in California unconstitutional.[15] On the heels of *Anderson* came the United States Supreme Court's decision in *Furman v. Georgia,* which found some aspects of the death penalty in Georgia, as exemplified in three cases, unconstitutional.[16]

Of the two decisions, *Anderson* was by far the more extreme. Save for one dissenter, the justices found that California's death penalty was "impermissibly cruel. It degrades and dehumanizes all who participate in its processes. It is unnecessary to any legitimate goal of the state and is incompatible with the dignity of man and the judicial process."[17] The justices relied on a linguistic difference between the U.S and the California constitutions, finding that

PHOTO 1. *Los Angeles Times,* front page, January 26, 1971.

California had higher constitutionality standards because its constitution forbade cruel *or* (rather than *and*) unusual punishment.[18]

Furman, by comparison, was much tamer; decided by a 5–4 majority (albeit per curiam), it did not completely repudiate the death penalty. Only Justices Marshall and Brennan found the death penalty unconstitutional in all its applications; the remaining concurrences limited their conclusion to particular deficiencies—specifically, the concerns about "uncontrolled discretion of judges or juries" leading to racial and class disparities in its application.[19]

That a decision *lamenting* unfettered discretion would set in motion a series of events that would end up creating a de facto death penalty *through* unfettered discretion was of course still unknown. But it was *Anderson* that provoked most of the public furor in California. The majority in *Anderson* declared their decision fully retroactive, an outcome upheld in *Aikens v. California.*[20] The consequence was the commutation of 174 death sentences, a group colloquially known as the "class of '72." In addition to Manson and his followers, this group included Sirhan, the murderer of Senator Robert Kennedy; Dennis Stanworth, sentenced to death in 1966 for the brutal kidnapping, rape, and murder of Pinole teenage girls Caree Collison and Susan Box; and Robert Massie, who would later be paroled and commit a second murder while on parole.

The *Anderson* commutations evoked furor, considerably fueled by the sole dissenting justice, Marshall McComb. Incensed by the breadth of the

The Death Row Inmates

By George Draper

CHARLES MANSON
In Los Angeles

PHOTO 2. Manson and other famous San Quentin death row inmates, *San Francisco Chronicle*, February 19, 1972.

decision and by the audacity of abolishing the death penalty while *Furman* was pending before the Supreme Court, McComb violated the pledge to keep the decision secret and called a press conference the day before the decision was to be read.[21] Governor Ronald Reagan, an avid supporter of the death penalty, vowed to do all in his power to change the ruling.[22] The *Santa Cruz Sentinel* reported Reagan's disappointment in Chief Justice Wright, his own appointee, referring to Wright as "the Earl Warren of California."[23] Reagan was quoted as saying the court "had placed itself above the will of the people Friday when it declared the death penalty in California unconstitutional."[24] Indeed, after a brief period in the late 1960s when most Americans were opposed to the death penalty, at the time of *Furman* and *Anderson* the majority of Americans supported it again, by a margin of 50 to 41, a gap that would continue to grow well into the mid-1990s.[25]

In practice, the furor was misdirected, for *Anderson*'s bark was worse than its bite. As the *Press-Telegram* reported just prior to the decision, even if the death penalty were to be upheld, no executions were expected. Since 1962, only two executions had been carried out at San Quentin; a barrage of successful appeals and retrials had led to fifty removals from death row; and save for a handful of inmates, the entire death row population at San Quentin had pending postconviction proceedings. The director of corrections estimated that it would be "many months, at least" before execution dates would be set for Manson and his "clan."[26] In addition, even though the outcome of

Anderson was that these inmates would be let out of death row, many of them would be housed in security conditions for years before joining the general population.

The public uproar about *Anderson* and *Furman,* and particularly about Manson and his followers, is therefore best understood as reflecting a sentiment that the decisions reflected top-down, elitist sensibilities. In *Executing Freedom,* Daniel LaChance highlights the inverse relationship between "the amount of trust Americans placed in the federal government" and "their level of support for capital punishment." With this trust shaken by the Vietnam War, Watergate, and the end of hippie-era innocence, Americans' support of the death penalty rose above their trust in their government, just at the moment when their Supreme Court found key aspects of the death penalty unconstitutional and effectively halted its use. LaChance identifies "[a] growing crisis of confidence in the nation's moral integrity, stoked by a rising awareness of white psychopathy and a sense that it was a symptom of cultural decadence, [which] contributed to what followed: tumbling support for a prevention- and rehabilitation-based approach to criminal justice and a dramatic uptick of public support for capital punishment." He quotes Cornell University professor Walter Berns, who, writing in support of the death penalty, hailed it as a supportive message to the "good people," who "vastly outnumbered the Charles Mansons of the world, and . . . an affirmation that they, not the psychopath, embodied what it meant to be human."[27]

The public's disdain for *Furman* and especially for *Anderson* was evident in California voters' enthusiastic approval of Proposition 17. The bill, explicitly designed to circumvent the court's decision by amending the California Constitution, stated that "the death penalty provided for under those statutes shall not be deemed to be, or to constitute, the infliction of cruel or unusual punishments within the meaning of Article I, Section 6."[28]

Despite the proposition's passage, no executions were held in California until 1992, due to the nationwide effect of *Furman.* In addition, death penalty opponents challenged the proposition's constitutionality in courts—a debate that would resolve itself only in 1978, when the court declared, in *People v. Frierson,* that Proposition 17 was constitutional.[29] By then, Robert Hendrickson's 1973 documentary *Manson* had been released, including chilling footage of Manson Family life and interviews with Manson and his followers, such as Lynette "Squeaky" Fromme and Sandra Good, which did not endear them to the American public;[30] a considerable majority of Americans supported the death penalty;[31] the Supreme Court had decided

Gregg v. Georgia, approving capital sentencing statutes that complied with the Eighth Amendment;[32] and Manson and his accomplices had become eligible for parole, a situation which, given the average terms served for homicide at the time, evoked panic and rage among Californians.

THE RETURN OF THE DEATH PENALTY AND THE BIRTH OF
THE EXTREME-PUNISHMENT TRIFECTA

Georgia's legislature had clearly read *Furman* carefully and internalized its lessons. In *Gregg* the Supreme Court found that the state's new legal provisions—enumerating several aggravating circumstances that would need to be proven beyond reasonable doubt to a jury before a death sentence could be meted out—met the constitutional threshold.[33] The 6–3 decision still allowed Georgia to inflict the death penalty for nonhomicide offenses, albeit in rare circumstances.[34] In addition, a jury's plea for mercy could not bind the court, a policy whose approval by the Supreme Court has led to many cases of judicial override and imposition of the death penalty, especially in Southern states.[35] But the approved Georgia framework was adopted by several states, including California.

Proposition 7, placed on the California ballot on November 7, 1978, while Proposition 17's fate was still hanging on the balance, was a *Gregg*-compliant death penalty statute, which increased the penalties for first- and second-degree murder, created life without parole as a punishment for murder, and thoroughly revised the lists of mitigating and aggravating circumstances in a way that made the new punishment viable and appealing.[36] As such, it was a considerably bolder move than the mere upholding of the death penalty in Proposition 17—and, by creating an intermediate option of extreme punishment, it would plug the "hole" between Manson's original death sentence and his actual fate, life with the possibility of being paroled that very year. Conservative politician John Briggs, who recruited former New York prosecutor Donald Heller to draft the proposition, tapped into the political sentiment about *Anderson, Gregg,* and the hoped-for aftermath for Manson and the Family. In an interview for the *Desert Sun,* he criticized the inefficiency of the existing death penalty statute: "If a man like Charles Manson were to again order his family of drug-crazed killers to slaughter a family, he would not receive the death penalty because the Legislature's death penalty bill does not apply to the mastermind of such a plot."[37]

Briggs correctly read the public's sentiments: Proposition 7 passed with 71.1 percent approval. It was impossible to undo the commutation of the class of '72's sentences, but the proposition was carefully crafted to address Manson-like cases in the future. Not only did it expand the reach of the death penalty and create life without parole—a sentence that would be far more comforting to the public than the one inflicted on Manson and his followers—but it also set the minimum sentence for first-degree murder as twenty-five years to life and for second-degree murder as fifteen years to life.[38]

The public support for these reforms was hardly a lucky guess on Briggs's part. Proposition 7 arrived on the heels of a monumental change in California's sentencing structure, which reflected similar sentiments. While the force behind the proposition explicitly mentioned the Manson case as a catalyst, the concern about sentencing the Charles Mansons of the future and their followers was at the forefront of California's Uniform Determinate Sentencing Act of 1976.[39] In fact, the expansion of life without parole in 1978 came shortly after its wholesale creation as part of the determinate sentencing scheme.

DETERMINATE SENTENCING AND THE POLITICIZATION OF PUNISHMENT

The new determinate sentencing bill was the response to a widely held sentiment that judicial and parole discretion led to disparate and unpredictable sentencing outcomes. In addition to its most renowned feature—the shift away from judicial discretion in sentencing to rigid "triads" set by the legislature[40]—the law introduced other important changes to the criminal justice system in California, which reflected a shift away from the bureaucratic and professional administration of corrections by experts and civil servants, hidden from the public eye, to its administration in an expressive, public, and emotional way by politicians and wealthy private citizens. The extent to which this change—which was reflected in the introduction of life without parole and in the diminished role of the Board—stemmed from strong reactions to violent "redball" crimes and a gripping fear that parole boards could release their perpetrators, cannot be overstated.

Scholarly commentary on determinate sentencing describes it as the outcome of a bipartisan push, a description that dovetails with recent literature highlighting the contribution of liberals and professionals to mass incarceration.[41] But in fact, the bill generated considerable—and prescient—opposition from the left and even from within the system. Numerous organizations predicted that determinate sentencing would lead to harsher sentencing across the board, and they submitted letters to Governor Brown, then in his first term, urging him not to sign these changes into law. For example, California Attorneys for Criminal Justice predicted that redball crimes, such as the Manson murders, would trigger increasingly harsher responses from the legislature, and in September 1976 the group wrote to Governor Brown: "The inescapable reality of this change is the absolute certainty of never-ending effort to increase terms. Every sensational crime with widespread publicity will be the subject of legislation to increase the base terms for the particular crime involved. The resulting pressure that will be placed on the Legislature as a whole, and key legislators in particular, will inevitably result in penalty increases."[42] Similarly, the ACLU of Northern California wrote: "Sentence escalation will become a popular legislative pastime once SB 42 becomes law. Discussion in Assembly Ways and Means indicated with what vulture-like rapacity certain legislators will look forward to sponsoring even more draconian provisions."[43]

Several opponents were specifically concerned with the parole process. In a prescient telegram to Governor Brown, Harold Vogelin, chairperson of the Law and Justice Committee of the Los Angeles Chamber of Commerce, observed that this law "does much more by drastically changing the penal code in other areas."[44]

The California Probation, Parole, and Correctional Association (CPPCA) was keenly aware of the effect the new law would have on the Board's composition: "The bill neither specifies that the Community Release Board be composed of professionals trained to make such important release or sentencing decisions (judges, experienced corrections officials) nor requires recommendations by professional staff. We fear the result will be poorer performance and increased danger to the community."[45] The CPPCA also expressed concern that the new requirement to transcribe parole hearings, and make them publicly available, "shall have a dampening effect on parole actions, resulting in overly conservative decisions. Parole boards cannot guarantee positive citizenship on the part of the parolee."[46]

Even nonpartisan policy experts and some law enforcement agencies expressed concern about the weakening of parole. The City of Los Angeles Legislative Analyst's Office wrote: "The Los Angeles Police Department has indicated that under the existing system wherein there is a sentence with established limits, qualified individuals in the corrections system can best decide the length of prison sentence within the set limits. These qualified individuals within the corrections system are better able to evaluate specific prisoners and make recommendations for release."[47]

Rather than the traditional right versus left, the proponents and opponents of the Determinate Sentencing Act reflected a different dichotomy: On one side stood politicians and prosecutors, elected officials who felt accountable and vulnerable to the public on public safety matters. On the other stood professional parole officers, therapeutic professionals, and other employees in the gigantic California rehabilitation machine, who until then could toil in relative obscurity, relying on their professional legitimacy and immunity from critique. To these professionals, who perceived parole decisions as complicated matters requiring education and expertise, the idea of public accountability was terrifying. A public swayed by redball crimes such as Manson's would demand increasingly severe punishment—an appetite that could never be curbed given the few basic constitutional limitations on the death penalty that remained under *Gregg*. Ideas of rehabilitation and utilitarianism, which the opponents of determinate sentencing thought relevant to personalized parole decisions, would give way to abstract notions of proportionality and retribution.

Framing the determinate sentencing revolution as a struggle between professional bureaucrats and elected public officials also explains the role of life with parole and life without parole under the new sentencing regime. Technically, these two types of sentences appear to be outliers—open-ended sentences that did not conform to the new rule of the felony triads. But consider how these sentences would be applied under the new sentencing regime. Life without parole, the newcomer to the extreme-punishment "family," offers its own version of certainty: a person sentenced to life without parole never leaves prison, period. As for life with parole, consider the changes made to the parole process itself. The parole board would no longer be composed of professionals with therapeutic expertise, but rather of gubernatorial appointees (the following years would see a change in the Board's composition to an almost exclusive slate of law enforcement personnel). The Board's decisions would be public and therefore subject to critique. These extreme sentences, therefore, rather than offering an island of judicial and professional discretion in the sea of legislative and prosecutorial power, would in fact conform to said power and maintain the pull toward harsher sentences.

The rise to prominence of these two types of sentences—the newly introduced life without parole and a rougher, longer, politically vulnerable version of life with parole—reflects how well these two sentences fit the general intent behind the 1976 reform. By 2012, lifers with and without parole constituted more than 30 percent of all inmates in California prisons.[48] The California version was a harbinger of things to come in other states and federally. Between 1971 and 1990, twenty-six states enacted life without parole statutes (before 1971, only seven had such statutes).[49] Nationwide, the number of lifers rose from 34,000 in 1984 to 69,845 in 1992, reaching 159,520 in 2012. Both categories of lifers rose at about the same rate: in 1992, there were 12,453 lifers without parole, and by 2012, there were 49,081.[50]

The developments in the Manson Family cases in the late 1970s contributed to this shift in penal policy. To the public's shock, all the defendants, whose sentences were commuted following *Anderson,* would come up for parole as early as 1978, per the existing timetable for parole hearings. Moreover, one of the convicted defendants, Leslie Van Houten, succeeded in obtaining a second trial, which was set for 1978 as well. In the Tate family memoir, Doris Tate describes this period: "Between Manson, Atkins, Watson, and Krenwinkel's annual hearings, one of them surfaced in the news just about every three months."[51] The victims felt that, given the average terms for lifers, keeping the murderers behind bars would be an uphill battle. Doris Tate came to see Stephen Kay, one of the prosecutors in the case, to express her concern: "Leslie Van Houten has a parole hearing coming up, and she plans to present nine hundred signatures supporting her release," she said. "If I don't counter that support they might give her a parole date."[52] And in 1979, the public concerns about violent crime and parole would be vindicated by Robert Massie, who received commutation as part of the class of '72 for a murder he had committed in 1965. Just as the Tate family geared up for what they perceived as an uphill battle against the Manson killers' releases, Massie, still on parole in 1979, killed a store employee and wounded another in the course of a liquor store robbery.[53]

The Sentencing Reform Act and Proposition 7 were the first in a series of reforms that would solidify the notion of the Board not as a valve to reward rehabilitation and alleviate overcrowding, but as a gatekeeper protecting the public from dangerous criminals. These changes were characterized by two trends: the increasing politicization of the Board and the growing power of the victims' rights movement.

Most experts agree that, by the early 1980s, the public perception that violent crime had increased manifold was at least partly based on facts. Whether this sentiment arose from grassroots victims' movements or was the outcome of top-down racialized messaging from the Reagan administration is debatable.[54] Also, given the lack of automation in compiling crime rates in the 1960s in various local jurisdictions and consequently the difficulty in fully relying on FBI crime statistics earlier than the mid-1970s, it is hard (albeit not impossible) to extrapolate just how much crime increased during those decades.[55] Be it as it may, in the early 1980s, people in general, and crime victims in particular, perceived crime as rising and threatening.

This perception proved fertile ground for the awakening of the victims' rights movement. The Tate family became active in the new organization Parents of Murdered Children, which emerged in 1978 in Cincinnati and quickly found a solid foothold in California.[56] President Reagan convened a Task Force on Victims of Crime in 1982, which recommended over a hundred reforms aimed at making the victim heard at all critical stages of the criminal process.[57] In the same year, California voters approved Proposition 8, known as the Victims' Bill of Rights, which required reaching out to the victim for an impact statement prior to sentencing and at parole hearings.[58] This was not the first time that victims' perspectives were allowed in court and at a hearing: since the 1920s, various jurisdictions had introduced victims' statements through probation officers' reports,[59] and some California counties, such as Fresno, allowed victims to speak even before victim allocution became part of the state's penal code.[60]

Another change to the tenor of the parole hearing was the prosecutor's presence. Stephen Kay, committed to attend each and every parole hearing in the Manson Family's cases, pioneered a program to encourage prosecutors to attend parole hearings.[61] The Tate family memoir relates Patricia Krenwinkel's surprise at meeting Kay for the first time after her conviction at her parole hearing; she asked the board, "Is he allowed to be here? . . . He's just come to harass me."[62]

Media restrictions on contact with inmates were still lax, and in the 1980s, Manson gave four interviews, none of which improved his public image or chances of parole. The first, an interview with Tom Snyder that aired in June 1981 on NBC's *The Tomorrow Show*,[63] was recorded at California Medical

Facility in Vacaville and features Manson with an unmistakable swastika tattoo on his forehead. In March 1986, Charlie Rose interviewed Manson for CBS News *Nightwatch* at San Quentin, winning the Emmy award for best national news interview.[64] In 1988, Geraldo Rivera interviewed Manson for his prime-time special on Satanism.[65] And in 1989, Nikolas Schreck interviewed Manson for his documentary *Charles Manson Superstar,* where he concluded that Manson was not insane, but merely acting out his frustrations.[66]

Against the backdrop of solid, unchanging public opinion against Manson and his followers, a surprising minor news item appeared on page 30 of the *San Francisco Chronicle* in May 1986. Steve (Clem) Grogan, a "former Charles Manson follower [had] been paroled and [was] working as a house painter after serving 14 years in prison for fatally stabbing a Hollywood stunt man." Grogan, who had been convicted of murdering Donald "Shorty" Shea with Bruce Davis, "[had been] released November 19[, 1985] from the California Medical Center at Vacaville and has been living in the San Fernando Valley with his family, state prison officials said Wednesday." The article did not report Grogan's address, but assured readers that "it [was] not in the Chatsworth area, where Shea was killed and buried on Aug. 27, 1969."[67] The article also reported that Grogan, a former drug user, visited his parole agent weekly and had passed drug tests.

That the release of a Manson family member did not evoke furor is perhaps understandable in light of the special circumstances. Grogan was presented by Vincent Bugliosi in *Helter Skelter* as a very minor participant of limited intelligence, evoking less punitive zeal from the prosecutorial team. His death sentence was not commuted by *Anderson* but rather reduced by a judge, who found that Grogan "was too stupid and too hopped on drugs to decide anything on his own."[68] Moreover, Grogan's parole was the result of his cooperation: in 1985, he had led the authorities to Shea's burial site.[69] Grogan remains the only Manson family murderer to have been paroled.

The politicization of the parole process, with the Manson cases as a perpetual cautionary tale, continued in 1988, when California voters approved Proposition 89, which shifted the final parole decision power from the Board to the governor—an additional layer of review required by only two other states.[70] The proposition amended the California Constitution to allow the governor to "affirm, modify, or reverse the decision of the parole authority on the basis of the same factors which the parole authority is required to consider."[71]

Even prior to the initiative's passage by a 55 percent majority, the governor was not without power: his authority extended to offering pardons and commutations. The animus behind the initiative was expressly punitive and calculated to allow governors to exercise their authority in the opposite direction. Supporters of the initiative, lawmakers and prosecutors, explicitly and extensively relied on redball crimes, including those of the Manson Family and other members of the class of '72 as the raison d'être for the initiative. The point of departure was Governor George Deukmejian's unsuccessful effort to block the parole of William Archie Fain and the need to "correct that court decision by expressly giving the Governor the power to block the early release of convicted murderers." The voter information guide's argument for the proposition argued that current law did not "protect the public," that "first-degree murderers who were paroled last year averaged less than 14 years in state prison," and that "in the next three years, over 500 convicted killers are due for parole hearings and possible release, including . . . Manson Family followers Tex Watson, Bobby Beausoliel [sic], Leslie Van Houten and Patricia Krenwinkle [sic]." Proponents presented the proposition as a restoration of balance: "The procedural safeguards of the system are designed to protect defendants. The Governor can act on behalf of more lenient treatment of convicted criminals. We believe the state's top elected official should also be given the power to protect the public from the early release of still dangerous killers."[72]

This emotional appeal contrasts with the opponents' argument, written by the Prisoners' Rights Union, echoing the professionalism-versus-emotion debate over determinate sentencing. The opponents warned about unnecessary politicization and hailed the professional skills of the Board. They reminded the public that the governor "will not have any different information than his nine-member parole board would have had. It will simply allow him to grant or deny a parole date when it is politically expedient." They also sought to correct the factual inaccuracy regarding Fain's release, explaining that the proposed initiative "would have made no difference in the William Fain case. The Governor tried to block Fain's parole years after his parole date was granted by the Board of Prison Terms." The opposition expressed confidence in the Board's professionalism: "The Board of Prison Terms commissioners are prosecutors, sheriffs, police officers, and probation officers. They represent hundreds of years of experience in law enforcement. Their main job is to protect the public. If they give a parole date it is only when all doubt has been removed. Any question about the advisability of a parole date is cause for them to take it away. Proposition 89 will only politicize the parole process."[73]

Implied in the opponents' argument is evidence of the professional shift that the Board had undergone. By the 1980s, the Board was composed of commissioners from law enforcement backgrounds—correctional officers, police officers, sheriffs, or prosecutors. Such a Board would already be fairly cautious about releases, and the passage of Proposition 89 meant that controversial decisions to grant parole would be reversed. Media coverage of a governor's decision to reverse a parole grant would, naturally, present the governor as responsive to the public concerns and would shed a negative light on the overly permissive Board.

Ironically, the odds of release on parole for high-profile inmates decreased further just as the inmates' public presence might have rendered them worthier of parole. In 1989, Susan Atkins published her memoir, *Child of Satan, Child of God,* documenting her journey to evangelical Christianity with the support of fellow born-again Christian Bruce Davis.[74] Her subsequent book, *The Myth of Helter Skelter,* was written with her husband James Whitehouse, a Harvard-educated attorney who represented her at the hearings.[75] Charles "Tex" Watson's *Will You Die For Me?,* reflecting his own religious conversion, appeared in 1978,[76] and a following book, *Manson's Right-Hand Man Speaks Out,* also relied heavily on religious themes.[77] By contrast to Manson's scandalous media appearances in the 1980s, his followers' forays into the news were few and universally disavowed their former mentor. In 2002, Leslie Van Houten appeared on CNN's *Larry King Live.*[78] She called Manson "an opportunist of the cruelest, most vicious kind." She also accepted blame for her role in the LaBianca murders. Similarly, in 2004, Charles "Tex" Watson, who once called himself Charles Manson's "lieutenant for killing,"[79] referred to Manson in a radio interview as "manipulative" but added, "I take full responsibility for my ignorance, lack of identity, emptiness and choices in life, which left me prey to his deceptive plan. My actions were my own."[80]

These repudiations and public expressions of accountability, however, would not win the day for Manson's followers. Another legal development was to impact their parole schedule.

CRYSTALLIZING "LIFE DE FACTO": MARSY'S LAW AND THE TRIUMPH OF THE TATE FAMILY

In 2008, California voters approved Proposition 8, a "victims' bill of rights," Also known as Marsy's Law, the proposition bore the name of Marsy

Nicholas, a twenty-three-year-old college senior murdered by her ex-boy-friend Kerry Conley in 1983.[81]

The transformation of the Nicholas family's tragedy into punitive law is emblematic of California's political culture and of the power of the victims' rights movement. Marsy's brother Henry became a billionaire tech entrepreneur, injecting over $4.8 million of his own fortune into the political war to advance Marsy's Law.[82] His impetus stemmed from the cruel taunting to which Marsy's murderer subjected the family: in a newspaper interview, he recalled that the murderer stalked his mother in the supermarket, "staring her down. He would also drive around our neighborhood in a convertible, flaunting."[83] Conley was later convicted and sentenced to life with the possibility of parole, and the Nicholas family made the drive to Soledad for each of his parole hearings.[84]

Henry Nicholas channeled his grief and frustration into a victims' bill of rights that largely replicated its 1982 legislative predecessor. The novelty was in its particular focus on the parole process; its stated purpose was "to spare homicide victims the ordeal of prolonged and unnecessary suffering, and to stop the waste of millions of taxpayer dollars, by eliminating parole hearings in which there is no likelihood a murderer will be paroled."[85] In addition, its numerous changes to victims' rights were designed to significantly influence the hearing process. For example, Marsy's Law required the Board "to admit the prior recorded or memorialized testimony or statement of victims when making the decision to grant or deny," and directed the Board "to consider the views and interests of the victim when setting deferral periods for inmates denied parole."[86]

Capturing over 53 percent of the California vote[87] with promises of victim participation, Marsy's Law did not yield substantial benefits to victims. Pursuant to the 1982 bill and long-standing county practices and largely unbeknownst to the voters, many prosecutorial offices in California already had a victim advocate on staff and practically provided these rights before Marsy's Law was enacted.[88] Laura Richardson's 2011 study of the impact of Marsy's Law found inconclusive evidence that the bill had increased victim participation at parole hearings, and no conclusive evidence that the law had impacted the quality of victim participation at parole hearings.[89]

What the law *did* do was alter the framework for parole deferrals—a punitive proposal marketed as a victims' rights one.[90] The former statute directed commissioners to deny parole for only one year, reserving the option for the Board to deny parole for up to five years if it concluded that "it was not reasonable to expect that parole would be granted at a hearing during the following years."[91] The statute further presumed that the Board would "adopt procedures that relate to the criteria for setting the hearing between two and five years, thereby signaling that the legislature intended for the decision to set a denial period to be a separate and additional choice from the decision to deny or grant parole."[92] But now, the Board would be required to disassemble these two decisions and focus on the "public and victim's safety" as the "overriding consideration, not simply when the inmate will be rehabilitated." Most importantly—and least related to victims' rights—Marsy's Law extended the wait periods between hearings, even for low-risk defendants, with each denial setting a presumption of denial for fifteen years before the next hearing, unless "the [Board] finds by clear and convincing evidence that the criteria relevant to the setting of parole release dates . . . are such that consideration of the public and victim's safety" does not warrant such an extended deferral period.[93] Laura Richardson's aforementioned study analyzed 211 randomly selected parole hearing transcripts in California both before and after Marsy's Law's implementation and found that the initiative's passage nearly doubled the period set by the Parole Board between parole hearings.[94]

By 2009, the Tate family's battle to keep the Manson Family members incarcerated was victorious. Speaking to CNN, Debra Tate explained that the slayings were "so vicious, so inhumane, so depraved, that there is no turning back. . . . The 'Manson Family' murderers are sociopaths, and from that, they can never be rehabilitated. . . . They should all stay right where they are—in prison—until they die. There will never be true justice for my sister Sharon and the other victims of the 'Manson Family.' Keeping the murderers in prison is the least we, as a society who values justice, can do."[95]

Indeed, Susan Atkins's last parole hearing confirmed that the Board shared Tate's perspective. By then, Atkins was suffering from a brain tumor and was wheeled into the hearing room on a gurney, immobile and nonresponsive; her husband helped her deliver the Twenty-Third Psalm for her statement.[96] Debra Tate asked the Board not to free Atkins, stating, "There has never been any hate in my heart for these people. I am incapable of hating. I commend them—always have commended them—for their good deeds that they have managed to accomplish within the walls of confinement. However, I do believe that the death of my sister, my nephew—which would be turning 40 years old right now, this week—is not an irrelevant cause." The Board denied Atkins's request.[97] At the time of her death, she was California's longest-serving female inmate. In the Tate family memoir, Brie Tate, Sharon

Tate's niece, writes: "While my heart aches for any suffering human being, I forced myself to look away from photos of the pathetic and dying Susan Atkins and remember the young and vibrant Atkins who with callous disregard unjustly murdered eight people and watched them beg for their lives, fall down into their own blood, and die without an ounce of dignity. The parole board must have agreed because at her last hearing in 2009, with full knowledge that she had only months to live, they gave her a three-year denial."[98] She adds: "I believe that with the final court denial of Susan Atkins's plea for compassionate release from prison, it's a safe bet that the rest of Sharon's killers will never leave prison alive. The parole hearings will continue, but I believe that the need to attend those hearings to give a victim's impact statement has finally been laid to rest with my mother's generation. If that situation changes, you can be certain that I will be the first one in line to oppose their release because I figure I'm Nana's and then some."[99]

Marsy's Law and its aftermath—a parole denial of a terminally ill woman on her deathbed—reflect not only the triumph of the victims' rights movement. They reflect the moment in California's correctional history in which the three harshest sentences in the state's penal system—death, life without parole, and life with parole—converged into a virtually indistinguishable regime of extreme incarceration. The process that began with the outcry over the suspension of the death penalty came to its logical conclusion. The California correctional apparatus was now one in which not every single lifer would die in prison, but the Board could allow that to occur with impunity, even for inmates who posed no risk at all to public safety.

Each step on the journey toward the trifecta of extreme punishment was heavily driven by the emotional response to redball crimes. The series of crimes committed in 1969, their details so horrifying that they shook the nation, resurfaced whenever new legislation further politicized the process and placed furor and fear over precaution and professionalism. The first of the perpetrators to die did so behind bars, and the possibility of release, already made remote by years of fear-driven voter initiative process, vanished with her last breath.

THREE

The Triumph of Helter Skelter

HOW THE MANSON FAMILY CASES CAME
TO REPRESENT THE SUI GENERIS
ULTIMATE EVIL

> O nobly-born, if thou dost not now recognize thine own
> thought—forms, whatever of meditation or of devotion thou
> mayst have performed while in the human world—if thou hast
> not met with this present teaching—the lights will daunt thee,
> the sounds will awe thee, and the rays will terrify thee.
>
> *The Tibetan Book of the Dead*

The Museum of Death in New Orleans is located in a quiet corner of
Dauphine Street.[1] The entrance features merchandise and prints emblazoned
with skulls and bones. In the museum's first room is a reclining human skeleton, its left foot in the mouth of an alligator skeleton, with nearby taxidermy
mounts of various animals on display.

Not much prepares me for the second room, shielded from the eye by
a white curtain. It amounts to what can only be described as a shrine to
serial killers. Twenty-six hand-drawn posters, listed from A to Z, depict
serial killers, accompanied by nursery rhymes about their crimes. Displayed
below, on the walls and in a glass cabinet, are letters written by the featured
killers to friends and admirers, professing love, asking for porn. The letter *M*
is devoted to Manson, who is drawn with Susan Atkins and Leslie van
Houten by his side. The nursery rhyme reads, "M is for Manson, from
Charlie's clan, with Leslie, Cupid, and Sadie, too; no creepy crawling in the
cells."

About a sixth of the entire collection is devoted to the Manson murders.
Toward the end of the exhibit, a large wall is covered in photos from the Cielo
Drive murder scene, photos from the trial, and newspaper headlines, accompanied by large posters for the film *Beyond Helter Skelter,* "guaranteed to
never be shown on TV." Artifacts connecting the defendants to demonic

cults and souvenirs from prison, as well as pamphlets compiled by Manson fans portraying him as an innocent political prisoner, are in abundance.

Museum exhibits, like books, movies, and conversations, tell stories; narratives, Roland Barthes tells us, are "present at all times, in all places, in all societies."[2] The story I was told at the Museum of Death echoed the authoritative narrative of the Manson crimes: bizarre, gruesome murders of strangers committed in service of an outlandish ideology by psychopathic monsters. Given the prevalence of this narrative, the considerable impact of the Manson cases on the landscape of extreme punishment in California is understandable.

But any narrative is only "one way of recounting past events,"[3] a combination of content and structural conventions.[4] It is a way of arranging facts into a coherent story that allows us to make sense of a series of events.[5] Most importantly, a narrative gives voice to its particular narrator, thus exposing the absence of a single, objectively apprehended truth.[6] Patricia Ewick and Susan Silbey argue that narratives can be strategic, deployed in the service of legal and social goals, and the context of the situation might dictate which narratives will be successful in a legal setting.[7] Ewick and Silbey distinguish between hegemonic and subversive stories. In the former, "the structure, the content, and the performance of stories as they are defined and regulated within social settings often articulate and reproduce existing ideologies and hegemonic relations of power and inequality." Hegemonic stories are further enhanced by the narrative's ability to colonize social consciousness.[8] By contrast, subversive narratives root the experiences they relate in the context of the structural and institutional world, particularly structural inequalities and disempowerment.[9] The tension between hegemonic and subversive stories can often explain the success or failure of a narrative either in the narrow sense of a legal victory or defeat or in the broader sense of public acceptability.

In the context of the Manson family murders, the juxtaposition of hegemonic and subversive narratives can explain how one narrative, which I refer to as the "Helter Skelter" narrative, came to prevail over the public and legal discourse of the crime. As this chapter shows, a powerful narrator—prosecutor Vincent Bugliosi—deployed this narrative for strategic legal purpose, and as early as 1971 established hegemony over the conversation that would turn the crimes into sui generis horror tales. In the process, two complementary but subversive stories of the murder, which I refer to as the "cult" and the "common-criminals" narratives, became muted and subsumed in the legal and cultural chatter about the cases. The triumph of the Helter Skelter narrative had a circular effect: as these cases, perceived through the Helter Skelter lens, played a pivotal role in shaping California's extreme-punishment trifecta, they were shaped by the same trifecta in return, setting the stage for decades of unforgiving parole processes.

THE HELTER SKELTER NARRATIVE

The quintessential narrator of the Manson Family crimes is prosecutor Vincent Bugliosi, whose bestselling memoir *Helter Skelter* is widely regarded as the authoritative account of the crimes.[10] Bugliosi is the protagonist of his own narrative, which lends him considerable authority, and his story heavily relies on the trope of the triumph of good over evil after a protracted uphill battle.

After describing the murder scenes and police bafflement about the perpetrators, Bugliosi dramatically reveals how he uncovered the motive for the murder through a conversation with two young Manson disciples. The girls explained that Manson, inspired by the Beatles' song "Helter Skelter," instructed his disciples to commit grisly murders and craft the crime scene in a way that would incite a race war: "Judgment Day, Armageddon, Helter Skelter—to Manson they were one and the same, a racial holocaust which would see the black man emerge triumphant. . . . That Manson foresaw a war between the blacks and the whites was not fantastic. Many people believe that such a war may someday occur. What was fantastic was that he believed he could personally start that war himself—that by making it look as if blacks had murdered the seven Caucasian victims he could turn the white community against the black community."[11] According to Bugliosi, Manson inculcated his followers in the race-war story, assuring them that, after the blacks killed all the whites, they would turn to Manson as their leader. Much of the military organization of the Family around that time—acquiring dune buggies and looking for hiding places—was aimed at preparing for this apocalyptic scenario. Since Helter Skelter failed to materialize, Manson plotted the murders, as well as the writings on the murder scene, to cast blame on blacks so as to hasten its arrival.

Bugliosi openly admits that he strategically chose to highlight his narrative. He was, after all, a prosecutor in search of a theory of criminal culpability. The Tate-LaBianca murders presented him with two legal difficulties. First, Manson himself was not present when the murders took place (though he arguably was on the scene before the murders occurred, tying up the victims, as he had been at Gary Hinman's residence before his homicide). To obtain a conviction, Bugliosi would have to convince the jury that Manson was the mastermind behind the murders, contrary to the defense's argument that Manson's followers committed the crime on their own, without his knowledge. That would require a strong showing of Manson's powerful hold over the perpetrators' will and his hand in planning the murders. On the other hand, Bugliosi could not afford to present the followers as mindless robots ordered around. In that respect, he was somewhat aided by the fact that knowledge about cults, mind control, and brainwashing was not part of the zeitgeist in 1971; however, Bugliosi was determined to seek the death penalty for all defendants, and that called for proof of premeditation on their part. The doctrine of felony murder was not as developed.

Bugliosi is open about his conscious choice of the Helter Skelter narrative. In this section, he reveals his rejection of what he terms a "secondary motive" involving musical producer Terry Melcher, who refused to offer Manson a contract after auditioning him. But this motive would not suffice, as it would portray Manson and his disciples in a more ordinary light:

> We knew there was at least one secondary motive for the Tate murders. As Susan Atkins put it in the Caballero tape, "the reason Charlie picked that house was to instill fear into Terry Melcher because Terry had given us his word on a few things and never came through with them." But this was obviously not the primary motive, since, according to Gregg Jakobson, Manson knew that Melcher was no longer living at 10050 Cielo Drive.
>
> All the evidence we'd assembled thus far, I felt, pointed to one primary motive: Helter Skelter. It was far out, but then so were the murders themselves. It was admittedly bizarre, but from the first moment I was assigned to the case, I'd felt that for murders as bizarre as these the motive itself would have to be almost equally strange, not something you'd find within the pages of a textbook on police science.[12]

In presenting the crimes as stemming from a bizarre, apocalyptic motive, Bugliosi achieved another important goal. He made Manson and his followers into sui generis, otherworldly characters, with a peculiar and universally unacceptable perspective on life. In the aftermath of the race riots of the late 1960s, a deliberate effort on the part of white people to start a race war using blacks as scapegoats would have been utterly excoriated.

Indeed, Bugliosi's demonology extended not only to Manson himself, but also to his female followers. His descriptions of the women and men differ dramatically. In his accounts of conversing with Paul Watkins and Juan Flynn, he is portrayed having reasonable conversations with reasonable, sensible people. Even Tex Watson, presented as having feigned insanity, eventually sees reason. By contrast, the women are presented as dreamlike, floaty, seemingly unaware of the circumstances, their sunny demeanor eerily contrasting with their unspeakable deeds. The miniseries *Helter Skelter* confirmed and intensified this portrayal. The dramatic cinematography and music amplified the terrifying, otherworldly portrayals of Manson, Atkins, Krenwinkel and Van Houten; the actor portraying Manson often opened his eyes wide, as in the iconic depictions of Manson at his most demonic.

Following swiftly in the footsteps of *Helter Skelter* was Ed Sanders's book *The Family.* Sanders, a counterculture insider and former rider on Ken Kesey's famous Furthur bus, plants the Manson murders deeply in the context of various other countercultural groups but does so not to normalize them but rather to shock and titillate. He mentions Manson's prison-time acquaintance with "so-called devil worshippers,"[13] as well as his re-creation of a crucifixion ceremony in which "Charlie would put himself on a cross. And . . . a girl would kneel at the foot of the cross and . . . he would moan, cry out as though he was being crucified, and . . . they would also sacrifice animals and drink their blood as a fertility rite. Oo-ee-oo."[14] Sanders mentions another cult, The Fountain, as the inspiration for these crucifixion scenes.[15] One story, quoted as "internally consistent" with known facts, tells of "the involvement of Manson with a 'death cult'" in the summer and fall of 1968 that "operated out of the notorious Waller Street Devil House in the Haight District."[16] And, like Bugliosi, Sanders implies Family involvement with additional murders.[17]

A similar scandalous revelation is available in *Manson, Sinatra and Me,* the tell-all memoir of Virginia Graham, the inmate who first heard Atkins's confessions in the Sybil Brand Institute. In the book, Graham, a Hollywood brothel madame, reveals her liaisons with movie stars and oil magnates. Her self-professed worldliness fails her when she hears Susan's confessions:

> For the next few days, Susan kept referring to the leader as Him and finally she told me that his name was Charlie. She said that Charlie had given her the name "Sadie Glutz" and that he was a beautiful person with God-like qualities, and she spoke of him as Jesus Christ. She talked about life at the ranch

and how at night around a campfire Charlie would preach to them about the plans he had to lead them to better lives.

She said that he had been in several prisons and that those experiences had only made him stronger. Everyone at the ranch lived under Charlie's orders—nobody ever questioned his authority. He was their leader—their father.

Then she told me how he would often put himself on a cross and "we would all kneel before him "and then very quietly she added, "Charlie is our love. He is Jesus Christ!"

At that moment I remember saying to myself, "You are crazy, Sadie!"[18]

Graham expresses her shock clearly, delineating clear lines between Atkins and her horrible deeds and the other people she meets in prison, made even more demonic by her sweet, hippie affect:

By this time my knees were trembling, and I kept trying to put this sweet looking hippie together with the horror she was relating to me. But Susan was still caught up in her grisly story, chatting amiably and hurrying on as if she were some high school girl telling another girl about the first time a boy put his hand under her dress. She also kept watching me for a reaction.[19] . . .

"Hey, dig this:" Susan said to me. "You know that beautiful cat I was telling you about the other day? Well, dig on this, listen carefully now. His last name is Manson. Think about it. M-A-N-S-O-N. Man's son, isn't that fantastic? He's so . . . " and she made a worshipful hand gesture. . . . She had told me how he was going to take the Family to a hole in the center of Death Valley that only he could find. A civilization was living there, solely in wait for the Manson Family to come and lead it. There would be a world revolution she said, and only their underground people would be safe."[20]

Graham's narrative and Bugliosi's reaffirm and augment each other: "Vincent Bugliosi, the district attorney who prosecuted the killers said to me, 'It's amazing—this whole case. Your chance of being where you were was a million to one.' He said the more he investigated the more bizarre it became."[21]

It is, of course, not surprising that some of the strongest affirmations of the Helter Skelter narrative come from the family members of the murder victims. Brie Tate and Alisa Statman's *Restless Souls* tells the story of the trials from the perspective of the Tate family. They quote from Bugliosi's opening statement:

"The evidence will show that one of Manson's principal motives for the Tate/LaBianca murders was to ignite Helter Skelter. In other words, to start the black-white revolution by making it look like the black people had murdered the five Tate victims and Mr. and Mrs. LaBianca. Thereby causing the white community to turn against the black man, and ultimately lead to a civil war between blacks and whites, a war Manson foresaw the black man winning.

"Manson envisioned that the black people, once they destroyed off the white race and assumed the reins of power, would be unable to handle the reins because of inexperience and would have to turn over the reins to those white people who had escaped from Helter Skelter. That is, turn over the reins to Manson and his followers."[22]

To the victims, one particularly demonic and gruesome aspect of the murders was the gender of some of the perpetrators. Tate's father is quoted in *Restless Souls:* "On another day, I entered the courthouse men's room still thinking about Virginia Graham's testimony. She recounted Susan Atkins' confession in which Atkins provided details of how she'd killed Sharon. I'd always believed that my gentle disposition made it impossible for me to ever raise a hand to a woman. But Atkins was doing a great job challenging that belief. Given the opportunity, I wouldn't have hesitated to make her suffer tenfold for what she did to my baby."[23]

The narrators of *Restless Souls* are heavily invested in the Helter Skelter narrative for important strategic reasons. The portions of the book that are narrated by Doris Tate see her initiate a series of meetings between victims and murderers (but not the murderers of her daughter). Later, Debra Tate will describe her own assistance to parolees (but not the parole candidates who murdered her sister) in her victim impact statements. By highlighting a narrative that places these murders in a class of their own, the Tate family members present themselves as reasonable, compassionate people and at the same time staunch objectors to the murderers' release.

Manson's fans and those who seek to capitalize on his crimes perpetuate the Helter Skelter narrative in true-crime books. Many of these are poorly researched, self-published works reproducing material found elsewhere.

One such example is *The Manson File*. Its opening passage is full of over-the-top jargon, presumably in an effort to demystify Manson, but actually enhancing his dark mysticism: "Charles Manson has been transmogrified by the electronic thaumaturgy of mass media into a mythic creation, a larger-than-life hieratic emblem of evil. Manson has become the favored brand name for murder and madness, the very archetype of everything the popular mind understands as anti-social, crazy and criminal. He is one of the last true heretics of our time."[24] The book delves deeply into Manson's presumed involvement in other occult and malevolent organizations, referring to him as an "occult messiah"[25] and, in the fashion of Sanders's *The Family*, connecting him to the Symbionese Liberation Army, which famously abducted Patty Hearst.[26]

A testament to the enduring power of the Helter Skelter narrative is the NBC series *Aquarius*,[27] a period police procedural featuring a smorgasbord of 1960s culture: revolutionary characters, the Vietnam War, the Nation of Islam, homophobia, closet homosexuality, and the early days of second-wave feminism. The show's story arc revolves around the Manson Family, and many of its characters—such as Manson, Mary, Sadie, and Katie—are fictionalized versions of real people. The first episode introduces Manson as a diabolical character through his charm and charisma, predatory behavior, grandiosity, mystical talk, and "pull" with the Los Angeles upper crust. The following episodes see Manson enchanting girls with two-bit New Age speeches and then controlling and domineering them. Manson's origin story in the series is offered as explanation for these traits: "I learned there and then," he says of his mother's abandonment, "that it's better to be the thing people are afraid of than to be afraid." But far from humanizing him, the story is merely background for his terrifying violence toward the women, particularly Mary, which is shown in explicit and grisly detail. Moreover, the show supplements the real events with utterly fictional crimes that almost "out-Manson" Manson. In one of these, an encounter with his mother ends with Manson selling her to the Straight Satans. In another, Mary Bronner gives birth to a dead son, and Sadie somehow procures a live one for her to replace him, partly to curry favor with Manson. Whether the fictional embellishments add to Manson's demonic image or merely diminish the show's credibility, they certainly support the Helter Skelter narrative and show its continuing appeal.

THE CULT NARRATIVE

As the Helter Skelter narrative came to hegemonic prominence, a subversive narrative, which focused on Manson's young female followers, began to emerge. Importantly, this narrative—the cult narrative—converges with the Helter Skelter narrative in portraying Manson as a toxic, charismatic, authoritarian figure; the difference lies in the cult narrative's focus on the followers, particularly the women; it sheds a mitigating light on their culpability because of Manson's control over them. The early roots of the cult narrative lie in Leslie Van Houten's diary from her Spahn Ranch days, which tells of her enthusiasm in finding a family, people who felt "together" and comfortable where they were, and her pleasure in communitarian eating, playing, and lovemaking. Van Houten's intelligence and conventional beauty make her a sympathetic narrator, and it is no coincidence that her likeness tends to appear on the cover of cult narrative books.

The most reliable narrator of the cult story is Karlene Faith, who, in the early 1970s, conducted research on incarcerated women as a graduate student at the University of California, Santa Cruz.[28] The warden, faced with the commutation of the Manson girls' sentences, asked Faith to serve as their tutor. Faith, who was more invested in working with poor women of color, had little interest in the girls, but reluctantly agreed. For several years, she maintained a strong friendship with the three girls, who were held in isolation at a remote unit in the prison.

Faith's subversive narrative of the crime directly undermines Bugliosi's hegemonic narrative, explicating it as biased and self-serving:

> It was a best-seller, and is still in print today, replete with inaccuracies due to the defendants' false testimony in court and their own propagation of sensationalized myths. One reviewer describes this book as a "morality tale of the highest order, with the crusading prosecutor battling a demonic Manson on one hand and the bumbling of the Los Angeles Police Department (LAPD) on the other." One of Manson's messages, like St. Augustine's, was that he (and everyone) represented the perfect dialectic of God and the Devil, life and death, good and evil, sacred and profane. The symbolism was perfectly geared to a Hollywood sensibility. Through the lenses of the prosecutor, a woefully tragic set of murders became mythic owing to their perversely formulaic entertainment value. Bugliosi went on to oversee the 1976 CBS-TV version of his story, and to make $2,500 per speech (a large sum at the time) on the lecture circuit. The case brought him a celebrity career, but in the process he compromised his reputation as a serious attorney, and his lost a political bid for public office.[29]

By contrast, Faith pays attention to her charges, marveling at the incongruence between their innocence and the horrific acts in which they participated: "I appreciated their talk because I wanted to understand it. I wondered for a time if they had actually been involved in the murders at all, if the whole thing was someone else's doing, and the women were sacrificing themselves as martyrs to their faith in Charles Manson. In effect, that is what happened, even though they were physically present and tried very hard to be good soldiers."[30]

Confronted with her charges' childlike innocence and inability to shake Manson's influence, Faith attributes their attitude to a subversion of their free will. She identifies them as cult members that have been brainwashed: "Cults accomplish brainwashing in several ways. Initially, fasting, meditation, and any form of sensory deprivation result in physiological changes that affect perception. These changes may have positive spiritual effects but they may negatively affect the individual's practical judgment. Certain neurological brain patterns commonly occur among those converted to cults.... Poor diet, erratic sleep patterns, giving sex on demand, coping with sexually transmitted diseases, physical stresses, drugs, and isolation from the world coupled with nonstop Manson influence would certainly have weakened their judgment."[31]

More confirmation of the cult narrative, complete with a self-absorbed and disturbing undercurrent of sexual desirability, is found in Peter Chiaramonte's 2015 memoir *No Journey's End*. Chiaramonte, a Canadian professor of education, is also an unreliable narrator: the book is a tell-all narrative of his love affair with Van Houten in the course of her appeal and retrial, marketed under the slogan "the book Van Houten's attorneys don't want you to read."[32] Chiaramonte, who became fascinated with Van Houten after reading Bugliosi's book, began corresponding with her and described the process of her conversion into a Manson follower: "When Manson first met the pretty brunette Beausoleil brought with him this time, he dropped what he was doing to study her closely. Charlie had plenty of experience handling runaway teenaged girls like Leslie before. First, he tacitly implied he possessed insight into all of her lonely disaffections. For example, he used a common theatrical device to mirror her moods. By copying each changing expression or gesture Leslie made, Manson intended to show how well he could identify what she was thinking and feeling. That's why they call guys like him 'con artist.'"[33] Chiaramonte's subversive narrative identifies inconsistencies in Bugliosi's theory of the murders, asking, "Why was this man so intent on reducing them all to pawns of Charlie Manson with no will of their own and then equally intent on reconstructing them as mindful, capable individuals acting out of their own volition? Bugliosi seemed as nuts as the rest of them."[34]

Faith and Chiaramonte evoke a language beyond leader and followers; they rely on notions of cults and mind control, which were not part of the cultural lexicon during the original trials. This is not to say that cults were not in existence during Manson's heyday; on the contrary, in the late 1960s the Haight-Ashbury was teeming with self-styled gurus and their devoted followers. Nor was Manson unique in his hodgepodge of pseudo-Asian philosophy and apocalyptic prophecies; he picked these up from the fertile petri dish of similar ideas that were floating about San Francisco at the time of his release from prison. But the public was slow to recognize the power of charismatic leaders to subjugate and command obedience.

The idea of "brainwashing"—a subversion of a Chinese term—was connected in the public imagination to Communism and to the Korean War.[35] In 1951, journalist Edward Hunter wrote a book first describing brainwashing as "a process of abrupt attitudinal change that was used in the People's Republic of China."[36] The 1962 film *The Manchurian Candidate,* based on Richard Condon's 1959 novel, told the story of an American prisoner of war "programmed" by his Korean captors to assassinate on command upon his release, and puppeteered by his mother, a covert Communist agent.[37] The novel and film exploited a rich array of contemporary tropes: fear of communism as well as of powerful women on the political stage. Brainwashing was thus regarded as an extraneous technique, used by foreign enemies, and was not at the time linked to the many experiments in communal life, in California and nationwide.[38] Some doubters of the hippie lifestyle were nonetheless impressed with their selflessness and willingness to share their property and resources,[39] which were as foreign to the mainstream American ethos as their use of hallucinogens.[40] But while young participants in these countercultural communes and groups were fascinated with this new way of life, their parents gradually grew less enthusiastic.

It is perhaps not surprising that the push to "import" the notions of cults, brainwashing, and mind control, into the domestic scene, happened not in the context of home-grown groups like the Manson "family" but in the context of one imported from Korea: the Moonies, named after their leader, Korean priest Kyung-See Moon. As Moon gained young American followers, books that familiarized their parents with the cult's beliefs and practices warned of the followers' subjugation, even as they soothed the parents' anxiety about their children's vegetarian diets.[41] Moonies were not the only source of concern. Several Christian Evangelical cults operated in California at the time, including the notorious Alamo Christian Foundation. These groups, especially their isolationist stance toward relatives of their followers, were a source of increasing concern among parents of the disciples.

It was this parental concern and pressure that finally broke ground with the California legislature. On August 24, 1974, the California Senate's Select Committee on Children and Youth held a hearing on "the impact of cults on today's youth."[42] The committee chair, Mervyn Dymally,[43] addressed "concerned citizens" by explaining the difficulty to distinguish between "groups of individuals democratically joined together to seek a better way" and "authoritarian groups demanding total mindless obedience and a total break with family, friends and previously held beliefs." As Dymally remarked, the committee was about to embark on the search for a delicate balance:

> Ours is a society in which freedom to practice one's religious beliefs is guaranteed—no matter how far-out, weird or unconventional that belief may seem to the majority. Yet how far can the demands of blind obedience in the name of religion go, before such demands in effect deny the individual the very religious freedom that he is guaranteed by the Constitution? How far can religious practices go before they infringe on the other freedoms which all are guaranteed? Is there a feasible way to decide what on the one hand is the advocating of religious belief and on the other, becomes brainwashing?
> Should the legislature, law enforcement and other governmental agencies be taking a harder look at such groups, since some of the practices reported and methods used in such groups raise disturbing questions?[44]

Dymally chose to tread lightly, stressing that the hearing would yield no legislative action or policy consequences. The goal of the hearing, he explained, was to hear both sides of the controversy; if a real threat to the youth would be detected, the hearing would identify it, and if not, it would "put our minds at ease."[45]

The committee heard a diverse range of opinions. Some speakers were representatives of new religions arguing that "if a child willingly on his own is allowed to join a group, take what is good for him, reject what he feels is not good for him, and then walk out, I see nothing wrong with it personally."[46] Others, relatives of cult members and former members, told harrowing stories of squalor and neglect.[47] One family member testified that she had initiated legal proceedings against a cult, leading to threats and even a beating by her daughter and another cult member when she visited the group; she stated, "I love my daughter and would like to see her out of a prison environment, believing whatever she chooses and getting her whatever help is necessary in order to live a normal existence—to be able to think for herself."[48]

One notable witness was Ted Patrick, the pioneer of "cult deprogramming," whose extreme actions to remove young adults from cults against their will brought him admiration from the parents as well as run-ins with the law. Patrick voiced the parents' frustration ("no one will listen to us") and turned the constitutional-freedom argument on its head: "Now, freedom of religion—this is what we are fighting for. I will fight and die and do anything to defend those rights, the freedom of religion. But these victims do not have freedom. Anytime a person destroys your free will, your mind to think, and makes a dummy out of you, you don't have a free will. The only thing we do is restore their free will."[49] Some of Patrick's descriptions of charismatic leaders strongly evoke Manson's leadership style: "They can be singing or playing a guitar and the only thing they want you to do is look them straight in the eyes for five or ten minutes and you believe everything and go with these people."[50] At one point, he explicitly refers to the Manson case:

> [Young people in cults] hate their parents. In destroying a person's mind, they destroy the family influence. They hate their parent's guts. You can ask anybody who has been deprogrammed, "If your leader would have told you to kill your parents, would you have killed your parents?" Every last one of them say, "I would have killed my parents or anyone else." It is identical . . . the same as the Manson Family. The Manson Family shouldn't have been convicted. Manson should have been hung! But the Manson Family should be out of jail because they are innocent as anyone in this room, because they were under his mind control, they had all his books . . . they knew where he learned this mind control, in prison. They even say he had the inmates brainwashed, but they made no mention in the trial of Manson.[51]

Throughout the hearing, cult opponents received loud and lengthy applause, which Dymally tried to cut short for fear of appearing biased. He repeatedly attempted to clarify the committee's bipartisan status ("We don't want the committee to be used for any forum to criticize any single group") and to remind the parents that "the question of over 18 leads to some very serious problems for us."[52] An audience member's request to bring the testimonies before a grand jury would present, according to Dymally, "an impossible problem for the legislature."[53] These careful words did little to assuage the frustrated parents and deprogrammers, who felt that they faced an uphill battle in bringing the problem of brainwashing and cults to the attention of policy makers.

Were these concerns overblown? David Bromley and Anton Shupe argue that the brainwashing metaphor was marshaled to usher a moral panic about cults.[54] Moral panic, which has been studied in the context of public upheavals against alcohol,[55] witchcraft,[56] drunk driving,[57] or adolescent skirmishes, refers to a situation in which "a condition, episode, person or group of persons emerges to become defined as a threat to societal values and interests,"[58] which then produces a disproportionately hostile social reaction.[59] Some of the anti-cult concerns, such as the worry about vegetarian diets, seem quaint and overblown now, but even by Bromley and Shupe's own account, families were understandably disturbed by their loved ones' extreme lifestyle changes, alienation from family members, and dramatic changes in character.[60]

If concerns about cults were exaggerated, perhaps it is because of the role the Manson murders played in the awakening anti-cult movement and the birth of deprogramming. This movement, according to Shupe and Bromley[61], emerged as a reaction to those murders, the Patty Hearst kidnapping, and the violence associated with the Synanon drug rehabilitation organization, together with "popular culture and folklore, from Hollywood's fright-film zombies and the innocent little girl victimized by the devil in *The Exorcist* to beliefs in demonic possession, which can be found in virtually every major religious tradition since antiquity."[62] In the spirit of this cultural fear of new religions, "the Manson Family was dubbed a cult, and Patty Hearst became an example of the kind of mindless violence that could be expected from brainwashed cult members."[63] All these "served as dramatic illustrations of the extent to which people presumably could be manipulated for anti-social purposes."[64] Moreover, even though these incidents were unrelated to each other, coupled with the later mass suicide at Jonestown, they were cited to suggest that "cultic" organization was prevalent, dangerous, and due to brain-washing.[65] Indeed, when

youthful recruits of the new religions allegedly began to manifest striking changes in demeanor, attitudes, and even personality, parents began to for-mulate explanations for these changes which drew on this imagery. At first, the psychiatric evidence collected after the Korean conflict was heavily cited; later, the testimonies of psychologists and psychiatrists as well as the accounts of apostates from the new religion were used as evidence to demonstrate that manipulative coercive procedures akin to brainwashing had been employed to effect these "undesirable" behavioral and attitudinal changes.... What the brainwashing metaphor did was to provide a secular equivalent to this archaic religious theme, reshaping it into a form more acceptable to twentieth-century rational man and documented with "scientific" evidence which would account for such radical individual changes in a fashion more consist-ent with dominant paradigms of human behavior.[66]

The Manson murders directly inspired the deprogramming profession. Shupe and Bromley describe a successful deprogramming facility, the Freedom of Thought Foundation, established in 1976 by Michael Trauscht. Trauscht, special attorney for Pima County's finance department, heard concerned parents complain about the association of their adult sons with a new religious organization called The Body. "Posing as a pair of backpacking hikers, Trauscht and a police officer located the group in the nearby Tucson Mountains where Trauscht was reportedly 'appalled' by conditions he observed at The Body's encampment. Shortly before this excursion Trauscht had been reading Vincent Bugliosi's *Helter Skelter,* an account of the Charles Manson cult, and noticed similarities between the regimented lifestyle of The Body and Manson's 'Family.'"[67]

Other cult scholars also explicitly referred to the Manson cases as influence. Harvey Cox and George Harris cite Robert Heinlein's *Stranger in a Strange Land,*[68] which heavily influenced Manson and others, as being among the books that Cox's students "were really hooked on" because they featured a transcendental form of knowledge or understanding, "in a way that we earthlings have trained ourselves not to do."[69] Jacob Needleman cites an essay by Marcia Cavell that denounces the romantic Eastern flavor of Manson's doctrine: "Guilt, as Manson says, is a figment of the imagination. . . . A lesson to be learned from the Manson cult, I think, is that dreams of heaven often pave the road to hell."[70] In an introductory essay by Edward Heenan in the same collection, the witchcraft elements of this doctrine are highlighted: "In California in 1969 actress Sharon Tate and six others died in a brutal, ritualistic murder. Later it was revealed that convicted murderer, Charles Manson, as well as his victims had been involved in the occult. As shocking as this case was, it was merely the most publicized example of the witchcraft, Satanism, and occultism that have been moving like a dark shadow over America."[71] And, for Patrick Morrow, other elements of this spirituality include rock music, and particularly "three recent major musical productions, all of which usually are considered to be dangerous and subversive antitheses to spirituality, Jesus, the Messianic calling, and Christian conversion"[72]—including the Beatles' album *Sergeant Pepper's Lonely Hearts Club Band.* Morrow does not explicitly mention "Helter Skelter," but he does refer to numerous other Beatles' songs, arguing that their alternative morality was a forerunner to the rise in apocalyptic Jesus fervor.

In *The Lure of Cults,* an anti-cult publication aimed at Christians, Ronald Enroth takes pains to distinguish cults from mainstream Christian organizations, warning that "the attempt to package, conceal, mollify, and modify their message must be viewed as just another dimension of the deception that is at the heart of all false religion."[73] Enroth's categories of these false movements include eastern mystical groups, aberrational Christian groups, psychospiritual or self-improvement groups, eclectic-syncretistic groups, and psychic-occult-astral groups. It is easy to find elements of Manson's spiritual universe in this adverse description.

Some modern versions of the cult narrative, such as Emma Cline's novel *The Girls,* highlight its gendered aspect. This fictionalized account of the Manson murders is written from the perspective of a former female disciple who escaped the cult. Evie, living an ordinary and melancholic life, is attracted to the camaraderie of the girls, who seem like "they were sure of what they were together."[74] Hungry for love and belonging, Evie is drawn to the girls, who introduce her to Russell, the Manson character. Here, Cline, writing for a 2016 readership deeply familiar with the cult lexicon, can rely on easily recognizable tropes of grooming and calculation:

> Russell had put me through a series of ritual tests. Perfected over the years that he had worked for a religious organization near Ukiah, a center that gave away food, found shelter and jobs. Attracting the thin, harried girls with partial college degrees and neglectful parents, girls with hellish bosses and dreams of nose jobs. His bread and butter. The time he spent at the center's outpost in San Francisco in the old fire station, collecting his followers. Already he'd become an expert in female sadness—a particular slump in the shoulders, a nervous rash. A subservient lilt at the end of sentences, eyelashes gone soggy from crying. Russell did the same thing to me that he did to those girls. Little tests, first. A touch on my back, a pulse of my hand. Little ways of breaking down boundaries. And how quickly he ramped it up, easing his pants to his knees. An act, I thought, calibrated to comfort young girls who were glad, at least, that it wasn't sex. Who could stay fully dressed the whole time, as if nothing out of the ordinary were happening. But maybe the strangest part—I liked it, too.[75]

Cline cleverly weaves in Russell's violence toward the girls with Emma's disbelief of what she witnesses ("He couldn't have hit her—the stupid blare of sun made that impossible, the hour of afternoon. The idea was too ludicrous."[76]). She also paints a complicated picture of complicity in the character of Suzanne, who is simultaneously a subservient follower of Russell and "not a good person." Evie reasons that "Suzanne and the other girls had stopped being able to make certain judgments, the unused muscle of their ego growing slack and useless. It had been so long since any of them had occupied a world where right and wrong existed in any real way. Whatever instincts they'd ever had—the weak twinge in the gut, a gnaw of concern—had become inaudible. If those instincts had ever been detectable at all."[77]

But even though the Manson murders ushered in an understanding of cults, their perpetrators—even the women—never benefitted from this new sensibility. In *Creepy Crawling,* Jeffrey Melnick discusses the widespread runaway crisis in the 1960s, remarking that the crisis never translated into pity for the "Manson girls," whose personal histories could evoke similar compassion or protectionism. "That these young women were generally construed as spoiled dropouts—as opposed to vulnerable runaways—is one of the many tragedies of the Manson phenomenon."[78] Only a year after the California Senate hearings, the Runaway and Homeless Youth Act of 1974 was enacted,[79] growing largely from the horrors of the killings of at least twenty-eight young boys in Houston by Dean Corll. But no consensus emerged about the source of the runaway crisis. Melnick remarks that "the culture surrounding the Manson Family was open to the possibility that young women runaways were misguided but not irredeemable,"[80] and he opines that the girls' unwillingness to offer a "public renunciation of Manson's power over them" immediately banished them from the realm of cultural concern over runaways. While these women would later receive sympathy from anti-cultist activists and researchers, such as Faith, Chiaramonte, and Cline, the idea of their vulnerability came too late to aid them at trial and the question of their personal agency was too ambiguous to subvert the powerful Helter Skelter story.

THE COMMON-CRIMINALS NARRATIVE

Buried in Bugliosi's Helter Skelter story hides a third narrative, which portrays Manson not as an otherworldly dark prince of violence and mayhem but as a ruthless but not uncommon drug dealer operating in the context of a racialized underworld.

The best exposition of the common-criminals narrative is Jeff Guinn's *The Life and Times of Charles Manson.*[81] Narrating the crimes from an objective, journalistic perspective and from the vantage of time, Guinn starts with Charles Manson's personal background of neglect and deprivation. In portraying Manson's history as grim but not unique, Guinn is obviously less motivated to paint Manson as an evil aberration than Bugliosi was in *Helter Skelter,* as well as less motivated to portray him as an innocent victim of horrible circumstances than Manson himself was.[82] Born on November 12, 1934, in Cincinnati, Ohio, to Kathleen Maddox, a sixteen-year old girl,

Manson was shuttled between family members, especially during his mother's incarceration. Beginning in 1951, Manson was in and out of prison and would eventually spend half of the first thirty-two years of his life behind bars, mostly in federal prisons. During his incarcerations, Manson was exposed to various Eastern philosophies and mind control communities, learned to play the guitar, and at least appeared to be motivated to pursue a musical career.

Released on March 21, 1967, after a ten-year stint in prison, Manson arrived in San Francisco's Haight-Ashbury neighborhood. The Summer of Love had recently ended,[83] leaving the neighborhood ravaged by drugs and violence.[84] The hippies, whose legacy is now part of the city's history, were not embraced by the neighborhood at the time, to the point that there was serious political opposition to the inauguration of the first free clinic in the neighborhood, despite dire need.[85] Manson was by no means the only violent man in the neighborhood; even writers who relished sensationalizing his crime, like Ed Sanders, have provided accounts of vicious and frequent violence.[86]

Guinn regards Manson's philosophy as "a hybrid, cobbled together from Beatles song lyrics, biblical passages, Scientology, and the Dale Carnegie technique of presenting everything dramatically. . . . He offered nothing radically different from hundreds of other would-be Haight gurus with the exception of his presentation."[87] Even the deep interpretation of Beatles lyrics was not unique: the release of *Sergeant Pepper's Lonely Hearts Club Band* was celebrated in the Haight, and "its desperate denizens took *Sgt. Pepper* as a sign that the Beatles *understood*."[88] Manson's charismatic and manipulative personality attracted women to his enterprise, and the idea of women scavenging for food as he gave the orders appealed to him, just as it did to other misogynists of the time.

Guinn extensively describes the racial tensions of the late 1960s; in 1966, while Manson was still incarcerated, Bobby Seale and Huey Newton formed the Black Panther Party.[89] For Manson, whose racism ran deep, "the Black Panthers demanding donations by the Cal-Berkeley gates were the equivalent of the militant, intimidating Black Muslims that he'd seen inside McNeil and Terminal Island, but the Panthers were armed and loose in the free world. Angry black men with guns meant that white people were going to die. From the moment when Charlie first encountered them in Berkeley, the Panthers impressed and scared him."[90]

Indeed, Manson's fear of the Panthers echoed the sentiments of many whites in he late 1960s, rendering the apocalyptic Helter Skelter scenario, which Bugliosi had sensationalized as a motive for the murders, less bizarre and unique and more grounded in the context of the times. More importantly, these fears played a role in the events leading to the murders.

Manson's hopes for his musical career, which he pinned mostly on musical producer Terry Melcher and the Beach Boys, were quickly shattered. His much-hoped-for audition for Melcher was a disappointment; while Manson's followers thought "the audition had been a tremendous success," Melcher left the ranch "feeling certain that Charlie Manson had nothing to offer musically" and gently rejected him.[91] Manson's disappointment and rage ended up being channeled into the Family's "creepy crawling"; the Tate-Polansky residence, scene of some of the murders, had been Melcher's home until shortly before the murders.[92]

With no source of income in sight, Manson had to resort to a drug deal, this time turning to a different contact: a girlfriend of Tex Watson, one of Manson's followers, who was tasked with finding someone who would pay $2,500 in advance for twenty-five kilos of nonexistent weed. The plan was to "burn" the girlfriend and the buyer. But unfortunately, the buyer was "a tank-sized black dealer named Bernard Crowe, whose street nickname was Lotsapoppa."

> Tex got the $2,500 up front, but Lotsapoppa and his boys said they'd keep Luella until they took delivery of the weed. They told Tex in graphic detail what would happen to her if they were stiffed. Tex swore he was on the up-and-up, then took the money back to Charlie at Spahn. Lotsapoppa soon guessed that he'd been swindled, and called the ranch demanding to talk to Tex. Charlie stuck to the plan, telling him that Tex was gone and he had no idea how to contact him. Lotsapoppa described what he was about to do to Luella. Charlie didn't care about that, but he was terrified by what he heard next. Lotsapoppa declared that he was a member of the Black Panthers. If he didn't get his weed or his money, he was going to gather an army of his Panther friends, come out to Spahn Ranch, and kill everybody there.[93]

Manson, who was terrified of the Panthers, took the threat seriously and set out to Crowe's home in North Hollywood with family member T. J. Walleman. On the way, Manson ordered Walleman to shoot Crowe at his command. At the apartment, "Walleman lost his nerve and Charlie had to pull the gun himself. Walleman told Tex Watson later that the pistol misfired on the first try, but then Charlie managed to shoot Lotsapoppa in the chest. The big black man toppled over."[94]

Unbeknownst to Manson, Crowe survived the shooting. But Manson, despite bragging to his followers of having shot a Black Panther, feared that the Panthers would attack the ranch, demanding their money as well as avenging their friend. The need to pay the attackers was the motive behind Gary Hinman's murder: Hinman, a musician, had helped the group in the past, and Manson tried to extort money from him. When Hinman claimed to have no money, Manson slashed his face, leaving his victim at his residence with Susan Atkins and Mary Brunner, who tended to his wound. Eventually, Hinman was killed by Robert "Bobby" Beausoleil, a promising musician and actor and loose associate of the Family. Hinman's murder was quickly solved and Beausoleil was placed behind bars.

According to Guinn, the Tate-LaBianca murders were an effort to clear Beausoleil of Hinman's murder by creating "copycat" murders that would suggest a different perpetrator. Indeed, the scenes of both later murders were crafted to resemble the Hinman murder scene, with political slogans written on the wall with the victims' blood. To Manson's dismay, the Tate-LaBianca and Hinman murders were handled by different police departments, and the connection between the crimes was not made.

Bugliosi did not dispute this motive and its place in the sequence of events that led to the Tate-LaBianca murders. Indeed, in *Helter Skelter* he discusses the copycat aspect of the scenes, if only to discredit the Tate-LaBianca police investigations, portray the detectives as bumbling and confused, and reserve the glory of solving the crime for himself. But relying primarily on the common-criminals narrative would make the murders seem more ordinary and would not serve the purpose of tying Manson to crime scenes in which he was not present while preserving the criminal culpability of his followers.

The common-criminals narrative, while not as exculpatory as the cult narrative, situates the crimes in a more ordinary context and features, unsurprisingly, in books written by two of the murderers, Tex Watson and Susan Atkins: Watson's *Will You Die For Me?* and *Manson's Right-Hand Man Speaks Out* and Atkins's *Child of Satan, Child of God: Her Own Story* and *The Myth of Helter Skelter*.[95]

Watson, careful to reserve his own accountability for the murders (meeting Manson "had everything to do with my own weaknesses") interweaves the Helter Skelter and common-criminals narratives:

> Manson thought he had to take things into his own hands when he saw that his prophetic philosophy, Helter Skelter, wasn't happening on its own. He needed money to finance Helter Skelter, you know, for guns, knives, dune

buggies and the like. He tried to get money from musician Gary Hinman, but ended up having him killed instead. When one of the family members, Bobby Beausoleil, was arrested for the murder, I was shocked! Then, a few days later, when Helter Skelter still wasn't "coming down," Manson thought a copycat murder would spring Bobby, and bring down Helter Skelter at the same time. He had built the Helter Skelter philosophy, and when it didn't happen, the copycat murder idea just gave him an excuse to start it. And at the same time, he thought the police would think the real killers of Hinman were still free to commit the Tate-LaBianca murders. Therefore, they would let Bobby go.[96]

He also espouses a version of the cult narrative, explaining that Manson "believed" his philosophy and "took pride in it" and at the same time "used both fear and love to control his followers,"[97] reminding his readers that "we were all ignorant about cults back then." A born-again Christian, he distinguishes his past and present spiritual beliefs: "We should watch out for these things, and always compare them with mainstream Christianity where our total devotion is to God, our Heavenly Father, not man."[98]

As early as 1978, Susan Atkins even more strongly endorsed the common-criminals narrative. While she acknowledges that "to us, Helter Skelter was real," she clarifies:

> I believe most of the analysts of the Manson family and its crimes failed to appreciate the impact the shooting of the black man had on future events. Vincent Bugliosi, the deputy district attorney who later prosecuted several of us, in my view gave Charlie more credit for criminal intelligence than he deserved. Bugliosi seemed convinced that Charlie was leading some grandiose plot against the world, when from where I was, Charlie was merely reacting for the most part to a situation that flew under control. Initially, he was reacting to the supposed killing of the black man. He already felt a black-white "armageddon" was coming and then feared that the Crowe case might trigger it. Charlie was not, in my opinion, trying to initiate the black-white showdown, but was merely reacting to it.[99]

In Atkins's later book, she repudiates the Helter Skelter narrative as a "myth" and explicitly points the finger at Bugliosi for mischaracterizing the murders. Having received a letter from young people who "wrote to tell me how 'cool' they thought my commitment offense was," Atkins explains that "criminals are simply fallible humans who make very bad decisions in their lives. They aren't anything worth admiring." Her concern is that the Helter Skelter narrative contributes to the glorification of the murders: "Unfortunately the fictionalization, exaggeration and media marketing of this crime and of the participants produces the very real risk of turning Charles Manson into a fictitious horror-movie character, or a comic-book villain no one really believes in. And it produces the risk of making Charles Manson a hero to misguided young people who don't actually know anything about him."[100]

Atkins casts the Helter Skelter narrative as a cover story for the common-criminals narrative:

> He needed men to deal his drugs, make his connections, rob and steal to raise money . . . and now for protection. But he could hardly admit he had just killed a Black Panther and the entire brotherhood of Black Panthers was about to come screaming into Spahn Ranch to wipe us all out. If he had said that, everyone would have left. The Panthers weren't looking for any of the rest of us, just Charles Manson.
>
> So Charles Manson had to figure out how to turn Spahn Ranch into a fortress without letting anyone know the real reason.
>
> And then it came to him. The answer was right before his eyes. It was right there in the apocalyptic sermons he had used to spellbind the drug-enfeebled minds of the young men and women all the way back to the San Francisco days.
>
> The beautiful part about it was that any amount of arming and prepara-tions could be covered by the explanation that they were preparing for Helter Skelter. And Charles Manson's constant talk of a black/white race war pro-vided excellent cover for telling his young idealistic followers to keep an eye out for blacks sneaking around Spahn Ranch. It all worked to perfection. His long, repetitive sermons every night began to be remolded to reinforce the militant preparations.[101]

A cynical reading of Atkins's and Watson's books would regard their adherence to the common-criminals narrative as a self-serving effort to nor-malize their crimes without appearing to "minimize" their accountability, as the cult narrative would imply. But both Atkins and Watson became born-again Christians in prison, which suggests that these narratives were an effort to demystify their crimes in an effort to "minister" to the young people who were sending them disturbing fan mail.

CONCLUSION

That new works, such as *Aquarius, The Girls,* and Quentin Tarantino's antici-pated *Once upon a Time in Hollywood,*[102] attest not only to the enduring public fascination with the murders but also to the continuing cultural struggle to make sense of them. Examining the narrative in these works, as well as in their predecessors, shows that the three narratives are not exclusive and are all supported by the facts. Which narrative takes center stage depends on the narrator's identity and purpose.

The prevalence of the Helter Skelter narrative can be attributed to Vincent Bugliosi's narrative authority; his account is widely regarded as the quintessential version of the events, despite its subjectivity and self-interest, and is strongly supported by the victims. As such, it trumps accounts by narrators of lesser social capital: the inmates and their sympathizers. But there are other explanations for the sui generis, ultimate-evil portrayal of Manson and his followers. In *Creepy Crawling*, Melnick argues that the Manson Family—or, more accurately, the idea of it as a family unit—constituted a serious threat to the already crumbling notion of the traditional American family. The notion that the Tate-LaBianca murders could have emerged from an ethos of love and loyalty—the wish to protect Beausoleil, who had recently been arrested for the murder of Gary Hinman, by providing a copycat crime—would have suggested feelings of care and nurturing, which was an unacceptable and frightening notion to the mainstream. Indeed, as Melnick shows, the early 1970s were rife with cultural artifacts juxtaposing "good"—normative, traditional families—with "bad," murderous, and sometimes cannibalistic families, as in the classic horror movie *The Texas Chainsaw Massacre*.

In order to support this declining institution against such subversion of the family model, it was crucial to present these crimes as outlandish, irrational, and dramatically out of the ordinary. Indeed, as we have seen, any narrative of the murders that casts doubt on the hegemonic notion that the Manson Family murders were in a class of their own faces an uphill battle. Melnick argues that influential commentators like Joan Didion and others were deeply invested in the Helter Skelter narrative and in the notion that Manson "killed the sixties":

> The stunning amount of investment that has been made in this construction should remind us above all that plenty of people were really eager to shut the door not just on Manson but on all the hippies, Yippies, and freaks he came to stand for. For sheer destruction of human life, the Tate-LaBianca murders do not rise to the level of the daily horrors inflicted at the same time by American forces in Vietnam, but we do not have the same tendency to imagine that this war "killed the sixties." The uncomfortable truth is that Manson was quickly converted into a weapon used to discipline the unruly generation in which he had immersed himself.[103]

The prevalence of the Helter Skelter narrative explains not only the influence of the Manson murders on the California penal scene; it also explains the parole board's subscription to this narrative and its resistance to alternative, or even complementary, narratives. The next chapters, which turn to the parole hearings, show how this narrative is reaffirmed not only by the commissioners but also by the prosecutor and victims and limits the inmates' ability to paint a broader picture of their crimes.

FOUR

Revisiting the Past

FROM FACTS TO EMOTION IN UNDERSTANDING
THE CRIME OF COMMITMENT

O nobly-born, (so-and-so), listen. That thou art suffering so
cometh from thine own karma; it is not due to anyone else's. . . .
The Good Genius, who was born simultaneously with thee, will
come now and count out thy good deeds [with] white pebbles,
and the Evil Genius, who was born simultaneously with thee,
will come and count out thy evil deeds [with] black pebbles.
Thereupon, thou wilt be greatly frightened, awed, and terrified,
and wilt tremble; and thou wilt attempt to tell lies, saying,
"I have not committed any evil deed." Then the Lord of Death
will say, "I will consult the Mirror of Karma." So saying, he will
look in the Mirror, wherein every good and evil act is vividly
reflected. Lying will be of no avail.

The Tibetan Book of the Dead

It's 9 a.m. and my students and I have just arrived at UC Berkeley to attend
Lifer School offered by UnCommon Law, a nonprofit focused on lifer representation in the context of parole hearings. Its website declares: "By providing high-quality advocacy and education, we equip prisoners and their supporters to transform their life prospects and to bring about the world in
which they want to live. Our ultimate aim is to reduce the number of adults
and children entangled in the criminal justice system."[1] The nonprofit pur-
sues this goal in three ways: by providing direct representation to parolees
before the Board, partnering with legal clinics at nearby law schools, and
challenging the Board's and governor's decisions before the court in individual and class actions. Keith Wattley, UnCommon Law's executive director, offers trainings at least once a year to dozens of attendees, mostly practicing lawyers or law students.

Wattley is a tall, broad-shouldered African American man with an infec-
tious smile and a quiet demeanor. His careful, well-spoken descriptions of the

process and his deadpan humor belie a razor-sharp mind, very aware of the backstage politics of the parole process. On occasion, Wattley hosts special speakers: former lifers with an insider's perspective, family members of lifers who can speak about helping and supporting from the outside, and representatives from various organizations and nonprofits that offer reentry resources.

We start the day with a round of introductions. Many of the attendees either work, or are hoping to work, as panel attorneys. Wattley tells me later that, although the payment per meeting is paltry, representing multiple clients on parole is not a bad way to make a living. The problem is that the list is long and it is difficult to get appointments.

Even those who are appointed panel attorneys or who manage to get parole cases via their private practice (representing the few lifers who can afford to pay attorney's fees) face difficult challenges: representation on parole requires a more muted persona than the attorney. If the attorney has to speak at a parole hearing, things are already going quite badly: the attorneys must meticulously prepare their clients to present their own case to the Board, minimizing their own participation. This is, of course, antithetical to ordinary representation,[2] which often consists of rendering the clients' lay discourse in legalese.[3] Parole representation does require legal skills, such as determining the relevance of information and sometimes greasing the wheels of the legal machine to smooth the way for cases.[4] But this is not, by far, the greatest difference between parole work and trial work.

"First," Wattley explains, "you have to remember: you are no longer a criminal defendant. That part was over with the trial, a long time ago." One should not walk in with a criminal defendant's mentality, because the Board's point of departure is that the facts as established at trial—not just the bare conviction—are true. Denying or minimizing them suggests that the inmate does not possess "insight."

Insight, Wattley explains, is the key concept in parole hearings and represents the attitude expected of a successful parole applicant. The idea of insight permeates the entire parole process from beginning to end, but what it actually means is fairly nebulous. In the context of the inmate's past, it requires demonstrating a deep understanding of the factors that led to the crime, as well as profound and sincere remorse. In the context of the present, the inmate is expected to show that he or she is no longer the same person who committed the crime; in other words, that the inmate's path since the crime—in terms of discipline, rehabilitation programming, and other activities—shows a profound awareness of personal failings and a genuine and successful effort to correct them. Concerning the future, the inmate is supposed to show a concrete plan for a law-abiding, stable life—complete with housing, employment, and a network of support—as well as a comprehensive plan to prevent the internal failings that produced the crime. Victor Shammas, who conducted qualitative analyses of some parole hearings, points out the required nexus between the inmate's understanding of his or her crime and his or her subsequent efforts at reform:

> In essence, the inmate must be able to show why a crime occurred, that is, to produce a causal account of the crime, and show how those causes have been curbed by a labor of self-improvement. If anger is seen to be a cause of their history of violent crime, for instance, the inmate must be able to demonstrate an ability to control their emotions, which must in turn be validated by participation in programs such as anger management classes and a "clean" prison record. If gang membership is considered a central cause of their "life crime," a record demonstrating freedom from entanglements with prison gangs could be suggestive of appropriate levels of insight.[5]

Shammas quotes a commissioner explaining the concept to an inmate at one of the hearings he attended: "This insight issue, it's a concept. There's no such thing as perfect insight. But more insight is required than what you were able to demonstrate today. Everyone in this room agrees you had a horrible childhood. We know that. But the hard work about saying well, how does that affect me and how does that translate into my extreme rage and my issue of anger and violence against women."[6]

Every hearing starts with a discussion of the inmate's past: the crime of commitment and other precommitment factors, such as the inmate's criminal history. A longitudinal examination of the Manson Family hearings reveals four important developments in the Board's treatment of the past:

1. the crystallization of the court record as the ultimate representation of the facts surrounding the crime (in the early hearings, the Board had been open to discussion and negotiation of the truth with the inmate; from the mid-1980s onward, the Board has recited the court record, offering the inmate little to no opportunity to provide alternative or complementary narratives);

2. the transition from a professional-therapeutic emphasis mostly on the present and future circumstances of the inmate to an emotional, introspective emphasis on the inmate's relation to the crime of commitment (initially, through the term "remorse," and since the early 1990s, "insight," a much broader and vaguer term);

3. an evolution in the role of the prosecutor from either nonexistent or cursory to being a central player with a large, strategically timed speaking role, assuming (increasingly in tandem with the victims) the role of the "moral memory" of the original crime; and

4. a gradual but dramatically increased role for the victims, from nonexistent to being central players, whose interests are represented by multiple people, including support people and political advocates, melding with the role of the prosecutor to constitute a solid bloc of "moral memory."

This chapter discusses each of these developments in turn. Though I saw strong echoes of each shift in all the cases I studied, for the sake of convenience I rely on one or two inmate hearings to make each point. I then argue that these transitions reflect more than the mere idiosyncrasies of the cases I studied; rather, they characterize many parole hearings. Moreover, they do not just reflect the natural timeline of a particular case, but rather they echo the developments in California's approach to corrections and extreme punishment discussed in chapter 2.

THE COURTROOM TRANSCRIPT BECOMES KING: THE CRYSTALLIZATION OF THE FACTUAL PAST

A room full of attorneys listen attentively as Wattley warns that by "factors of the crime," the Board does not mean the broader socioeconomic, cultural, and political context of crime; rather, insight is all about accepting personal responsibility for one's failings. This is unsurprising: the parole process does not differ in that respect from countless rehabilitative programs and workshops I am familiar with. Most of the inmates with whom I interacted, with the exception of those who claim innocence, are very careful to start any general critique of society, their circumstances, and the criminal justice system by vocally and vehemently taking responsibility for their own contribution to their predicament.

This tendency, which is hammered into them in prison, manifests itself even after release. In 2011, Alessandro de Giorgi conducted ethnographic research on reentry in Oakland.[7] Expecting to document the "significant expansion of the penal state," de Giorgi was surprised to find mostly "chronic poverty and the daily struggle for survival in a neoliberal city . . . the daily struggles of stigmatized people scrambling to disentangle themselves from the treacherous grips of chronic poverty, sudden homelessness, untreated physical and mental suffering, and the lack of meaningful social services."[8] Despite these very real problems, "the main services offered to reentering prisoners are aimed at restructuring their personalities along the coordinates of an idealized neoliberal subject: a self-reliant entrepreneur of the self, constantly at work to accumulate human capital and eager to compete with his/her peers in the lowest regions of a deregulated labor market."[9] This narrow focus on accountability is echoed by de Giorgi's interlocutors, who "appear to have internalized the neoliberal narrative of personal responsibility that is constantly inculcated in prisons, rehabilitation centers, and reentry programs. They wholeheartedly embrace the dominant rhetoric of free choice, as well as hegemonic definitions of social deservingness and undeservingness."[10]

The pressure to assume responsibility at the parole hearing presents various dilemmas for attorneys and clients, such as the innocence problem. What insight is a parole applicant expected to display about a crime he or she claims not to have committed? Wattley patiently explains that the parole hearing is no place for innocence. Anyone deemed guilty by the courts *is,* for all intents and purposes, guilty, and any effort to dispute guilt is the business of criminal defendants, not of parole hopefuls. The audience becomes impatient: what, then, are their prospective clients supposed to do? Wattley suggests a way of displaying insight in this case: show the board the deep understanding of the situation in which you would have committed the crime *had you done so.* For example, if the inmate was convicted of a drug-related murder he claims he did not commit, he should explain how he became involved with drugs and thus in a situation in which he *could* have committed the murder— but didn't. Incredulous, I raise my hand: But what if there was no context? What if the inmate's conviction is the result of mistaken identity? Wattley shrugs his shoulders: the only way to dismantle the master's house is with the master's tools.

Parole attorney Charles Carbone, in his newsletter *Parole Matters,* explains that "for those innocent of the life crime, this first bit of insight can be difficult to deal with." But for those guilty of their crimes, it boils down to agreeing with the court's version and remembering (to the best of your ability) exactly what happened. For example, the Board can find lacking insight when an inmate cannot remember essential facts of the crime that he or she should know despite being (perhaps) intoxicated during the commission of the crime. Here it is crucial to agree with the court's version and to be able to recall those facts with as much detail as possible. The Board is basically testing your honesty and acceptance of responsibility. If you are conveniently forgetting key facts, the Board may conclude you are minimizing, or your memory is self-serving with an eye toward remembering the crime in a way that makes you less accountable or less involved. It's best to agree with as much of the court's version as you can, and to recall as much of the crime as you can. That's insight.[11]

The problem of remorse and innocence is not unique to parole. In *I Was Wrong*, Nick Smith enumerates fourteen factors of a complete apology, the first and second of which are a corroboration of the factual record and an acceptance of blame.[12] In *Showing Remorse*, Richard Weisman discusses two kinds of people for whom these factors would be challenging: innocent defendants and defendants who believe that their actions were right.[13] Indeed, even inmates who do not fully claim innocence but merely dispute some facts in their court records face a variant of this uphill battle. This places lifers, whose crimes were invariably severe, in a tricky position. On one hand, embracing an extremely negative version of the facts does not endear one to the Board;[14] on the other, quibbling with the court record can make one seem argumentative and detract from a show of insight.

Before 1980, the Manson hearings did not include a summary of the facts, perhaps because the crimes were still fresh in the public consciousness, but experienced panel attorneys have told me that they saw the same in other old transcripts of their clients. At the time, inmates were active participants in the discussion, sharing the story from their personal perspective, and they were not directly challenged by the Board. Between 1980 and 1984, the Board gradually increased its references to the court record. Going beyond the convicting jury verdict, which offers no detail,[15] the Board followed the narrative proposed by the prosecutor in the original trial, assuming that the conviction unreservedly affirmed this narrative. By 1984, at least a third of all hearing transcripts were devoted to a recitation of the court record, and prosecutors were also invited to repeat these facts at the closing argument toward the end of the hearings. By contrast, the inmate's input into the fact determination decreased to the point that any deviation from the courtroom narrative was perceived as "minimization" of responsibility and thus evidence of lack of insight.

An example of the Board's early flexibility with the facts is Patricia Krenwinkel's 1978 hearing. She states that, during the prosecutors' presentation, "there was a whole lot of little things that I felt that the man said that are all just little incorrect things. . . . I don't want to go into it." Board member DeLeon explains, "Don't lose sight of the purpose of this hearing. This is not a trial. It's a hearing to determine whether you are suitable for parole."[16]

Similar flexibility about the facts in the early years can be found in Charles Manson's hearing from 1980. At a prior hearing, in 1978, the original prosecutor in the case, Stephen Kay, had provided a lengthy version of the Helter Skelter narrative (discussed in depth in chapter 3). This narrative, as explained above, was essential for the conviction of Manson, who had not directly participated in the murders. At the 1978 hearing, Manson rejected this narrative, objecting multiple times and arguing that he had not ordered anyone to kill and was not the leader of any group. Note the neutral, even conciliatory, way in which Board member Pizarro frames the debate:

> Mr. Kay . . . his feeling was that Mr. Manson was the leader of the group, that he dominated the group, that he ordered the killings, and the reason being that Mr. Manson wanted to start a race war, and thereby was responsible for the nine killings and was convicted thereof. Mr. Manson, on the other hand, denied it, denied that he ordered the others to kill, denied that he was the leader of the group, denied that he had followers, and, more or less, expressed the feeling that the others did what they did because they wanted to do it and not because he ordered it. . . . I might state to all concerned, though, we must deal with the fact that the court has convicted Mr. Manson and that if there are any problems in that regard about whether Mr. Manson did or did not do it, that's between the prisoner and the courts and not necessarily between the prisoner and this panel.[17]

Bugliosi's narrative of the Tate-LaBianca murders emerged from Susan Atkins's boastful stories to fellow inmates about stabbing the pregnant Tate even as her victim begged for the life of her unborn baby. Atkins repeated this narrative at her trial. However, prior to the trial, at the grand jury hearing, she distanced herself from this act, confessing that she was at the scene but attributing the actual stabbing of Tate to Tex Watson.

At Atkins's 1978 hearing, she and her attorney, Richard Caballero, adhere to her version at the grand jury, rather than at the trial. Atkins explains that she had lied at the trial because "my state of mind at the time was I was betraying my so-called comrades . . . and I was having to deal with guilt for doing that."[18] She explains that she was still in thrall to Manson, who "had given me a message through the prison system that he wanted to see me. . . . I was still very, very much influenced by things that he had said to me. And he told me . . . that I needed to retract what I said."[19]

The Board listens attentively to Atkins's explanation, and then Board member Rushen says, "All right. Do you want to tell us what did happen?"[20] Atkins proceeds to provide her version of the events, in which Tex Watson was responsible for the stabbing of Sharon Tate. Throughout this inquiry, the Board members ask detailed questions, expressing interest in Atkins's version. Atkins's narrative closely follows the common-criminals narrative, portraying the murders as a "copycat" effort designed to free Bobby Beausoleil, who had been apprehended for Hinman's murder. The Board restricts its commentary to clarifying questions, and Atkins walks a thin line between rejecting her previous version and maintaining accountability: "I want you to understand. I take responsibility for my actions. But I'm asking you to try and understand where my state of mind was at the time that I took those actions. It's not where it is today."[21] After a five-minute break, DeLeon and Atkins have an exchange about which factual version would be the determinative account of the murder.

> DELEON: I understand what you're going through now, and what is happening now, but you understand also that we have to make a decision, you know, based upon fact . . . under those conditions where you had a great deal of notoriety, which may be contributing to lie telling, and you had the somber atmosphere of the courtroom, which ordinarily is believed to be conducive to truth telling, and you have statements under oath in that much more formal atmosphere than this is—
>
> ATKINS: Yes.
>
> DELEON: —which is conducive to truth telling. And under all of those conditions, you know, and you've explained well the reasons, but you made statements totally contrary to the statements you are making here. Now, ordinarily, our decisions aren't tempered or influenced by the fact that a person is not the active or inactive aggressor in a killing—
>
> ATKINS: Yes, I understand that.
>
> DELEON: —as opposed to where a crime partner is the aggressor and does the killing, you know, a person who is an active participant as opposed to crime as your counsel states, as an aider and abettor in that particular role.
>
> ATKINS: Yes.
>
> DELEON: So, naturally it would serve one better, you know, under these conditions to come out as an aider and abettor, which would be self-serving, you see.[22]

DeLeon presents the dilemma before the Board as a judicial dilemma—one that requires a truth determination and frames Atkins's testimony before the court not as a definitive account in itself, but just as an alternative account that possesses indicia of reliability. "Arriving at the truth" is seen as within the ambit of the Board—and "difficult to do."

Kay launches into an emotional rebuttal, stating that "the eight murders in which she participated are considered to be among the most vicious, brutal murders in the history of American crime."[23] His take closely follows the factual determination at court: "She just kept stabbing Sharon Tate until Sharon Tate stopped screaming."[24]

In 1979, there is still room for Atkins to debate Kay's Helter Skelter story:

> Just to repeat what I said last year, that I, in fact, did not take anybody's life, that I had lied at the trial. I had lied at the Grand Jury. And Tex Watson's statements in his recent confession of killing everybody verifies that.... I know that the facts that Mr. Kay presents, 99 or 90 percent of them are true. And I know that he must, in his position, present them according to the way they were presented in the trial as the facts. But because things that are presented in courts are presented as facts, they are not always necessarily facts. And I live with me, and I know what I did, and I know what I didn't do. And you can believe me, or you can believe Mr. Kay. That's up to you.[25]

Board member Risen reiterates the Board's commitment to the conviction, but also the members' curiosity as to the facts:

> Okay. Well, at this point it's not a matter of believing him or you. We have to rely upon the judgment of the court, or the jury. And you were found guilty. So, we have to go by that.... What we are doing is discussing it in an effort to find out actually what happened and maybe to mitigate some of the areas.[26]

But by 2005, this window of opportunity has closed, with Board member Perez stating at the beginning of the hearing:

> Okay, during today's hearing you're not required to admit the offense nor are you required to discuss the offense. However, it's important for you to understand that this Panel does accept [as] true the findings of the court. We are not here to retry your case. Okay.[27]

The extent to which Atkins's narrative deviates from the prosecutor's account of the crimes is openly discussed by professionals in her psychiatric evaluations. Upon observing that Atkins exhibits "credible insight and remorse," the psychiatrist says that "insight and remorse will probably always be clouded somewhat by the factual disputes that stem from her earlier versions of the crimes."[28] The factual dispute between Atkins and the prosecutor was taken to be detrimental to her insight.

Another example of the increasing futility in contradicting the official version of events is evident from Robert Beausoleil's hearings. In his early hearings, Beausoleil extensively disputes the facts, including the trial version according to which Manson had injured Hinman, and Beausoleil, who stayed at Hinman's home, eventually killed him. Beausoleil argues that "there was no incident between Gary Hinman and Charlie Manson" and adds, "I didn't testify and I didn't give any statement to the authorities at the time. I wish now that I had."[29] The Board then invites Beausoleil to tell them "what went down."[30] Beausoleil conforms to the common-criminals narrative and tells of a drug deal gone bad in which Hinman had participated and a motorcycle club had been swindled. He then explains that he went to Hinman to obtain compensation to mollify the club and, again, denies Manson's presence at the scene,[31] explaining Hinman's face injury as an imperfect self-defense scenario: "I went out in the living room trying to find something worth a thousand dollars. And the next thing I knew she is screaming that Gary's got the gun. And I came running into the kitchen, and he's got the gun. He's pointing it at me, and I'm in a stand-off situation. I got my knife out, and we're in just kind of a Mexican stand-off kind of situation. I didn't think—I took a chance. I didn't think that he would shoot if I made any attempt to get the gun away from him. And I was right."[32]

He then describes getting Hinman to sign off his cars and tending to the injury for a day, thinking that "his cheek would have healed up fine. It was closed; it was a real thin cut. . . . And I figured everything was—you know, we were square. . . . I was ready to leave the next evening. And on my way out he said that he was going to blow the whistle on me when I left for assault and whatever. And I just made a choice whether I wanted to take that chance."[33]

This version both maximizes and minimizes Beausoleil's accountability. On one hand, it enhances his criminality, as he ascribes Hinman's initial injury to himself, rather than to Manson (as in Bugliosi's Helter Skelter account). On the other hand, it distances Beausoleil from Manson and excludes some of the more bizarre elements of the crime, such as Manson wielding a sword. Beausoleil explains that the previous attribution to Manson was done to assuage his parents, who "immediately assumed that I was an innocent young man. . . . And I just didn't have the heart . . . to shatter that illusion at the time."[34]

The Board expresses interest in this story, as does Ross, the prosecutor, who expresses agnosticism about the facts. Although Ross argues that "there do seem to be a number of aggravating factors in connection to the case,"[35] he adds, "the ear was severed by some large instrument. It could have been a knife; it could have been a sword. No one knows for sure."[36]

At Beausoleil's subsequent hearing, the Board repeats the Helter Skelter version of the events. In response, Beausoleil presents a letter from Ross confirming his agnosticism. The Board confronts Beausoleil with the trial testimony of Mary Brunner, a Manson follower who was at the scene of Hinman's murder with Beausoleil and Atkins, according to which Manson was present at the house; Beausoleil repeats that Manson was not involved,[37] and that he had originally claimed otherwise because he wanted to spare his parents knowledge of his guilt.[38]

At Beausoleil's 1980 hearing, the Board relegates the facts to the court process ("The Board, of course, is relying upon the testimony presented in court")[39] but asks him to clarify some ancillary matters, such as his emotional state at the time and the fate of the car he had extorted from Hinman.[40]

In 1981 Beausoleil, for the first time represented by an attorney, resumes his contestation of the facts. Board member Patterson resists: "The panel cannot be in a position of saying that didn't happen, when a court of law says it happened."[41] And at this point, the Board is no longer receptive to Beausoleil's alternative version:

> PIZARRO: It puts us in a situation where you are saying something at one time; you're saying something else at a different time. You are saying, well, it wasn't true then, but it is true now, this kind of thing. In fact, you— part of your pitch, of course, is that you want to divorce yourself from the Manson family as much as you possibly can.

> PATTERSON: The Statement of Facts, as has been read into the record over the last years, is the District Attorney's case that went to the jury or his theory that went to the jury, that the jury bought and found you guilty of. Now, if, you know, ever since you have been coming to the Board, you have told a different story, which you say is what happened. It's part of the record. But what found you guilty is the facts as we have them now. And that's what the court sentenced you on, and that is what the jury found you guilty of.[42]

Board member Coronado adds a remark about the importance of the court record: "I—Mr. Patterson, I wish to—for the record, to reflect that in no way will this amend the circumstances of the offense as they are reflected in the official version of what we have been dealing with in the past."[43] Beausoleil tries to interject, but the Board interrupts him. Beausoleil's attorney, Amos, interjects and explains that Beausoleil is not trying to avoid responsibility "that his convictions in any way are a mistake or incorrect. . . . The thrust of his argument is that: I really am fully responsible.'"[44]

By 1983, the crystallization of the court record becomes part of the standardized introductory comments:

> LEDDY: You're not required to discuss any of the matters and you're not required to admit guilty [sic]. But the panel must accept true and [sic] any facts or findings of the court.[45]

In 1984, Beausoleil modifies his version to include a phone call he made to the ranch to consult with Manson, in which Manson reportedly told him "'you're on your own.' In so many words—he says you know as well as I do what to do. He didn't want to have anything to do with it."[46] Board member Epperly refers back to the court record, citing from the probation officer's report (POR) that Beausoleil was associated with the Manson Family and resided with them at the time of the murder. Beausoleil rejects this.

> EPPERLY: Well, this is part of the court's official documents that were part of your trial, and at the time of your sentencing provided an opportunity for your counsel to have any facts or statements in the POR refuted. Were statements in the POR challenged by your defense counsel?
>
> BEAUSOLEIL: I don't think they were brought up until after the trial. I don't think—
>
> EPPERLY: Okay, they're all part of the court proceedings at that time.[47]

By 1985, the dispute between Beausoleil and the prosecutor over the facts of the case becomes crystallized: the prosecutor and the Board adhere to the court record, and Beausoleil continues to dispute it.[48] In 1992, Commissioner Koenig prefaces the hearing by saying to Beausoleil, "You must realize that the panel accepts as true the court findings in the case."[49] Subsequent questions about the crime cover ground already covered in the dispute, but they are asked by commissioners who are unfamiliar with the case. Beausoleil refuses to answer questions.[50]

At that point, however, Beausoleil accepts the Board's version of his crime, including Manson's complicity in the injury done to Hinman. He explains he had omitted Manson from the description of the crime because he wanted to distance himself from Manson,[51] but he insists it is a small detail: "Since 1976 the only fact that I hedged on was the fact of Charles Manson showing up at the residence. Because I thought it would be to my advantage to take full responsibility."[52]

At his 2003 and 2005 hearings, Beausoleil reads into the record a "statement of facts" prepared by his attorney. The facts essentially reiterate the facts from the 1992 hearing, and Beausoleil acknowledges that the Board accepts the courtroom version as the only true account of the crime.[53]

The Board recurs to the court record even when it does not offer proven facts. At Bruce Davis's trial for the murder of Donald Shea, the body was still missing; the court relied on statements by Davis to others in which he had reportedly said that the body had been mutilated, which, upon the discovery of the body in the early 1980s, turned out to be untrue. At Davis's 1982 hearing, the Board prefers the court's conjecture to the later forensic facts, prompting Davis to protest: "I'd like to say one thing about where my head was when I talked to Allan Springer when I said we cut his arms and legs off. Okay? Obviously not true. Are you aware that the Coroner found his body, and they said that there had been no mutilation and decapitation?"

CHADERJIAN: How many stab wounds were in the body?

DAVIS: I don't know.

CHADERJIAN: More than ten?

DAVIS: I have no idea.

CHADERJIAN: No idea? You have never heard during the course of the trial?

DAVIS: No, sir. In my trial, when I was at trial, the body had not been found, so there could be no—there was no real testimony.

CHADERJIAN: And subsequently you have never heard?

DAVIS: No. All I heard was—you remember when I had my rehearing at Folsom—

CHADERJIAN: Yes.

DAVIS: —because we found—when Steve told where the body was, Mr. Noguchi . . . went to check it out. And he said that there was no decapitation or mutilation. I don't think he told—well, I don't know. I never heard how many stab wounds there were.[54]

Davis's foray into the area of criminal minimization does not bode well, and he is perceived as unrepentant. He explains he caved to peer pressure: "If three or four people decided to do something like this and it's not that serious, it's rather—it's not a healthy thing to do, uh, to say, "No, I don't think we will," when several people seem to have their mind made up in a certain direction."

> LANDER: Nobody was holding you there, were they?
>
> DAVIS: They sure weren't. You know—when I first—when I first returned from Europe and saw Charlie and then again after the first time, I knew that . . . for several days at the ranch, I knew, I said, "No, I'm gonna leave here. This pla—it's really—it's not right." You know? Everything had changed a lot. But I didn't go. I see now, a lot of, you know, misplaced ideas about who my friends are, what was important, what wasn't important. Anyway, I didn't leave. I—I can still see the wisdom in should have left but I didn't.[55]

The Board tries to make the most of the evidence on record against Davis, trying to push him to admit that his limited complicity in the crime is nonetheless meaningful:

> TONG: Okay . . . with regard to Mr. Schey [*sic*], if you just laid the neck against his knife [*sic*], and you didn't break his skin, you didn't puncture his skin at all, what are you guilty of?
>
> DAVIS: Well, I'm guilty of not doing anything to stop what happened. I'm guilty of associating in the presence of what was going on without, you know, really doing anything to help. I drove the people to where they were going. Now, I didn't know what was going to happen to Mr. Hinman, but I, I, I knew that it was not, you know, it wasn't something that was going to be good.[56]

Davis stops short of agreeing with what Tong suggests (that he is guilty of murder as an associate). The Board takes this to imply minimization and lack of acceptance of his role in the crime, declaring: "At this time it appears that Mr. Davis does everything within his power to depersonalize the entire sordid episode and thus develop the detachment that now seems delectable."[57]

Even sticking to the courtroom narrative can be seen as minimization and lack of insight when the inmate highlights mitigating aspects of the record. Here is the Board's decision in Patricia Krenwinkel's 2011 hearing: "[When] she admitted that she stabbed Leno LaBianca in the stomach with a fork, but maintains he was already deceased when she did this, we find that just minimization. That's mutilating someone that you've just murdered, and anything that sounds like minimization is of concern to this Panel, and so we have to go by the written word in this case."[58]

The transcripts, therefore, reveal a gradual crystallization of the courtroom version of the events. As legal truth becomes factual truth, efforts to debate factual events become evidence of lack of insight. Presenting one's involvement as less than central and distancing oneself from association with Manson are perceived as "minimizing" and thus making one unsuitable for parole. Some inmates conclude that the safest strategy is to refrain from discussing their crime. In *In re Rico* in 2009, the Second District Court of Los Angeles held that Rico's decision not to discuss his crime with the Board could not, in itself, constitute proof that he "lacked insight," because Penal Code Section 5011 and Title 15 of the California Code of Regulations, Section 2236, protected his right not to discuss the crime.[59]

FROM THE EXTERNAL TO THE INTERNAL: THE BIRTH OF INSIGHT

The early hearings until 1980s are focused on the inmates' adjustment to the prison environment and their steps toward rehabilitation. More emphasis is placed on their formal programming plans and rehabilitative adjustment than on their internal perspectives. An outlier is this telling exchange between Board member Sides and Bruce Davis in 1978, in which there is already an early effort to deduce Davis's state of mind from his nonverbal communication:

SIDES: As you think back to the lifestyle, do you think—are you nostalgic about it? Do you think back that it was a fantastic, great lifestyle?

DAVIS: Not—no. No, it was pretty destructive. Was nothing great about it.

SIDES: The reason I'm asking you, describing elements of it, I thought I saw a smile across your face, and I wondered if it was because of that or something.

DAVIS: You know, when—there was just such an element of absurdity in it. Just no reason for that. Like a clown, you know. And if it hadn't been so serious, it would have been kind of funny. But it was serious. But, I mean, there was just such elements that made no sense at all, and what was so bad is that people were doing it without asking questions, saying, "Why are we doing this?" They just—when I say, "they," I don't mean they exclusively. You know, I was involved in my mind, and I didn't say, "Well, we shouldn't do that." That never—and I would stand back and see it, and I'd ask myself, "What am I doing?" And yet there I'd be. But there wasn't anything great about it. It was really pretty bad as I see it now. I know it was. I mean, as I see it now.[60]

This short exchange reveals some interest in Davis's inner world, but the defense attorney's retort affirms that, at that point, the focus is on external factors: "As the Board has long since known, the whole story has never been told. In 1976, 1977, they indicate he had told his part in this thing, and he has told his part of it. It's not a pretty story. His part is certainly not a pretty part. He admits that it isn't. He accepts responsibility for this. Isn't this what this is all about? He's willing to accept what he has done, make what amends he can."[61] Indeed, the denial of Davis's parole in 1978 is ascribed not to his internal relationship with his crime, but rather to the brutality of the crime.

Subsequent hearings show doubts in the psychiatric evaluation as to the depth of Davis's remorse. The following exchange in 1982 sees Davis and Board member Coronado negotiating what an appropriate display of remorse would look like:

CORONADO: [quoting from the counselor's report] "There does not appear to be too much remorse from subject over his involvement in the committed offenses."

DAVIS: You know—okay. When I read that, I took note of that. And even in the psych report they said the same thing. And, you know, I wish I could do something that would bring those lives back, but I can't. And I realize that there are some lives that are being affected in an ongoing way even now because of things that happened. And if I ever get a chance or there is ever a way for me to do something beneficial in that area, well, I certainly will. I'm sorry for what happened.

CORONADO: Let me ask you a question. Is this perception on his part perhaps because of the way you characterize what happened and your involvement?

DAVIS: Well, okay. There is the point that says, "He makes himself a minor character." Well, what I did, as far as quality of the offense, is bad. I don't mean to say, "Well, what I did wasn't so bad," because what I did was bad. It was bad. And I don't have any—you know, I'd make no defense. What I did was wrong. It was very wrong. It was as bad as anybody—you know, with Hinman, if I'd have been there and blew his brains out, I wouldn't have been more wrong than I was to have participated in this and done nothing to stop it.[62]

This is especially interesting in Davis's case because, as opposed to the other Manson Family crimes, at this point there was still a paucity of evidence, so the facts were still under dispute. Revealing more damning aspects of Davis's involvement in the crime would, perhaps, render him more credible, but it would also make his crime more heinous. On the other hand, painting himself as a "minor character" in the crime could tame the extent of his depravity in the eyes of the Board, but could also be read as lack of remorse.

Davis is acutely aware of the fact that his version of the events, albeit not contradicting the court record, could be read as minimization. In 1986, he explains:

> I'm not—I mean, you know, when I look at all this stuff that happened, I'm guilty of what I was charged with. You know, I'm guilty of knowing that we were—that Gary was going to be put in some trouble. From the beginning, I didn't know how much. I'm guilty of knowing that I saw Charlie hit him with the knife. I didn't do a thing to stop Charlie. And I could have. I mean, I had a gun. But I didn't. I took the guy's car. When I found out a few days later that he was dead, I didn't do a thing about it. So, you know, I'm not—I paid. I'm not fussing about—you know, I know I'm guilty of what you're saying.[63]

Davis is not alone in these dry, matter-of-fact displays of remorse. At her early hearings, Patricia Krenwinkel does not seem to think that the Board is looking for a long, soul-searching soliloquy. Instead, she offers this: "Well, there is no way that I can bring life to those people that are now dead. I don't think that—I know that I have like, losses, but I may never have money that I could pay back. . . . The only thing that I could possibly do is try to live my life daily as best that I can and try never to bring harm to anyone again. . . . I don't know exactly what you're asking."[64]

At Robert Beausoleil's 1980 hearing, the transcripts reveal Commissioner Pearson's curiosity about Beausoleil's internal understanding of the murder:

> But I think the question that is still in my mind is I really have not seen anything in any of these files that really answers what made Mr. Beausoleil commit the killing itself. In other words, what actually internally triggered this? This may not be answerable by him, and how do we know as he sits here now that whatever it is that triggered that doesn't still exist within him? I see nothing in the reports that really identifies what caused it and tells us that doesn't exist. That may not be answerable.[65]

Over the course of the next few years, it becomes gradually clearer that this introspection is not an invitation for the inmate to understand the social and cultural context of his or her crime. Beausoleil learns this bitter lesson when he responds first in 1978 and then in 1980:

> When I was first arrested, I was 21 years old. And this was at the end of the sixties. A lot of—there was a lot of problems in the world, and like a lot of youth at the time I was rebellious, resentful. I have done a lot of growing up since then.[66]
>
> I was put in a situation that was totally beyond anything I had experienced. . . . A threat of a loss of freedom can be just as threatening to a man or some kinds of men as a threat against your life . . . and that just—I'm telling you, man—just scared me to death.[67]

In the 1978 hearing, he also resists the linkage with the Manson Family's later crimes: "It seemed like the whole world had caved in on me on this case, you know, being associated with the Manson family thing when in point of fact I was never a member of the Manson family. I have never done anything under orders from Charles Manson . . . The whole thing just—Man, all of a sudden I'm part of this bizarre cult, murder cult, you know, with some kind of god."[68] But the Board remains unimpressed, denying Beausoleil parole because of the heinousness of his crime. It is only later, at Beausoleil's 1983 hearings, that his reflections take the inward turn the Board comes to expect:

> I, perhaps maybe more than I should, do make attempts to diminish Manson's involvement in my life. And, the thing about it is that I have to live myself for the rest of my life. And the situation . . . I have a different kind of lifestyle and different type of orientation now and have had for quite a number of years, and I really—I don't want this stem [sic] to be a maelstrom around my neck for the rest of my life. I don't think I'd make a very good parole candidate if I was—still oriented the same way. And I'm not interested in having Manson or anybody that's associated with that—with all of that, Tate, Bianca [sic], the whole mess, that—I don't want them to play that large of a role in my life in the future.[69]

As can be noted from these examples, the Board's interest in remorse is still cursory and nascent, and the inmates themselves are not yet expected to perform insight for the Board. In 1981, as the Board walks an unrepresented Bruce Davis through their plan for the hearing, Pizarro describes an inventory of issues, of which remorse is only one:

One of the things we talk about when we talk about suitability or unsuitability is a juvenile record, some stability on the outside or prior to the time you came to the State Prison. We talk about remorse. We talk about whether there were any significant stresses in your life immediately prior to the offense. We talk about and we search for violent priors especially. We consider your age and we wonder whether or not because of your age that this would reduce any further criminal involvement. Realistic parole plans are certainly a consideration. Your institutional behavior, what you do within the prison, is certainly considered. We will also consider any kind of sadistic sexual offenses or sexual offenses that are violent. Certainly the psychiatric factors are taken into consideration.[70]

This list reflects a therapeutic-professional perspective on parole. Present in the room (in this hearing and in others from the same era) is the correctional counselor, who disappears from the parole stage in the mid-1980s. The emphasis is on external recidivism predictors: Davis's age and the existence, or lack thereof, of violent or sexual blemishes on his criminal record. Davis, fairly taciturn at his early hearings, accepts this and barely responds to the Board's questions.

Still, another aspect of curiosity emerges later in the hearing, when Davis observes his roles as leader and follower. Davis expresses interest in the fact that, even after having driven Manson to Hinman's home and taken part in the murder (by pointing the gun at Hinman), he did not go to the Tate residence despite being there when the group prepared to go and invited him to join them. His soliloquy on the subject is not required, but when freely offered, it evokes interest in one of the Board members:

CHADERJIAN: Mr. Davis, as long as you saw fit to inform the panel of your feelings in retrospect, why on the evening of the Tate matter, did you decline to go with them?

DAVIS: You know—well, now I believe that I just knew that was just, wow, I couldn't do that.

CHADERJIAN: You couldn't participate in another murder, is that what you're saying?

DAVIS: Well, at that point, I had already, I had driven—I had been involved in the Hinman thing.

CHADERJIAN: I understand.

DAVIS: And when they, when they said, "Let's go do this." And I just said, "No. I'm not going to do it. I'm just not going to do it."

CHADERJIAN: Well, if we could look at this in view of the parallels that were discussed earlier. . . . What you're losing sight of is the analogy [according to which Davis follows leaders; he followed Manson, then an American Nazi group when he first came to prison, and subsequently joined a Christian ministry,] how you include that interim "following the leader" if you will, following the superior will . . .

DAVIS: Well, I—

CHADERJIAN: Obviously, you didn't have these flashes of insight until very recently.[71]

Toward the mid-1980s, the prosecutor begins to comment on the inmates' absence of remorse. Even before the birth of the concept of insight, remorse already proves slippery and difficult to express, especially for heinous crimes. Epstein, Susan Atkins's attorney in 1985, expresses frustration with the vagueness of remorse: "Just for Mr. Kay to say it doesn't exist because she hasn't talked about it—has anybody asked her about it? How does she speak to that? When—when you ask her if she has parole plans, should she say, 'I have a lot of remorse here'? Or should she it [sic] perhaps correctly at the closing of these proceedings when it's appropriate to tell you how she really feels about this?"[72] Atkins herself says in 1988:

Remorse is not a tangible emotion. I cannot pull it out and put it on the table. If I could, I don't know that it could be recognized, or would be recognized or be acknowledged. What I've tried to do to show how I feel is to live my life in the opposite direction, by doing good, by changing, by growing, and I will continue to do that. I've been told I feel nothing for why I'm here, I've been told I deserve an Academy Award for my performances, excuse me, there are nine people that are, are not alive in this . . . and it, today, because of me.[73]

The term *insight* emerges for the first time in the 1984 hearing of Bobby Beausoleil. At this point, it is not a buzzword or a term of art, but merely part of a conversation:

JAUREGUI: Did you gain any insight as to why you committed the crime?

BEAUSOLEIL: Well I know why I committed the crime. Because I allowed myself to be influenced, put under duress, to look up to people who were into things I had no business being involved with.

JAUREGUI: And how do you feel now?

BEAUSOLEIL: . . . I like myself a lot. I don't like myself for what I did then. You know, it's the thing that I am most ashamed of. And I'm trying to out, outlive that. I'm trying to overcome that and be something that I can be proud of.[74]

In Davis's case, we see the 1984 Board express interest, for the first time, in his affect as a barometer for the sincerity of his remorse: "The psychiatric evaluation from that year concludes that Davis's regrets 'seemed insincere and the way he tells his story, one can only wonder why there was any guilt at all. He portrayed himself as following the Manson teachings because they met his needs at the time. . . . He lacked affectual attachment to his statements and had a distinct cold and intellectual presentation.'"[75]

In 1992, the word *insight* still does not categorize the conversation. But at Beausoleil's hearing that year, the prosecutor, Jonas, expresses concern that Beausoleil has not renounced his former beliefs: "The thing that troubles me [is that] he has never acknowledged buying in so deeply to Manson, he has never in any way, shape, or form rejected outright any if not all of those things for which at least somebody believes Manson stood. Whether it is free sex. Whether it is abuse of drugs. Whether it is the exploitation. Whether it is, quote, a nonconformist attitude where you can rise above society. Whether it's anti-establishment, whatever or however you view that in the context of illegal conduct."[76] Beausoleil's attorney, Russo, tries to resist: "I think the most serious charge that Mr. Jonas levels at Mr. Beausoleil is that Mr. Beausoleil was a typical '60s mush brain. That he had held values that were held by a lot of teenagers in the, excuse me, in the 1960s. . . . For him to say that some bizarre beliefs that a 20-year-old held 24 years ago somehow indicates the beliefs of an adult, it just boggles the—it's just mind-boggling."

Beausoleil himself evokes the theme of maturation:

When I first came to prison at the age of 21, I was a troubled young man who was living in a time when social values were very much in a state of flux, making it a time in which it was particularly difficult and confusing to be a young man. . . . Compounding the extreme difficulty of learning how to survive in prison, I was overcome with shame and guilt for having taken another human life for selfish reasons, while at the same time struggling with bitterness and anger, because I felt in some obscure way that I was the victim of circumstances and actions beyond my immediate control. I was, in other words, in denial.[77]

Krenwinkel's 1980 statements echo the same theme:

It came up about '65. It was the beginning of the marches. It was the beginning of the civil rights movement. It was the beginning of all the movements of the late sixties, which eventually involved entering the war. . . . I found that I couldn't seem to find my bearings in this world at that time. . . . I couldn't seem to find where there was any, on my own—seem to find any reinforcement for doing anything other than kind of letting myself go with the time of what at that time was tune-in and drop-out, as Timothy Leary so put it. I mean, it's hard to say. There were so many components. I was a child of the sixties. And there definitely is something to be said about the sixties. It was an incredible time in the period of our history. It's something that I look back on and I see, because there's thousands of people out there that were not much different than myself.[78]

Unsurprisingly, the prosecutor, Kay, turns this reasoning on its head:

I feel that it's kind of hard for me to accept Miss Krenwinkel's statement that she was a child of the sixties, and there were thousands of others like her out there in the sixties. I myself went to law school at Berkeley during the time of Mario Savio and could observe some of these children of the sixties. And they characterized themselves as flower children. Their slogan was "make love, not war." They weren't into murdering people.[79]

In the late 1980s, the transcripts reflect a shift away from external markers of rehabilitation and remorse to internal self-flagellation. In 1988, Board member Castro browbeats Patricia Krenwinkel into fully maximizing the heinousness and sui generis nature of her crime:

CASTRO: Let me ask you, do you think that this is one of the worst crimes committed in the history of California?

KRENWINKEL: My personal belief, that any life that is taken is equal to another life that is taken. Therefore, I think any murder is equal to the other, because I feel that anyone's life is just as valuable as the next.

CASTRO: I don't, I don't understand your, your answer to my question. My question was do you think that this is one of the worst heinous crimes committed in California?

KRENWINKEL: Yes.

CASTRO: Do you? Do you think therefore . . . [Krenwinkel confers with her attorney.] Do you think that an ahh . . . an individual who commits a most heinous crime, should he be given the right by law to be released?

KRENWINKEL: I think it would depend on that person, and I think whether or not there has been sufficient adjustment and sufficient turnaround in their life.

CASTRO: Okay. So any person regardless of the number of murders and regardless of the number of the ahh . . . the aggravation, can be subject and should be considered to be released on parole, given a rehabilitation process, is that your position?

KRENWINKEL: Yes.[80]

This exchange reveals Castro's perspective, which is antithetical to his role as a presiding Board commissioner: that some crimes are so heinous that their perpetrators should not be considered for release (even, presumably, if they are eligible for parole).

This trend of turning inward is even more evident in Bobby Beausoleil's 1997 hearing. At the beginning of the hearing, which he attends via telephone from Oregon, he is asked, "What would you do with your life if you had to do it over again?" Beausoleil replies:

> I would learn to make much more responsible decisions and be far more con-science [*sic*] of the consequences of the decisions that I make. . . . I made some really, really bad choices when I was young. I guess I wasn't conscience [*sic*], I really wasn't conscious of and aware of how one person's actions can affect another person's actions. And had I been aware and made different choices, then there would have been a lot else. There would have been a growth pattern from that point which would have been much more responsible and productive and beneficial, I think, to society as a whole.[81]

Beausoleil's subsequent hearings reveal gradually increasing efforts to portray his psychic excavation. In 2005, he explains the reasons for the murder:

> I'm ashamed to admit, even though I'm now 58 years old and I'm no longer the kid that I was and I understand that if I were faced with similar circum-stances, certainly I wouldn't be driven by the same impulse or need. It still shames me to say that the reason I killed Gary was because I was so unsure of myself, so inadequate, that I felt that the only thing I could do to [*sic*] was to bring myself up to the esteem of the people that I wanted to be accepted by, to—as Charlie Manson said when he came in there—he was showing me how to be a man. . . . I was left with a problem, totally out of my depth and, I must say, manipulated by people older than me, who I looked up to, who I wanted to be respected by, who I wanted to be accepted by.[82]

The inquiry then delves into the cumulative nature of Beausoleil's insight:

> FARMER: Sounds like that's a conclusion that you've arrived at after a con-siderable period of time and reflection.
>
> BEAUSOLEIL: Absolutely. In fact it was fairly recent that I realized the thing that was driving it up to that point, and a lot of my getting involved with those people in the first place, was . . . of my relationship with my father and my inability to gain his acceptance and approval. . . . It really came home to me when I started working with at-risk youth, about seven

or eight years ago. . . . As a result of this awareness that I gained through meeting with the young men who were like a reflection of myself, and all of them tried to prove themselves, tried to find a way to be accepted in doing horrendous things that their peers put them up to so that they could demonstrate that they were tough guys and that they are worthy of being accepted.[83]

By 2008, the focus on insight is somewhat simplified. Although Beausoleil repeats the same explanation for his crime, Commissioner Anderson begins asking questions that appear to be part of a formula of insight.

ANDERSON: Okay. So, you were a follower at the time. Why are you a leader at this time?

BEAUSOLEIL: A leader?

ANDERSON: Yeah. You've gone from being a follower to a leader. Are you a—Do you consider yourself a leader?

BEAUSOLEIL: I don't really think of myself as a leader, necessarily.

ANDERSON: Well, you're leading your life.

BEAUSOLEIL: Well, yes, I do.[84]

It is very difficult to make sense of this peculiar dialogue without assuming that "insight" is, at this point in time, sort of a term of art and that part of the process the Board expects the inmate to put on display is a follower-to-leader transition. It certainly does not trace along Beausoleil's personal journey as it emerges from the hearings, which, if anything, is more of a story of leader to follower—an admission that he was not the strong, self-sufficient man he purported to be in his early thirties, but rather a young and insecure man trying to impress the motorcyclists and Manson. But it seems that Beausoleil is trying to fit his narrative within a framework that the Board expects to hear.

But even this increasing introspection is interpreted negatively. The 2010 Board constructs Beausoleil's incremental expressions of insight as inconsistency:

ANDERSON: In my personal opinion because of his being self-centered, he's had the inability to gain the credibility that he needs to get out of prison. He says he takes responsibility, but he's just telling us that because he's a superficial individual. His statements are inconsistent, and he several times insulted this panel by his inability to follow the rules that I laid down for him. He's an individual who lacks insight into the causative factors . . . of why he did this in the first place. We've got too many versions. I'm not going to go over them; they're on the record. He's self-absorbed.[85]

Several themes emerge from these examples. First, showing insight requires a tight, causal narrative of human behavior. This is a very difficult thing to provide: human behavior seldom has one cause, or even a dominant leitmotif, that can neatly explain all the events in a person's life. The Board expects causality because its primary concern is with preventing future criminality, and the underlying assumption is that this is achieved by comprehending and treating its cause.

Second, the insight story has several scripted plot points. The inmate's life up to and including the crime is a "buildup" that encompasses the root of the criminal endeavor. This is why, as explained above, innocent inmates are still supposed to demonstrate insight for how they found themselves in circumstances in which they could have committed the crime. But the real turning point of the narrative is the crime of commitment itself, which is constructed as the consequence of the flaws and failings that preceded it.

Third, importantly, "perfect insight" is impossibly to attain, but the improvement of insight is considered a cumulative project. The commissioners expect repeated hearings to evince an incremental improvement in the quality of narrative, which is measured by deeper psychic excavation and an increasing tendency to attribute events to one's own agency. Efforts to contextualize the crime are perceived as "minimization" and lack of insight.

Fourth, insight has a strong performative element—it is something that is not only *felt* but *expressed*. The inmate is expected to possess mastery and expertise as to the details of his or her own life—a tall order, as Victor Shammas explains:

Inmates are asked to recall large amounts of information about their life crime, but the events lie decades in the past, thereby becoming subject to memory slippages or even involuntary acts of repression. Inmates are often unable to study the extensive paperwork detailing their case (including the Probation Officer's Report, court transcripts, police records, and witness testimonies), and they may have (unconsciously) developed rationalizations to survive institutional life during long decades spent in prison when release seemed like—and, objectively speaking, really was—an impossibility. On the opposite side of the table, the commissioners and prosecutor have access to the documentary record with the touch of a few buttons on their computer.

Strangely, then, inmates may speak less convincingly about the experiences of their own life—the commission of the crime, its circumstances and causes—than complete strangers who were never there but who have crucial access to their case files.[86]

Moreover, the inmate is expected to display some fluency—not complete fluency, which might make the performance seem inauthentic—in describing the causes of the crime. The buzzwords, of course, are crucial, but using them verbatim could be considered evidence of manipulation and deceit. The inmate must strike the right note of rehearsed authenticity with the Board, exhibit the right amount of humility and deference. Echoes of the need to do this can be found in Commissioner Anderson's statement at Bobby Beausoleil's 2010 parole denial:

> Now, Mr. Beausoleil, one of the critical parts of being involved in a hearing is to follow the rules. I gave you ample opportunity to follow the rules today. You didn't do it. In order to allow a Board an opportunity to sufficiently provide for your suitability and hear how you think, you got to follow the rules. The rules apply to you. We set the rules, you don't. And if you don't want to follow the rules, the next Board is not going to find you suitable either, because we've got to have you follow the rules in order to make a determination whether you're suitable for parole, and part of that is your presentation. Your presentation was poor today. And I read the prior transcript, which I was on, and it was poor last time. So, you've got a pretty good track record right now. I suggest you follow the rules, sir. It will be better for you.[87]

But it is also tricky to demonstrate sincerity about one's analysis of one's own shortcomings. When not characterizing an inmate's response as "minimizing," the Board will sometimes argue that the insight is not genuine. In doing so, they often rely on the psychiatric evaluation (see my discussion of these evaluations in chapter 5). Any aspects of the inmate's presentation that remain wanting are filled with blanks from the inmate's past, specifically the crime of commitment. Because of this, litigation from the mid-2000s to the 2010s—and particularly in the post-*Lawrence* era—shows the meaning of *insight* as contested territory between the parole board and the federal courts. What these cases largely reveal is a tendency, on the part of the Board and the governor, to use *insight* as a thinly veiled manifestation of the heinousness of the original crime.

One area of contention relates to the cumulative nature of the narrative. The Board and the governor sometimes disbelieve an inmate's insight if it is "too recent." The expectation is that these narratives develop gradually, and a quick enlightenment or gain in insight is deemed inauthentic. For example, in *In re Wen Lee,* the governor reversed the Board's grant of parole, claiming that the commitment offense was particularly heinous and that inmate's acceptance of responsibility was "too recent." The court reversed and held that the recent nature of the inmate's acceptance of responsibility is irrelevant to a determination of parole suitability as long as the acceptance is sincere.[88] Similarly, in *In re Barker,* the court reversed a parole denial in which the Board found that the inmate's extensive rehabilitative gains were "too recent." The court held that the suitability factors do not require that an inmate's gains be maintained over an extended period of time.[89]

Another disputed area concerns, as mentioned above, the relevance of guilt to the expression of insight. In *In re McDonald,* the governor reversed a grant of parole due to the inmate's "limited claim of responsibility," which demonstrated that he "lacked insight." The court reversed, holding that an inmate's claim of innocence is not probative of a lack of insight, provided that it is plausible in light of the evidence.[90] A similar reasoning was given in *In re Jackson,* where the court held that the Board's denial of parole due to a refusal to admit guilt was expressly forbidden by Title 15.[91]

There is also tension between the relative importance accorded to insight and dangerousness by the Board and the governor on one hand and the courts on the other. The courts expect insight not to be the be-all, end-all of parole denial; rather, they expect a causal relationship between the lack of insight and dangerousness. In *In re Twinn,* the governor reversed a parole grant due to his impression that the inmate "lacked insight" and minimized his responsibility. The court reversed, holding that the governor failed to establish a rational nexus between the inmate's alleged lack of insight and his current dangerousness; the fact the inmate did not have insight into the causative factors of the commitment offense in the past was not sufficient evidence that he was presently dangerous.[92] A similar reversal occurred in *In re Rodriguez,* where the governor found that the inmate "lacked insight, largely relying on the psychological report's conclusion to that effect. Here, too, the court reversed, holding that the governor had failed to show that inmate's "lack of insight" was related to a determination of current dangerousness, given the inmate's expression of remorse.[93]

In the post-*Lawrence* era, the heinousness of the crime is not, in itself, grounds for a reversal. But the Board has folded the original crime into the term *insight* and thus ensured its ongoing relevance. In 2009, in *In re Lewis,* the Sixth District Court of Appeal considered evidence from the Santa Clara County Superior Court that the Board found the crime "especially heinous" in 100 percent of cases in which parole was denied. While the superior court had ordered the Board to change its rules and to train its commissioners to end this practice, the court of appeal held that the superior court had gone too far, because there was no proof that the Board's finding of heinousness was the *only* reason for denying parole in all of the nearly three thousand cases reviewed.[94]

Finally, what is unique about insight and essentially awards the Board a carte blanche to deny parole is the fact that introspection can be a bottomless pit. It is always possible to ask a person to search deeper within himself or herself and find a crevice within, even if already extensively discussed, that merits further pondering. Granted, sometimes these are fairly obvious: in *In re Rozzo,* there was ample evidence of a racial motive, and Rozzo's refusal to acknowledge it showed a "lack of insight" sufficient for justifying the governor's reversal of his parole grant.[95] But insight cannot always be shown to the Board's satisfaction. *In re Singler,* the court rejected the Board's claim that Mr. Singler lacked "insight" into the crime because he couldn't explain exactly why he had killed his wife and what would stop him from acting violently in the future. The court found that Mr. Singler completely understood his crime and that he had taken steps to change his behavior and improve himself, even though he did not perform self-inquiry to the Board's satisfaction.[96]

The problem of the bottomless pit of insight is especially striking in Leslie Van Houten's case. By 2013, Van Houten had already undergone numerous hearings, hailed as a discipline-free inmate, active in rehabilitation, and contributing to the prison. Even then, in rejecting her parole, the Board mined her life in the mid-1960s for further self-exploration before it would grant parole:

> You only have one disciplinary write-up which isn't even a serious rules violation, and it's from 1981, a very long time ago. And that's why it's troubling to this Panel that after 44 years of this crime that you committed that you still demonstrate that material deficiency in your insight, in your insight into yourself. The question was posed, and it's been for the last 44 years: Were you a follower? Well, are you a follower? Are you a leader? Are you a manipulator? What kind of person are you? You were very popular when you were younger. That's the sense I got. You were the homecoming princess. You engaged in pro-social activities. Yet you have this event happen in your life. You become

pregnant. And then you feel that you've been manipulated by your mother. You were manipulated to get an abortion. You revolted and you joined a group of other people who had manipulative ways. . . . You also admitted to victimizing your own father, your family member. And he was the one who was supporting you when you were pregnant. . . . And you had racial hatred. . . . And you were a person in your family who—you weren't raised that way. So you need to demonstrate what made you that person to engage in those acts so long ago.[97]

These aspects of Van Houten's personal life had already been discussed to death in her previous hearings. It is unclear, after forty-four years, what the Board expected as her epiphany in the following hearing. Indeed, the 2017 hearing, in which the Board recommended her release, was laudatory about her insight, even though Van Houten's basic narrative had not changed from the already deeply introspective soliloquy she offered in 2013. The vagueness of insight offers the Board unfettered discretion, as their assessment of the inmate's performance is highly subjective and challenging for judicial review (see chapter 5 for an in-depth discussion of this issue, particularly in the context of disciplinary write-ups and rehabilitative program).

We now turn to two categories of participants that make it even more difficult to express credible insight before the Board: the prosecutor and the victims.

THE INCREASING ROLE OF THE PROSECUTOR: THE "MORAL MEMORY" OF THE BOARD

The prosecutor's active participation at the parole hearings, now part and parcel of any hearing, seems less remarkable now than it was in the late 1970s, when the Board was only beginning to deviate from its traditional rehabilitative function. At the time, since the decision to release an inmate was based on a clinical observation of rehabilitation rather than a retrial for the original crime, the prosecutor was irrelevant and unnecessary. Accordingly, several of the inmates in this study expressed surprise, on the record, when they saw a prosecutor at the hearing—particularly when the prosecutor was Stephen Kay, who coprosecuted the original Tate-LaBianca cases with Bugliosi.

Kay continued to attend the hearings for decades, and in his many media interviews in the years since the murder unapologetically reiterated that the murderers, whose sentence commutations were a legal anomaly, should never see the light of day. Much of the creation of the prosecutor's role at the hearing is Kay's work; as early as the 1980s, he saw it as his mission to "make sure the evil of the Tate-LaBianca murders is never forgotten."[98] Kay pioneered a program to encourage prosecutors to continue attending parole hearings of inmates they prosecuted at trial, making the prosecutorial presence at hearings one more example of the Manson cases' contribution to the construction of the extreme-punishment trifecta.

Kay's presence at Patricia Krenwinkel's first hearing appears to have been a surprise. The defense attorney was surprised to see him there, and Kay himself reported not having been notified of the hearing. Notice the conciliatory way in which Board member DeLeon explains Kay's role in the proceedings: "Now, we have a Deputy District Attorney present from Los Angeles County, and what we're going to do—this is not an adversary hearing. And so, we will permit the Deputy District Attorney to make a statement, whatever you would like, at the beginning and then at the close, before counsel for Miss Krenwinkel makes his final statement. But you will have the duty to make the final statement. Now is that satisfactory, Counsel?"[99] His presence surprised Krenwinkel as well, according to the Tate family memoir: "Yes, I knew this hearing would be held. I was just given notice only about five days ago, though, of my attorney, and I had no idea that Mr. Kay would be here at all. So, I had no—you know, I was not—I'm not prepared for that."[100]

Kay's presentation is very emotional and includes some creative, evocative authorship. He reminds the panel that Krenwinkel "had such a deep remorse" for participating in the murder that "the only thing she had to say was her complaint that her hand hurt because, when she stabbed the victim, she kept hitting her bones." Later, he says, she watched TV coverage of the murders "so she could see what a good job she had done."[101] Similarly, in 1979 Kay expresses indignation about Krenwinkel's lenient incarceration conditions and ventures to guess why she was absent from her parole hearing:

> So it might be one thing that she is functioning well as a lifeguard at the prison pool, and somehow, I don't quite understand why—a person goes to prison, and they have the ability to swim in the swimming pool, but aside from that, what happens when stress comes into her life? I mean, what happens if she would be placed in a free society? Look at today, we have a good example of what happens when stress is in her life. Does she show up for this hearing? No, she refused to come to this hearing. That's stress because she knew that the TV cameras were going to be here; the reporters were going to

be here; so instead of facing up to this stressful situation, she just refused to come. I think that's a very good indication.[102]

In 1981, he diagnoses her demeanor:

If you just look at her in the way she talks and the sharpness, there is a lot of deep-seated anger there which, of course, in the prison situation is suppressed. She wants to get out, and the way you get out is you have to be a model prisoner. We see this not only in Krenwinkel, but in Atkins, Van Houghton [*sic*], some of the others. They know that their chances are slim, if any, to get out, and the only way to get out is to be a model prisoner.[103]

And in 1989:

Having known Patricia Krenwinkel for 20 years, I can tell Doctor Armstrong that Patricia Krenwinkel has ice water running through her veins, and what she is missing is a heart and soul.[104]

Kay sees himself as fighting an uphill battle against the permissiveness of parole releases: "The public is very concerned about Patricia Krenwinkel and her codefendants getting out on parole. I think it would be a great deterrent value to show the public that not everyone who commits murder can automatically get out on parole."[105]

Kay's project to establish himself as the "moral memory" of the Manson Family murders was, indeed, an uphill battle in its early stages. At Charles Manson's 1978 hearing, the Board actually sustains some of Manson's objections to Kay's narrative, asking him to stick to the court record:

KAY: Mr. Manson would either himself pass out the LSD, or someone else would pass it out, and everybody would have to put it on their tongue and stick out their tongue to see that they were taking it.

MANSON: Can I object to the Board again?

DELEON: Yes.

MANSON: How is this man going to sit here and say who stuck their tongues out, and who was doing this, and who was doing that, and all of that? All of that was never entered into the court. That's all storybook.

DELEON: Okay. Objection is sustained. That is not a part of the record, Mr. Kay. If you will, please, restrict your remarks to that which is a part of the record.[106]

This exchange is notable because it precedes the solidification of the court record as the one and only source of truth about the crime. The Board seems as interested in Manson's point of view, does not exhibit a strong preference to Kay's narrative over Manson's, and on occasion, such as in the following exchange, virtually partners with Manson and his attorney in cross-examining Kay:

CHADERJIAN: Is there any direct evidence to indicate that Mr. Manson told Watson what to do?

KAY: As far as the evidence is concerned—and I said, of course, there is a dispute between Mr. Watson and Mr. Manson—but as far as the evidence is concerned, and as far as I am concerned, Mr. Manson told Mr. Watson to go to the residence and kill everybody there, but didn't tell him how to do t.

MANSON: That was not what was brought up in court.

KULLA [MANSON'S ATTORNEY]: That is also not the question that Mr. Chaderjian—he asked if you had any direct evidence. I'd like to have that answered.

CHADERJIAN: Your answer said—

KAY: Well, M. Watson states that Mr. Manson told him everything to do and how to do the murders, and everything. I don't believe Mr. Watson on that. Mr. Manson might have told him more than just kill everybody there, but how much more I don't know.

CHADERJIAN: Very well.

MANSON: May I offer this to the Board? Mr. Watson said in the trial that I was in that he didn't know whether he was his mother, or whether he was Charlie Manson. That was the extent of his testimony in the courtroom that I was in.

DELEON: Very well.

CHADERJIAN: Referring to you?

MANSON: That was the extent of his testimony, period.

DELEON: Very well. Proceed, Mr. Kay.[107]

Even when Kay limits himself to the facts, in the earlier hearings Krenwinkel's defense attorneys object, as in 1979:

GOMEZ: I believe that if there is some new information that Mr. Kay wishes to add, perhaps that would be something that is proper for consideration at this hearing. But merely rehashing of facts that have been brought out over the course of time . . . I don't think this is the appropriate place. We stipulated . . . that we could consider previous factual summaries that are contained within her file. . . . There's no need to . . . basically relive the crimes.

ROOS: . . . I think Mr. Kay does have the right to put on record what he feels are the highlights of the case. . . . I understand your objection, but he'll be allowed to proceed.[108]

And a year later, her new attorney, Haws, complains about Kay's prior presentations, which went beyond the trial record. He finds "a considerable amount of extraneous material that does not, in fact, go to the actual deed. It seems to be more of an attorney's argument before a jury."[109] The Board offers Haws the opportunity to "question your client so that whatever particular statement you would want in the record would be in the record," which is clearly not a solution to the problem Haws is describing. Subsequently, the Board overrules his objection.

As Kay becomes a fixture at the hearings and his status as moral memory is solidified, Krenwinkel's attorney makes efforts in 1985, 1988, and 1989 to disqualify his presence. She argues not having received sufficient notice of his presence under the regulations. Each of these objections is summarily rejected ("Okay, that's overruled"[110]).

While Kay's participation often served as an original source of information about the trial, the idea that the prosecutor is a living preservation of the trial record and of the original crime persists and becomes imputed to other prosecutors present at the hearings, even though they did not try the original crime. As early as 1979, Beausoleil unsuccessfully objects to the presence of a new prosecutor, Montagna, at the hearing, saying, "I do not know if he has something new that he could offer this panel or not."[111] These subsequent prosecutors assume the role of moral memory by becoming authorities about trials they did not personally prosecute. For example, Jonas, a prosecutor testifying at Beausoleil's 1984 hearing, intervenes in the proceedings to explain that Beausoleil's ties to the Manson Family were proven at trial by Mary Brunner. The commissioners ask him what he remembers of that trial, and the defense attorney objects: "I've got to object now, because we're going to be asking for Mr. Jonas's recall of what happened at the trial, when he wasn't there."[112] At the 1985 hearing, Jonas actually poses questions to Beausoleil about factual aspects of the crime, and Helbert, Beausoleil's lawyer, advises him not to answer them: "He's already responded to every one of those questions in previous hearings, and he's not going to offer any further response at this hearing."[113]

But the prosecutor's role expands beyond a purely preservative one. By 1986, Kay expands his role at the hearings beyond the official record keeper of the events and toward the present and the future—as shown when he interrogates Manson about his peculiar crafts in his cell: "What Mr. Manson does in his cell most of the time is to make scorpions—not, not dolls, but to make scorpions. And I would be interested to find out the significance from Mr. Manson of making scorpions." Manson's predictable response is that "the power to hurt is being given to people to try to save the air, the water, clean up the water, stop cutting the trees down, and redeem the wildlife from zoos. So in order to communicate to some people who are locked in their minds and death wishes, sometimes you have to get nasty with them. So the power of the scorpion gives a revolution to the heart of the people again."[114] Kay's intent—to lure Manson into mystical, dark speeches that will demonstrate his parole unsuitability—succeeds, and what's more, it cements Kay's authority to interrogate Manson at the parole hearing.

Kay's successors at the hearings proceed in similar fashion. Jones, the prosecutor at Beausoleil's 1983 hearing, comments about the inmate's lack of insight as it stems from an interview Beausoleil had given to Truman Capote.[115] By 1985, a subsequent prosecutor, Jonas, submits materials about the Capote interview, apparently conducted as background for an unreleased film about murderers on death row.[116] Back in 1983, Jones also acted as the moral compass of the Board, reminding them of Beausoleil's original capital sentence:

JONES: As this Board knows, Mr. Beausoleil, one point in time, was a condemned man on Death Row, and that was based upon the offense that was committed. And that is of great concern to the District Attorney's Office that a person that was considered that dangerous now sees himself, and perhaps others see him, as a candidate fit to be given a date.[117]

BEAUSOLEIL: I come to a hearing and the District Attorney's Office communicates 1969 [the year in which the crimes were committed] in the hearing, rather than if nothing has happened in the interim and no changes had taken place.[118]

Perhaps the most faithful follower of Kay's legacy is Patrick Sequeira, whose presence at the hearings becomes a defining feature of the transcripts in the 2000s. Like Kay's, Sequeira's discussion of the facts is highly emotional, and he does not limit himself to commenting on the crime of commitment; rather, he expresses his opinions about the inmates' sincerity and insight. At Susan Atkins's hearings, Sequeira comments on her psychiatric evaluations, expressing doubts at her 2005 hearing that the psychiatrist's favorable opinion about Atkins's remorse is valid. James Whitehouse, Atkins's husband and attorney, complains to the Board about Sequeira's mention of uncharged crimes, and about his doubts regarding Susan's finances and prison behavior: "2030(d)(2) states that the role of the prosecutor at these hearings is to comment on the facts of the case. For the last 20 years he's regaled us with stories about preincarceration history and postincarceration history. And I thought that was improper and in violation of this code."[119]

The Board rejects Whitehouse's objection, and Sequeira freely comments on present and future factors as well. In expressing doubts about a psychiatric evaluation that diagnoses Atkins as a low-risk inmate, Sequeira says, "I agree with Mr. Whitehouse . . . in that if this psychiatrist can miss something as obvious as her being married for 17 years, then how can one really feel that this psychiatric report is accurate."[120] At this point, Sequeira is considered a legitimate commentator not only on the inmates' records, but also on their flaws in the present and future.

Finally, the prosecutor's crystallized role at the hearings is also reflected by the gradual merging of his rhetoric and role with that of the crime victims, whose presence at the hearings increases in number and substance in the 2000s. This solidifies the role of the prosecutor as someone who speaks not only for the court but for the victims—even if some victims are present in the room to speak for themselves. At Atkins's last hearing, in 2009, members of both the Tate and Sebring families attend the hearing, and in addition two prosecutors—Sequeira and Purley—are present. The commissioners observe that there are two DAs and ask, "Who's going to be lead on this matter?" Sequeira explains: "I'm actually—will be representing the Los Angeles County District Attorney's Office. Mr. Purley is here as an observer and he's been asked to read a letter from one of the victim's family members. So his only participation will be to read this letter at the conclusion of the hearing."[121]

In the post–Marsy's Law world of parole, therefore, the prosecutors and the victims meld into a uniform punitive contingent; not only do they echo each other's rhetorical arguments, but they actually speak for each other, reading each other's letters and citing each other. We now turn to the victims and their presence in the room.

THE INCREASING ROLE OF THE VICTIMS AND THEIR ALLIES: FROM THE PERSONAL TO THE POLITICAL

In many parole hearings, and certainly those of the Manson Family inmates, there is a constant reminder of the crime present in the room in the form of the victim. Victims have been allowed in the parole hearing room since the Victim Rights Bill of 1982. The bill, which passed as a voter initiative added Section 3043 to the California Penal Code, which required giving a thirty-day notice of parole hearings to victims.[122]

Even before victim families were present in the room, their reputations were discussed and protected. For example, at Beausoleil's 1981 hearing, the Board balked at Beausoleil's suggestion that Hinman's murder was related to a "bad drug deal" in which the victim was complicit, seeing it as a form of "minimization" of Beausoleil's responsibility.[123] But in the mid-1980s, the victims' families began to speak for themselves. The Tate family memoir, *Restless Souls,* documents their involvement in the parole hearings starting in the late 1970s, but the transcripts show the first parole-hearing appearance of Doris Tate, Sharon Tate's mother, at Charles Watson's 1984 hearing. Doris Tate also attends Susan Atkins's hearing in 1985 and 1988; Paul Tate attends Watson's hearing in 1985. Throughout the 1980s and 1990s, the sole victim attendee is Doris Tate, with the exception of Suzan LaBerge (Rosemary LaBianca's daughter), who attends the 1990s hearing

As Table 1 shows, the 2000s brought three important developments to the victim presence at the hearings. First, we see an increase in the victim contingent beyond the Tate family. Second, many of these latecomer victims appear for the first time at hearings held decades after the crime, some of them having never personally met their slain relative. And third, Marsy's Law brings about multiple roles for victims and supporters. The law amended the Penal Code to allow "the victim, next of kin, members of the victim's family, and two representatives" to appear "personally or by counsel" and "adequately and reasonably express his, her, or their views concerning the prisoner and the case, including, but not limited to the commitment crimes, determinate term commitment crimes for which the prisoner has been paroled, any other felony crimes or crimes against the person for which the prisoner has been convicted, the effect of the enumerated crimes on the victims and the family of the victim, the person responsible for these enumerated crimes, and the suitability of the prisoner for parole."[124]

Marsy's Law's effect on the hearings was significant. For example, Charles Watson's hearings throughout the 1980s included only one victim: Doris Tate. By contrast, his 2011 hearing was attended by no less than seven people on the victim side: Debra Tate as next of kin; Michelle, Margaret, and Anthony Dimaria, next of kin to Jay Sebring, each of them reading letters from absent relatives; John Glick, a supporting person for a victim's next

TABLE 1 Victim presence at Manson Family parole hearings, 1984–2014

	Atkins	Davis	Krenwinkel	Manson	Van Houten	Watson
1982						
1983						
1984					Doris Tate, witness	
1985	Doris Tate, next of kin				Paul Tate, next of kin	
1986					Doris Tate, next of kin	
1987					Doris Tate, next of kin	
1988	Doris Tate, next of kin					
1989						
1990						Doris Tate, next of kin Susan LaBerge, next of kin
1991						
1992						
1993						
1994						
1995						Patricia Tate, next of kin Ellen Rediger, victim assistance Linda Senn, victim assistance Toni Wilson, victim services representative
2000				John Desantis, next of kin Louis Smaldino, next of kin Angela Smaldino, next of kin Mr. Bee, victim services coordinator		

Year					
2002			Debra Tate, next of kin Debbie Mitchell, victim services representative	Angela Smaldino, next of kin Louis Smaldino, next of kin John Desantis, next of kin Debra Tate, victim support	
2004				John Desantis, victim's next of kin Angela Smaldino, next of kin Louis Smaldino, next of kin Anthony Dimaria, next of kin support Debra Tate, next of kin support	
2005	Debra Tate, next of kin Anthony Dimaria, next of kin Margaret Dimaria, next of kin Marie Ford, next of kin June Jones, victim services advocate				
2006				Anthony Dimaria, next of kin Jamie Luna, observer John Desantis, next of kin Lewis Smaldino, next of kin Debra Tate, support/observer	Debra Tate, victim's sister Jean Weiss, victim escort
2007			Debra Tate, victim's sister Jo Klinge, support person for Debra Tate	Louis Smaldino, observer Debra Tate, observer Anthony Dimaria, observer	

(continued)

TABLE 1 *Continued*

	Atkins	Davis	Krenwinkel	Manson	Van Houten	Watson
2009	Debra Tate, next of kin Anthony Dimaria, next of kin Margaret Dimaria, next of kin Michele Dimaria, next of kin Nancy Gunn, victim services advocate					
2010					Louis Smaldino, victim advocate Deborah Tate, victim advocate spokesperson Jamie Luna, victim/witness representative, observer Barbara Hoyt, observer	
2011			Debra Tate, next of kin Anthony Dimaria, next of kin Jamie Luna, victim witness representative			Michelle Dimaria, next of kin Margaret Dimaria, next of kin Anthony Dimaria, next of kin Deborah Tate, next of kin John Glick, next of kin support Lynn Matthews, next of kin support Leslie Kowalczyk, victim advocate

2012	2013	2014
Debra Tate, next of kin	John Lamontagne, next of kin Leslie Lamontagne, next of kin Anthony Dimaria, next of kin and representative Lou Smaldino, next of kin and representative Todd Spitzer, next of kin and representative Debra Tate, next of kin and representative Jamie Luna, victim witness representative Barbara Hoyt, witness	Kay Hinman Martley, next of kin Debra Tate, victim representative Barbara Hoyt, victim representative Nate Brekke, victim services advocate
Debra Tate, next of kin representative Barbara Hoyt, next of kin representative Michelle Azpiroz, victim services Leif Brekke, victim services		

of kin; Lynn Matthews, another supporter of victim's next of kin, reading a letter from yet another relative absent from the hearing; and Leslie Kowalczyk, victim's advocate.

Importantly, opening the hearings not just to victims' next-of-kin but to advocates, representatives, and supporters of the victims, has allowed Debra Tate, who attends almost all the hearings, a sphere of influence far beyond the hearings concerning her sister's murder. Since 2002, Debra Tate has attended every single one of Leslie Van Houten's hearings, despite the fact that Van Houten was not involved in Tate's murder and, in fact, was unaware of it at the time. Tate attends these hearings under different designations; for example, in 2002 she is listed as "victim support,"[125] in 2006 and 2007 as "observer,"[126] in 2010 as "victim's advocate spokesperson,"[127] and in 2013 as "representative."[128] Other members of the victims' families similarly change designations throughout the 2000s, guaranteeing a powerful showing of people affected by the Manson Family at the hearings, tugging at the Board's conscience to see all the crimes—including those that do not involve their particular relatives—as actions of one heinous criminal enterprise.

The complicated designations of victim categories mean that efforts to object to their presence meet rejection, as there is always a legal justification, under Marsy's Law, to be present in the room. At Atkins's 2009 hearing, Whitehouse protests:

> WHITEHOUSE: In order for such persons to be admitted to the hearing the person requesting support shall advise the Board and the name of the support person at the time he or she informs the board of his and her intention to attend. . . . That has to be no later than 30 days prior to the date. And as you know, 10 minutes ago there were no support people when we talked about this prior to the hearing. . . .
>
>   What I'm understanding at this point is Richard Dallago is actually married or supporting Ms. Debra Tate. Is—am I wrong on that?
>
> PROSECUTOR SEQUEIRA: He's not going to present. He is simply supporting someone in their presentation today.[129]

Panel attorneys told me at interviews that objecting to the presence of particular victims or support people in the room can backfire. Even when the objection is made by the attorney rather than by the inmate, it can suggest downplaying the suffering of distant relatives or representatives, which could be imputed to the inmate to his or her detriment.

As with the prosecutor's presence, the victim's presence expanded over time in parole hearings, not only numerically but also thematically. At Bruce Davis's second 2012 hearing, Debra Tate and Barbara Hoyt (neither of whom is a victim of the crime) arrive only to find that the hearing has been postponed due to health reasons; the Board reports that Davis has collapsed, and his attorney requested a continuance. The prosecutor, Sequeira, expresses his doubts about Davis's illness (which is documented and occurred in front of the Board), and the victims chime in:

SEQUEIRA: Well, my comment is that I think it's an interesting coincidence that I was also informed today that defense counsel wanted to postpone the hearing for other reasons than his client's health, due to not being prepared, or having material that he hasn't reviewed. And that combined with the inmate's sudden medical issues raises a certain amount of suspicion in my mind. And if it were just me coming back, it's not so inconvenient so I can come back. But we are talking about victims' families and victims' families' representatives who expended quite a bit of expense to come here from long distances, and despite their own medical issues, you know, Ms. Hoyt here is a dialysis patient.

HOYT: I'm missing two dialysis sessions to be here.

FERGUSON: And we're very sensitive to that.

HOYT: I just believe that this is really convenient, and I do not believe these ethics [sic] at all.

FERGUSON: Well, the panel does not—does not share that suspicion because it happened during a hearing. Mr. Beckman was here and didn't know what had happened. It happened aside—apart from that. There was no way he could of [sic]—

HOYT: What was his discharge diagnosis? I'm an RN. I've been an RN for 38 years, so I would be very interested in knowing what the vitals were, what the EKG, if they did one, said. I would like to know—I would like to know the discharge diagnosis, and the admitting diagnosis, and, of course, the treatment, if I may.

FERGUSON: And we don't know.

HOYT: Well, I think those things matter.[130]

Note how Hoyt assumes the mantle of a medical expert to theorize about Davis's medical condition and request information.

The victims' statements evince repetitive thematical tropes, the most common of which is an equivalence between the murderers and their victims. This rhetorical device is, of course, not unique to parole hearings. In his book

Murder Stories, Paul Kaplan identifies the prosecutorial technique of rhetorically positioning the defendant and the victim side by side for the jury, evoking a sensation of imperfect retribution because the defendant is still alive while the victim is not.[131] Examples of this argument can be found in the transcripts of all seven defendants. Anthony Dimaria, Jay Sebring's nephew (who admittedly lost him as a child and barely knew him), speaks at Krenwinkel's 2011 hearing: "Patricia Krenwinkel and her attorney may believe that Ms. Krenwinkel has been rehabilitated and is a changed person. But I remind the Board that there are eight people that lie in their graves who remain unchanged, unrehabilitated, unparoled. I beg the Board to consider parole for Patricia Krenwinkel only when her victims are paroled from their graves, only when each of our families recover 40 years of loss and suffering, only when, only after the interrupted destinies of each and every one of her victims are restored completely."[132]

A related theme is the inadequacy of the present to compensate for the past. Such statements seek to focus the Board's attention on the original crime and away from the inmate's present circumstances. At Tex Watson's 2011 hearing, Dimaria reads a letter written by his uncle, Fred Cumber, brother of Dimaria's other uncle, murder victim Jay Sebring, paraphrasing: "It is devastating to listen today how a college degree or involvement in self-help groups and victims outreach programs are weighed against the value of my uncle's life or with the memory of my family happy and complete until these murders. . . . Is your mother's life or your child's life worth 30 years of NA, AA, and outreach programs or a college degree?"[133]

Another rhetorical theme is reiterating the anomalous, sui generis nature of the cases. Lynn Matthews, a victim representative, reads a letter from Janet Parent, Steven Parent's sister, at Watson's 2011 hearing: "Nothing can ever bring back my brother, but what we can do is ask that justice continues being served. None of the Manson Family members convicted of these crimes should ever go free. They have received mercy when the death penalty was overturned. Our loved ones though did not receive mercy from them."[134]

The overturning of the death penalty as an act of mercy is contrasted with the mercilessness of the impact of the hearings on the victims. Margaret Dimaria says: "I believe [the revocation of the death sentences in the case] gave them a second chance. They are alive. The victims have no second chance. At that time, my parents were assured that the people who killed their son would never get out of prison. I'm extremely grateful that my parents never had to endure one of these parole hearings. I thank God for that."[135]

PHOTO 3. Charles "Tex" Watson reads a prepared statement during his parole hearing at Mule Creek State Prison in Ione, California, November 16, 2011. (Associated Press/Rich Pedroncelli)

Such statements about the death penalty obfuscate the painful and traumatic effect of the death penalty *itself* on victims. The transformation of the death penalty into a de facto life-without-parole sentence, with or (almost always) without an execution at the end (a development traced in chapter 2), is arguably more painful for victims. And even when executions do occur, it is not rare to hear victims speak against the death penalty and reject the notion that the execution has brought them closure.[136] Many California victims oppose the death penalty and campaign against it.[137]

The victims' statements also reflect the sentiment that the perpetrators can never truly redeem themselves and that their very presence at the parole hearing is evidence of their lack of remorse. Dimaria speaks about Watson: "In my opinion, if Charles Watson has true contrition for the crimes that he has committed, I don't see how he can walk into this room and ask for parole."[138] Such statements suggest that the notion of remorse and the notion of parole are irreconcilable, a perspective somewhat reminiscent of the medieval water ordeals for witchcraft, in which suspected witches would be thrown into the water; if they survived, it was evidence of their wickedness, as the pure water had rejected them, and if they drowned, it was evidence of their righteousness.[139]

The Tate family's long involvement in the case is, in itself, a powerful statement. Debra Tate invariably tells the Board that she is the "last of my line," the guardian of her family's interest in the Manson Family's continued incarceration. Her commitment to attending the hearings as she ages, sometimes with other aging family members of the victims (Barbara Hoyt as a dialysis patient at Bruce Davis's hearing comes to mind) is a constant reminder that the wound is as fresh as ever, thus diverting attention away from the present and future of the inmates and toward the past of the victims. Like the inmates' lives, which are frozen in 1969 through these narratives, the victims' lives, too, are suspended as they revisit the decades-long crime and reopen the wounds by reciting its details.

In the post–Marsy's Law hearings, victim statements read like a Greek chorus: multiple statements from different victims revisiting the same themes. Victims attending as victim representatives—particularly Debra Tate, and sometimes a second prosecutor in the room—read aloud letters written by other victims, amplifying their voices. The merging of the victim voices in the room also has the effect of merging the four different crime scenes into one. Bruce Davis, a participant in Gary Hinman's murder who was not involved in the Tate-LaBianca murders, is confronted by Tate in her role as a victim representative, not as a direct victim. Leslie Van Houten, a participant in the LaBianca murders who was unaware of the Tate murders at the time, is also confronted by Tate. Beausoleil, who was under arrest for Hinman's murder at the time of the Tate-LaBianca's murders, is the subject of an antirelease petition initiated by Debra Tate. Any effort by the inmates to distinguish their crimes from those of their fellow Manson Family members is thwarted by the ever-present Tate family as the leader of the monolithic victim chorus, reminding the Board of the Manson context and strengthening the Board's tendency to regard any effort to discuss the crimes separately as "minimization."

Importantly, the Tates' control of the hearings powerfully, and sometimes aggressively, silences alternative victims' voices. Charles Watson's 1990 hearing was attended by Suzan LaBerge, Rosemary LaBianca's daughter. LaBerge, who had befriended Tex Watson through correspondence and through their shared evangelical Christian faith, came to the 1990 hearing to support his release. In *Restless Souls,* Doris Tate (as narrated by her granddaughter, Brie Tate) tells of her encounter with LaBerge:

A hand tapped at my shoulder. "Mrs. Tate?"

I turned to face LaBerge.

"Doris, why do you do this? Don't you think the time has come to get over this and move on with your life?"

"My dear, I will never get over this. I don't have that power. This man that you are here today to defend slaughtered my daughter—and your mother—without an inkling of humanity and a world away from the Holy Spirit."

"But God has forgiven him; why can't you?" LaBerge asked.

"That is between him and God; it has nothing to do with the laws of this state. We have to have deterrents whether God has forgiven them or not; otherwise we'd have nothing but chaos . . ." My voice trailed off as LaBerge glanced away, distracted. I closed my eyes and felt his presence behind. Dear Lord, grant me the courage to fearlessly confront the past and the demons that sealed this fate.[140]

Tate then proudly recounts verbally attacking LaBerge after the hearing:

At the parking lot, Steve and I ran into Suzan LaBerge. He blocked her path of escape. "You know, Suzan, that you dishonored your mother today."

"No I didn't."

I couldn't hold my tongue a second longer. "Oh yes you did. You were there today defending the man that stabbed your mother in the back forty-two times—that's beyond human forgiveness. Every mother within the sound of my voice would cringe if their kid went into a parole hearing to beg for their killer's release. You make me so sick I can't even stand to look at you, you dumb shit."

"You have no right to talk to me that way," she hissed. "It would be wonderful if you could be like my parents."

I got in the last lick right before the press came into earshot. "Oh, go to hell."[141]

Unsurprisingly, after this altercation, LaBerge never attended another parole hearing.

This narrative of the Tates—offered in Doris's voice through the writing of her granddaughter and her niece's partner—is deeply discomfiting. Tate essentially takes on the role not only of the quintessential victim but also of the *only possible* victim. Any nonpunitive victim position—any position that can accommodate notions of redeemability or rehabilitation—is perceived as dishonorable or inhuman, and, moreover, as outside the ambit of the Victims' Rights bill. This position would certainly be strengthened after the passage of Marsy's Law in 2008.

There are two serious problems with this construction. The first is that Suzan LaBerge is far from being the only victim of violent crime whose sentiments and worldviews differ from the Tates', and yet it is the Tates' perspective that comes to claim ownership of the victims' rights discourse in California. In *The Toughest Beat*, Josh Page discusses the collaboration and melding of the California prison guard's union (CCPOA) with one of the state's most powerful victim advocacy groups, Crime Victims United of California (CVUC).[142] Page shows how the two organizations share not only a strong adherence to extreme punitiveness, but also key personnel and organizational resources, and lobby together for more severe sentencing. In his analysis of CVUC, Page identifies them as a very specific category of victims: white, middle-class victims of violent crime, for whom the dichotomy offender/victim offers no shades of gray. Sharon Tate is the quintessential example of such a victim: a white, wealthy, famous, and beautiful woman, about to give birth to a cherished white child.

Absent from this narrative are countless victims who do not experience their own victimization as a Manichean struggle against the perpetrators, primarily victims of color in inner cities, for whom violence reduction and nonviolent dispute resolution are more important than increased, interminable incarceration. Many people who have taught lifers or interacted with them in prison, including myself, have learned that most inmates who are serving time for homicide have also been touched by homicide *as victims*. At the 2018 Violence Reduction Summit in the City of Sacramento, for example, African American mothers who had lost their children to gun violence spoke up about the need to introduce initiatives for violence reduction, including a considerable institutional and financial investment in educational and vocational opportunities for young people identified as deeply involved in gun violence.[143] The experience of victimization is far from universal, and yet the criminal justice system has strongly prioritized punitive models of victim participation over nonpunitive ones, such as restorative justice and victim-offender mediation. It is of interest to mention that, as explained in *Restless Souls,* Doris Tate participated throughout the 1980s in victim-offender meetings (albeit not, of course, with the murderers of her own daughter) and has argued that some people can reform and change (albeit not, of course, the murderers of her own daughter).[144]

This also means that the worldviews of victims who have the leisure, means, and inclination to participate at parole hearings, such as the Tates and their allies, overpower those of other victims, whose sentiments are less punitive and who are therefore less motivated to attend hearings. Visiting California prisons, where the hearings are held, is a lengthy and expensive experience on account of their remote rural locations, which also means that voices of poor victims of color, who are less likely to espouse punitive views, are also less likely to voice their perspectives at hearings.

The other problem with the Tates' irrevocably unforgiving stance is the immense suffering it seems to bring to the Tate family itself. The punitive position they present at the hearings does not seem to come naturally to them. In *Restless Souls,* Brie Tate describes how she "forced [her]self to look away from photos of the pathetic and dying Susan Atkins and remember the young and vibrant Atkins who with callous disregard unjustly murdered eight people and watched them beg for their lives, fall down into their own blood, and die without an ounce of dignity."[145] This forced effort to offer no forgiveness or possibility of redemption brings the Tates, by their own admission in *Restless Souls,* even more pain. The murders and the resulting grief and anger hold the victims, as well as the inmates, in a perpetual purgatory of "life de facto."

The question whether attendance and punitive statements are healing or destructive to the victims themselves is especially poignant given Marsy's Law's facilitation of late emergence of victims who had never, or barely, met the victims. Some of the victims that emerged in the late 2000s were young children when the crimes were committed and others were not even born. It would be presumptuous to assume that these victims attend the hearings to advance a punitive political agenda rather than to publicly voice their personal pain. But attending the hearings is costly and cumbersome, which should at least raise the question whether expanding the categories of victims, representatives, and support people exposes a broader population to an experience whose therapeutic value can and should be seriously questioned.

The victims' positions at the hearings are important not only in themselves but in their effect on the tenor of the hearings, including the performance of the inmates and their lawyers. The inmates facing the victims are placed in a difficult situation: anything said to counter the sentiments or facts expressed by the victims will be taken as disrespect, and thus lack of insight and remorse. The only acceptable response is to apologize to the victim, which the inmates are barred from doing: Marsy's Law states: "Neither the prisoner nor the attorney for the prisoner shall be entitled to ask questions of any person appearing at the hearing pursuant to subdivision (b) of section 3043."[146] Thus, even though the victims are present, the apology has to be offered to the Board, which lends an artificial quality to the conversation. For example, here is Patricia Krenwinkel's apology, after being told by the prosecutor that her very presence in the parole hearing is an expression of lack of remorse, because it suggests that she feels worthy of release:

KRENWINKEL: All I really have is an apology. I'm just haunted each and every day by the unending suffering my participation in murders caused the family and hurt my victims; the enormity of the grief I have caused fills me with intense sorrow. I'm so ashamed of my actions. I am ever aware that the victims who perished had so much life yet to live and their family and friends have been forever severed from those loving relationships. [inaudible] I'm sorry.

MELANSON: I'm sorry. I have to ask you to address your comments to the panel.

KRENWINKEL: I am also aware that for a period of time between the murders and my arrest, there was tremendous fear in the country, the state, and more specifically in Los Angeles, and to you, the citizenry, I apologize again, for the unbearable pain I caused to so many. I know the words are totally inadequate, but I am so deeply sorry.[147]

While addressing the victims at the hearing is forbidden, the Board criticizes Krenwinkel and the others for *not* addressing the victims in writing: "We heard Ms. Tate testify that not one of the perpetrators in the Manson clan have written a letter to the victims of this crime. And that really raises some concern with this Panel, why not. And that's a question that, Ms. Krenwinkel, I'd like for you to answer to yourself and think about and ponder on, because there's got to be a reason."[148]

One might wonder how conducive the hearing atmosphere, faced by a bloc of opponents the inmate may not directly address, might be to writing conciliatory letters to the victims. The hearings do not offer an opportunity for unscripted, spontaneous engagement, nor are they a container in which such engagement could have healing, productive effects. Given the setting, an expression of remorse at the hearing can only be suspected of insincerity (and be openly excoriated as such by the prosecutor and the ever-increasing group of victims and their spokespeople). In *Justice through Apologies,* Nick Smith argues against court-ordered apologies, whose very nature casts doubt on their authenticity.[149] The context of the hearings would likely render even letters written *outside* the hearing room insincere, as they could easily be interpreted as means to an end. The hearing transcripts, as well as the victims' memoir, suggest that the imperfect confrontation at the hearing room is

PHOTO 4. Patricia Krenwinkel appears at a parole hearing with her attorney Kevin Wattley and parole commissioners Susan Melanson and Steven Hernandez at the California Institution for Women in Corona, California, January 20, 2011. (Associated Press/Reed Saxon)

anything but healing and cathartic for the victims *or* for the inmates, and by its very nature it is designed *not* to produce the outcome that the Board ostensibly seeks: genuine insight and remorse.

Kathryne Young, who interviewed parole commissioners, found that her interviewees universally declared that their parole decisions were *not* affected by victim statements.[150] Moreover, most commissioners reported that victim presence and statements did not even impact the *difficulty* of making a suitability determination.[151] The only type of victim input that was found to be useful to the Board involved specific facts that would affect conditions of release.[152] At first blush, these findings appear to contradict studies conducted in Pennsylvania, Alabama, and California, according to which "when victims attend hearings, the grant rate is less than half the rate when victims do not attend."[153] However, as Young points out, the correlation between victim presence and grant rates is likely due to victims' tendency to attend initial hearings but not subsequent hearings; since inmates are less likely to receive parole grants at their first hearing, "the relationship between the two factors may not be causal at all."[154]

What the commissioners did note, however, was the deleterious emotional effect of the victims' statements on the hearing process itself. The commissioners did not limit the time allotted for victim statements; consequently, lengthy victim statements could take a hearing well past the two- or three-hour mark, and sometimes late into the evening. Young finds that "by and large, the commissioners viewed these long hearings not only as a major inconvenience, but as a threat to the integrity of the hearings process itself. They reported that it is difficult to keep themselves in top form for more than seven or eight hours in a hearings day."[155] Additionally, the commissioners reported that the victims' presence had an emotional impact on them, as victims directed their anger personally at them and monitored their expressions for signs of sympathy.[156]

Nevertheless, some of Young's interviewees believed that victim presence at the hearing was "good for the process." Some believed that forcing inmates to face their victims could be psychologically beneficial. There were mixed views on whether the victims' presence was good for the victims themselves; some thought that speaking at the hearings helped the victims grieve or gave them "closure," and others "believed that coming to parole hearings prevented victims from 'moving on.'"[157] One of her interviewees commented: "I've seen it as many times it being a cathartic thing for the victim's next of kin as it is a bad thing. Because you've got families who don't ever talk coming together just for this. And they relive it, they get all fired up, they get all animated, and it's some big to-do and the hate for this person. And they feed on it. It just doesn't get any better and they're not healing themselves. So that one works both ways."[158]

Young's findings dovetail with my own findings. Post–Marsy's Law hearings for the inmates in the Manson Family cases were considerably longer, with victim statements sometimes taking up a least a third of the overall length of the transcript. It is impossible, of course, to authoritatively say that the concerted effort to present an amplified, punitive victims' voice is the reason for the repeated parole denials. But the way in which these statements are offered raises serious concerns about due process as well as about the beneficial effect of this legal reform on everyone involved—including the victims themselves.

CONCLUSION

When I was little, my dad told me this joke:

> The fox and the wolf wanted to beat up the rabbit. They decided to go over and see whether the rabbit had a hat on. If it did, they'd say, "Why do you

have a hat?" and beat him up. If it didn't, they'd say, "Why don't you have a hat?" and beat him up. They went over and saw that the rabbit didn't have a hat on. So, they said, "Why don't you have a hat?" and beat him up.

The next morning, the fox and the wolf wanted to beat up the rabbit again. They decided to ask the rabbit for cigarettes. If the rabbit offered them cigarettes with a filter, they'd say, "Why did you give us cigarettes with a filter?" and beat him up. If the rabbit offered them cigarettes without a filter, they'd say, "Why did you give us cigarettes without a filter?" and beat him up.

They arrived at the rabbit's and said, "Hey, rabbit, give us some cigarettes."

The rabbit said, "With or without a filter?"

They said, "Why don't you have a hat?" and beat him up.

Even though the crime of commitment in these cases is far from funny, the transcripts suggest that the Board, like the fox and the wolf, has a particular outcome in mind and interprets the information before it accordingly.

Discussing one's past—a past the inmate tries to leave behind—at a parole hearing is a minefield. Even though, after *Lawrence,* the heinousness of the offense in itself cannot serve as a proxy for risk, the human beings on the other side of the table will naturally be horrified by heinous crimes and be reluctant to release their perpetrators, whether or not they acknowledge this as a basis for their decision. In addition to the natural tendency not to portray oneself at one's worst, there are habituations from trial, at least in the first hearings: thinking like a defendant, not like an inmate. It is a double bind: maximize your responsibility and appear a dangerous and unscrupulous person, or minimize it and display lack of insight.

The hearings also made me question the value of remorse as a predictor of desistance. On December 12, 2016, an Israeli parole board released a convicted rapist, Moshe Katsav, at his third hearing. His release put him in the minority of Israeli prisoners: while all Israeli prisoners receive a hearing after two-thirds of their sentence, only about 30 percent of them receive parole.[159] Katsav's release was remarkable because he was no ordinary prisoner: he had been the president of Israel. The offenses were committed while he had still been in high office, using the power of his distinguished position to forcibly rape several women who worked for him.

Throughout the trial, Katsav maintained his innocence, claiming that the women's complaints against him were fabricated and attributing the media onslaught against him to racism. Katsav continued to proclaim his innocence from prison, in the face of strong evidence against him. He participated in prison programming, which is more extensive in Israel than in California, but never expressed remorse for his crimes at the hearings. In the parole decision, the Israeli board said that expressing remorse was not a condition for release and that it was convinced by Katsav's record as a model prisoner and by the negligible risk he now posed that he was rehabilitated and safe to return to society.

Katsav's release provoked massive public outcry, especially from feminist organizations and victim advocacy groups. The fury about his parole was compounded by an unrelated event: On the same day, Katsav's successor, President Rubi Rivlin, declined clemency to a man called Yonathan Hailu, who had been convicted of manslaughter for killing a man who had raped and extorted him. President Rivlin reasoned that the purpose of the clemency process was not to replace the sentencing court's discretion, which already included a six-year "discount" because of the mitigating circumstances. This poor reasoning was excoriated by hundreds of commentators arguing that the purpose of clemency was *precisely* to provide mercy and hope where law could not reach. Katsav's release and Hailu's clemency denial were juxtaposed by critics and taken as a whole to argue that the state did not take rape seriously: it released its perpetrators and denied justice to its victims.

The outcry aside, the Israeli parole board's reluctance to require remorse makes sense: it is not obvious that remorse and reoffending risk are correlated. Stripped of the power of his office and his access to young women, Katsav would likely not rape again, and therefore would not pose recidivism risks. Whether his rehabilitation process was genuine or a sham, his personal record differed greatly from that of most other prisoners, who would face serious reentry hurdles due to poverty, lack of educational and vocational opportunities, and in many cases mental illness and/or substance abuse. Moreover, while Katsav's conviction rested on a solid factual basis, an alarming percentage of others who plead innocence do eventually turn out to be innocent. Many of those people, such as famed Israeli exoneree Amos Baranes and the three exonerees of the Danny Katz murder, were reviled for years for not admitting to crimes they turned out not to have committed. Had the public disbelieved the complainants' accusations against Katsav (and his family and supporters, indeed, claim to disbelieve them), we might be impressed by his willpower and valiant struggle to clear his name.

Between the discomfort with Katsav's denials and lack of remorse and the Manson Family members' repeated dialogues and monologues about their remorse and insight, I realized that David Ball's argument that the parole hearing is, in fact, an inalienable part of the sentencing process and should be treated as such is more than a creative academic polemic;[160] it reflects the very real weight the past, as discussed by the court and as processed by the inmate, bears on the inmate's present and future. The next chapter examines how the Board interprets and constructs the inmate's prison experience.

FIVE

Reinventing the Present

CRAFTING AND INTERPRETING THE
INMATE'S PRISON EXPERIENCE

O nobly-born, if thou hast not understood the above at this
moment, through the influence of karma, thou wilt have the
impression that thou art either ascending, or moving along on a
level, or going downwards. Thereupon, meditate upon the Compassionate One. . . . Those who are unendowed with meritorious
karma will have the impression of fleeing into places of misery;
those who are endowed with meritorious karma will have the
impression of arriving in places of happiness.

The Tibetan Book of the Dead

On the second Tuesday of every month, dozens of men and women arrive at
a nondescript building on Mission Street in San Francisco. After exchanging
pleasantries, handshakes, high fives, and hugs, they find a place to sit in a
crowded room. It is the monthly meeting of the PRNN (Peer Reentry
Navigation Network), and save for parole agents and a few guests, all attendees are formerly incarcerated lifers out on parole.

Some attendees have been out for a few days and some for many years;
most are still under parole supervision. But PRNN encourages people to
self-define in other ways, and so we introduce ourselves with our first names
and the foods we most enjoy cooking. Joe (Joseph) Calderón, a peer educator
and policy reformer who has been out of prison for years, runs the meeting
collaboratively with Martín Figueroa, San Francisco's first parole officer
assigned to lifer cases.

Joe, Martín, and others start the meeting by greeting the attendees:
"Welcome home." Martín tells the audience that his caseload, initially man-
ageable because so few lifers were being released by the governor, increased
exponentially after *Lawrence* and Jerry Brown's appointment, at which point
several other parole officers were added to the rotation. Martín emphasizes

that, counter to the assumptions of many new parole agents, the lifer population is the easiest to handle; they are, as he says, "a stabilizing force in the yard
and also on the outside." He and the other parole agents—most of them
former prison guards—express respect and confidence in the people in the
room and remind them that the most common parole violation is substance
abuse.

After a round of advice and information about housing and smartphone
tutorials, Cara, a young woman, steps to the front of the room to facilitate an
activity. She distributes blank pages and invites attendees to draw a picture
frame on the page. She then asks us to write or draw a picture of what success
means to us. We work in silence, occasionally sneaking a peek at our neighbors'
work and smiling at them. Cara then invites the audience to share. "Being able
to provide for my family." "Having a job, a stable place to live." "Finding someone to love and someone who loves me." One woman shares, "I want two dogs
and a Mercedes." Cara laughs. The woman jokingly adds, "What? You wanted
us to define success. Well, that's what success means to me."

Then Cara gives us the "bad news": If you are not actively working to
direct your life toward those goals, then perhaps you don't really want them.
For example, she says, if you want to save enough money for a down payment
on a house but you end up buying shoes and flashy outfits, then maybe you
are not really that driven to be a homeowner. You must pursue your goals
with real ferocity, she says.

For many of the people in the room, homeownership in aggressively gen-
trified San Francisco is a pipe dream. Since the rise of the tech industry, housing in the city has become prohibitively expensive, both for owners and for
renters. Even so-called low-income housing requires a considerable income,
as well as jumping through multiple bureaucratic hoops. Joe acknowledges
these difficulties but encourages attendees to overcome them. "If you want to
apply," he says, "I will help you. We'll work on your applications together." It
might take sixty applications, he says, but eventually one will succeed.

My ambivalence grows. On one hand, I admire the spirit of enterprise,
mutual aid, and community strength in the room. I recognize the importance of self-focused success and of belief in free agency. On the other, I'm
sure that my fellow attendees have learned all too well in the course of their
lives that, despite their best efforts, the reentry deck is heavily stacked against
them. I recall Alessandro de Giorgi's recently released subjects who attributed their immense difficulties and abject poverty to their own failings rather
than to the systemic difficulties that stood in their way.[1]

This mindset is so overpowering and pervasive that it is no wonder it follows people out of prison into their challenges on the outside.

In 2005, the California Department of Corrections (CDC) changed its name. In what activists saw as a victory, the department added the letter *R* to its name, for *Rehabilitation*. Reflecting back on this change in 2015, the CDCR secretary, Jeffrey Beard, commented: "It is not enough to incarcerate; one of our core public safety missions is to give inmates opportunities to live productive, law-abiding lives through programs that better prepare them for their return to our communities. CDCR's heavy investments in rehabilitation are paying off. . . . We now have a network of reentry hubs, and we are rebuilding our training, education and substance abuse programs to make the 'R' in CDCR a reality."[2]

This shift was, presumably, a change of direction back toward rehabilitation, after the decades of "nothing works" and a disbelief in rehabilitation.[3] But the tension between intentions and manifestation was palpable. As Michelle Phelps has demonstrated, no real changes in offering or funding rehabilitative programs were done nationwide in state prisons throughout the 1970s and 1980s.[4] Even long before the financial crisis of 2008, the California correctional system, accounting for more than 10 percent of the state budget, was in a dire financial situation. As late as 2000 and 2001, Joan Petersilia commented on the many unmet needs of parolees and on the lack of a continuum of care before and after release.[5]

The gap between the optimism embedded in "working toward" rehabilitation, release, or redemption and the scant resources allocated to support this work is palpable in the parole hearings as well, and my interlocutors assure me that it is generalizable beyond the Manson cases. As this chapter shows, the Board perceives the inmates as being on an individual path to redemption, offering them encouragement when they succeed, chiding them when they do not, and making suggestions on how to "course correct" when necessary. But this individual-driven perspective on inmates' prison performance does not acknowledge two crucial issues.

First, what counts as a success, or a step toward a goal, is subject to heavy interpretation by the Board. As this chapter shows, the Board has broad discretion in its "reading" of an inmate's write-ups and other disciplinary failings, down to coincidental minutiae, and tends to ascribe the worst possible meaning to these incidents. New relationships, religious discoveries, and professional milestones can easily be classified and interpreted as failures or errors of judgment—even when it is just as plausible to read them as successes.

Second, the idea that inmates can simply choose rehabilitative programs from an endless menu and, by following the Board's instructions, tailor their path toward rehabilitation is absurd. In California prisons, rehabilitative programs are limited, admission criteria can be extremely arbitrary, and the offerings' rehabilitative potential is largely unsupported by evidence. Worse, in numerous institutions, the Board requires that inmates attend programs that do not exist, relegating parole hopefuls and their lawyers to the task of seeking analogues in self-help books and therapeutic language.

Against this backdrop, several themes emerge in the parole hearing transcripts. Notably, the Board's discussion of the inmates' experience behind bars offers a window into various experiences in California prisons at the time: the horrific health-care system, which in the 2000s would throw the entire prison health-care system into a federal receivership and later lead to a rare order to alleviate overcrowding in California prisons.[6] But it also offers an opportunity to critically assess the Board's awareness of the realities of prison life and the reasonability of its expectations for inmates. The hearings reveal the following trends:

1. extensive review of disciplinary write-ups ("115s" and "128s"), including the discussion of minutiae and the rehashing of incidents from the distant past, through a lens of suspicion; the expectation that the inmate should express insight and introspection regarding these minute incidents, tying them to the personality flaws that produced the crime of commitment; and the expectation of a truly pristine record as a condition of release;

2. comfort with discussions of the inmate's personal, romantic, and sexual life, beyond the privacy and agency usually accorded to adults in such matters;

3. consistent downplaying of the lack of programs, the frequent unsuitability of existing programs for the inmate's needs, and institutional barriers that stand in the way of "going along with the program";

4. emphasis on substance abuse treatment as the preferred mode of programming for inmates, with clear preference for twelve-step programs, and a tendency to quiz inmates on the content of the steps;

5. suspicion of religious programs, evincing concerns about both insincerity of belief and overzealousness; and

6. suspicion of and a negative spin on vocational and educational endeavors that stem from the individual's own inclinations and talents, such as unrecognized programs, religious endeavors, and vocational enterprises, whether or not documented by "chronos" (laudatory memoranda from correctional staff or outsiders.)

Before discussing these findings, it is important to understand the source of the Board's information about the inmate's prison experience: the central file.

THE C-FILE

The inmate's central file, colloquially known as the "C-file," contains several categories of information relevant to the hearings. Essential to the discussion are the inmate's disciplinary proceedings, or write-ups, identified as 115s or the less serious 128s.[7] In addition, the inmate's rehabilitative and program life is documented in "laudatory chronos": documentation from staff, program directors, or outsiders positively noting the inmate's participation in a program or a work assignment. And, of course, the file contains psychological and psychiatric assessments, which over the years have morphed from being based solely on a clinical interview to relying on software-based risk assessment.[8]

The C-file is important because the "present" part of the hearing often opens with a technical debate about its availability and contents. Frequently, one of the parties will complain that documents are missing from the file or that they have not received notice about some of its contents. In the early 1980s, entire C-files had been purged, leading to incomplete and uninformed hearings. Patricia Krenwinkel's complaint about the purge was first treated incredulously ("The inmate indicates that she is quite unhappy about the hearing because seemingly her C-File has been, and I quote her, 'purged.'"). When she insists ("That's probably seven or eight years of paperwork. . . . That's an objection I lodge because it's just a fact"), the Board responds: "For a while, the Counseling Department of Corrections had purged files for a period of time, not only your file but all the files were purged. So the Board asked this be stopped. . . . It's something that is beyond our control."[9]

But this incident aside, as Valerie Jenness and Kitty Calavita note in *Appealing to Justice,* prison paperwork, including disciplinary write-ups and prison grievances, is characterized by bureaucratic chaos.[10] Jenness and Calavita's interviews with correctional officers reveal the cynicism and indifference with which inmate grievances are treated, especially grievances involving loss of paperwork, inappropriate disciplinary write-ups, and the like. This context matters when discussing the evidence of such occurrences before the Board. When inmates and the Board are disputing whether a disciplinary offense had, indeed, taken place or whether an inmate had refused an intervention, it is quite plausible that the written evidence for the institutional claim against the inmate is inaccurate or that challenging it was impractical or unsuccessful because of institutional flaws.

DISCIPLINARY WRITE-UPS AND THE UNATTAINABLE PRISTINE PRISON RECORD

It is hard to explain to those who have not experienced incarceration how difficult it is to avoid disciplinary write-ups in prison. As early as 1958, Erving Goffman observed that, in total institutions, "authority is of the *echelon* kind. Any member of the staff class has certain rights to discipline any member of the inmate class," including for minutiae such as "matters of dress, deportment, social intercourse, manners and the like."[11] Arriving at a parole hearing with several disciplinary write-ups in one's C-File is therefore not a rare occurrence. In his ethnographic article about California parole hearings, Victor Shammas found that the Board made absurd generalizations based on fairly minor events, including a decade-old write-up for drinking "pruno" (an illicit alcohol product) and a five-year-old write-up for possession of a cell phone. Shammas recounts the prosecutor's statement that "such behavior . . . evidenced the inmate's 'mental state today.' The prosecutor believed the inmate was duplicitous and dangerous, 'where he minimizes and tries to make himself look better.'" Shammas concluded that "time passed more slowly in prison than it did on the outside and seemed to be evaluated along a compressed time-scale."[12]

Indeed, at the parole hearing, the inmate's write-ups are examined with a magnifying glass—both old and new incidents are dissected and analyzed. The Board faces little risk of judicial review for its negative outlook on even minute offenses; disciplinary write-ups are one area in which the Board and the courts tend to see eye to eye. In *In re Reed,* the court upheld the Board's denial of parole due to continual disciplinary write-ups, finding that, even though the more recent violations were minor in nature, they constituted "some evidence" that the inmate was currently dangerous.[13]

In their study of parole suitability outcomes in California, Kathryne Young, Debbie Mukamal, and Thomas Favre-Bulle measured the impact of a disciplinary record in two ways: overall number of 115 write-ups and the existence of 115s and 128s in the recent year. They found that only the former variable appeared to influence suitability findings; an increase of ten 115s (not a rare occurrence for a lengthy incarceration period) halved the odds of release. The effect was "only marginally significant, and may suggest that commissioners are willing to overlook recent misdeeds but are less willing to overlook a longer history of more significant disciplinary infractions."[14]

The careful attention to disciplinary write-ups is not endemic to the Manson Family. If anything, the inmates whose transcripts I analyzed— especially the women—are outliers in that their records are remarkably clean. Their scant write-ups usually reflect the early years of their incarceration or the conditions of their incarceration. Nonetheless, in every hearing, the Board has at least mentioned, if not discussed, these early write-ups. Often, inmates have to repeatedly explain incidents they had explained in previous hearings, and sometimes facts that had been cleared up at one hearing were incorrectly reiterated in the following hearing. One of the most common problems was that the 115s often lacked clarity about the facts, and the documentation served more as evidence that "something" had occurred than as a comprehensive account of the incident. At Bruce Davis's 1978 hearing, for example, he explains a disciplinary write-up from 1973:

> DAVIS: Well, I'll tell you. We are allowed to paint—to do the painting in our own cells, and around the lavatory there is a lot of water, and the paint above curls up because of the moisture. And I had a spoon knocking the loose paint off. An officer walked by and said that I must be making a knife, and so that's how that happened. I think the report explains that.
>
> WAY: That report is here. That's the only incident then.
>
> DAVIS: Right.
>
> WHITE: Just a warning and reprimand.
>
> SIDES: It's not even a 115.
>
> WHITE: Yeah, it is.

WAY: But the penalty was just a warning and reprimand, so obviously—

DAVIS: They realized as soon as we got over to custody and Mr. Buchanan saw what happened, he told me, "Look, I know nothing happened, but the officer already filed a report. We cannot say that we don't know what he's talking about, so we're going to have to—

The incident of the spoon that was not a knife reappears in his 1979 and 1981 hearings, in which Davis repeats the same explanation.

Similarly, at Susan Atkins's 2005 hearing, the Board discusses her selling her prints, and her attorney and husband, James Whitehouse, corrects the record:

LUSHBOUGH: Okay, are you now not allowed to have your prints for sale or have you—are you continuing, but with a different representation?

WHITEHOUSE: Those were allegations that were investigated for a year and on the basis—in fact, the Warden here apparently thought that Susan had a court-ordered restitution order, not a civil judgment . . . and so when he heard that she was paying into this and couldn't find any paperwork, they investigated it. A year later, they gave her all her privileges back and she wasn't charged with anything. She wasn't even given a 115.[15]

The absence of a formal complaint (but nonetheless, the presence of a blemish on Atkins's record) requires explanations, which by virtue of contradicting the information in the file, are unappealing to the Board.

A typical engagement with a disciplinary record sees the write-up as a microcosm of the crime of commitment, with both incidents stemming from the same flaws. Leslie Van Houten's prison record, which is remarkably clean, showed two disciplinary offenses: "One, you had possession of marijuana in July of 1976. And the other, June 1976, possession of 50 cents."[16] Her explanation of the second incident delves into deep "insight" territory:

Yeah, that I had two joints and seeds on me at that time. And at that point, I—I was feeling like I really didn't have too much to look forward to. I was making, I think, bad judgments in a self-destructive way. . . . And it's taken me a long time to understand certain parts of me. And for quite a while— actually, it didn't really come clear until I was able to talk with the amount of psychiatrists I was in preparation for the second trial, because not only did I speak to them about the case and the upcoming trials, but I also spoke to them a lot about myself, because it became important to me to understand the different things in me that had led to this situation and my behavior. . . .

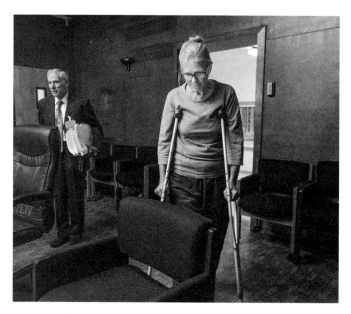

PHOTO 5. Leslie Van Houten and her attorney Rich Pfeiffer enter parole hearing room at the California Institution for Women in Corona, California, September 6, 2017. (Stan Lim/Los Angeles Daily News via Associated Press pool)

For a long time, I think rather than being able to directly cope with the guilt of what I had done, I would do things to set myself up for self-hurt. You know, like, I would have friends, and then maybe I would do something to where the friendship would become heated and ended. And to me, the marijuana thing was part in that area.[17]

Van Houten's take on the marijuana possession offense serves as a springboard for reflection about her character flaws and relationship patterns in general. Unsurprisingly, the Board ties this incident to her drug use in the 1960s, requiring her to attend drug abuse programs, and mentions that it is a serious offense that could result in denying her parole.

Even incidents in which the inmate was a victim, rather than an attacker, require explanation. Bobby Beausoleil explains to the Board a write-up in which he was "deemed to be a victim of the attack," which offers a window into gang alliances in prison and the dire straits in which he found himself:

A couple months previous to this the Aryan Brotherhood had offered me and a couple other dudes the opportunity to join their organization. And I couldn't agree with what they represented. Neither could any of the people that I was associating with at that time. And we told them no, denied their offer. A couple months later we found out they have got a contract on us. We tried to straighten it out with them. In fact, we did in fact straighten it out with them about three or four times . . . and then we found out that it was—it had come out, some orders out of the hole again, contracts on me and a friend of mine. And so we met them on the yard and confronted them.[18]

Against this backdrop, Board member Brown brings up a subsequent skirmish: "Then on 6/7/77 . . . you got involved in another disciplinary, which was a conduct, hitting a man with a baseball bat again. According to this, you were the pounder, this time with your feet."[19] Beausoleil explains that the attack was part of a gang feud with Nuestra Familia, denying that he ever held a baseball bat:

SMITH: The panel noted the CDC 115 on 6/6/77, in which you had a baseball bat and you did kick a victim on the ground.

BEAUSOLEIL: I did not have a baseball bat.

SMITH: I thought during the process of the hearing you admitted you had a bat, you were standing by the bat rack.

BEAUSOLEIL: No. I was deemed not to have a bat in the final hearing.

SMITH: Okay. But you did kick the victim on the ground.

BEAUSOLEIL: Yes, I did.

SMITH: And the bizarre nature of the commitment offense tied to that. We feel that there is a need for an extended disciplinary record to show control of aggressive impulses prior to projecting a parole date in your case.[20]

The baseball bat, whose existence was denied in 1978, makes a reappearance in 1979, and is subsequently mentioned in Beausoleil's parole denial decision.[21]

Beausoleil's refusal to join the Aryan Brotherhood, and consequently his precarious position in the prison's social ecology, comes up in many of his hearings. In 1979, the hearing reveals that, in an effort to protect Beausoleil from gangs, he was placed in protective custody: "I have never been able to get along with any of the inmate pressure groups. I can live with being under the authority of the Department, but I cannot live with being under the coercion or extortion of pressure groups. At San Quentin, I was found victim of an assault, but I would admit that I was standing up for myself at the time that incident occurred. When I was transferred here, I was immediately thrown into a hostile environment. I was trying to survive in some very precarious situations."[22] Board member DeLeon corrects: "Well, whether or not you were actually in fact a member of a clique, if the other population or members of cliques believed you to be a member of a clique, say, that was a particular White clique that was against the activities, say, of the A.B., then would that not be a reason to consider you Protective Custody subject?"[23]

At Beausoleil's 1980 hearing, he has to explain the social ecology of prison to the Board again, because his involvement in the incidents years ago is viewed as an example of his still-violent potential.

BEAUSOLEIL: I have earned the reputation over the years of being a man who stands up for himself and who will not be threatened or coerced by prison gangs.

CORONADO: Why would that reputation be so?

BEAUSOLEIL: Because I have always stood up for myself when confronted.

CORONADO: You mean you resort to any kind of violence to defend yourself?

BEAUSOLEIL: Only if it's projected at me.

CORONADO: But you resort to violence.

BEAUSOLEIL: Not if I have a choice. But if a man is threatening you with a knife or threatening your death, I would definitely stand up for myself.

CORONADO: So, it would be a matter of him or you.

BEAUSOLEIL: Well, I don't have any intentions of hurting anyone or killing anyone. I wouldn't try to kill someone because they threatened me, but I would definitely defend myself.[24]

In this exchange, the Board pushes Beausoleil to express insight as to his violence potential. That he does not do so (in contrast to Van Houten's discussion of her marijuana possession, above) is indication of his lack of insight.

At Beausoleil's 1982 hearing the Board reviews, yet again, all previous disciplinary offenses, finally arriving at a more recent 115 for possession of marijuana. Beausoleil's answer reveals something of prison conditions:

I wasn't trying to diminish my guilt. I—I did plead guilty to the charge. It was a small amount of marijuana, a couple marijuana cigarettes worth. Like I say, I don't want to diminish—I—I was in error. However, I can perhaps clarify, as far as my condition at the time, which has improved somewhat . . . [discusses his medical problem] . . . I was finally put into a physical therapy program by Dr. Solemean at C.M.C., who was a neurologist. And I have responded to the treatments, and have some improvement. But at the time there, you know, we have an infirmary at D.V.I. There's no—there's no hospital. There is one doctor for the entire population. I was taking about 15 to 20 aspirins a day. I was to a point where I couldn't get my bowels to move because of the aspirin intake. And I sought my own remedy, as best I could.[25]

This explanation is credible; it certainly reflects what we now know of health-care conditions in California prisons in those times, which were exposed in depth in the litigation that eventually led to *Brown v. Plata*.[26] The lawsuit, which had been brought in the 1990s, reflected years of suffering by patients who had agonized, and sometimes perished, waiting for relief from conditions that were largely iatrogenic.[27] But in the world of parole hearings, one cannot explain away one's involvement in any disciplinary infraction without prefacing it with a statement of full accountability.

Reading the transcript portions that address disciplinary hearings leaves one with profound discomfort as to the way the pressures and realities of prison life, including inadequate health care and programs, generate specks of dirt on people's files that are then looked at with a magnifying glass. But it was not as surprising as reading the portions addressing the inmates' romantic and sexual lives.

DISCUSSING THE INMATES' PERSONAL LIVES

Residence in a total institution, by definition, affects all aspects of life, including the most intimate and personal. Indeed, Megan Comfort's *Doing Time Together* documented the pervasive effect that incarceration had on one's family and romantic relationships, including the ability to express or display romantic feelings.[28] Prison regulations reflect a remarkable level of comfort with prescribing and proscribing inmates' relationships, ranging from prohibition of certain levels of physical affection with visitors to severe prohibitions on consensual sex among prisoners.[29]

The Board feels comfortable discussing inmates' relationships, marital status, and sexual and romantic feelings, and the transcripts reveal distinctly gendered patterns in these discussions. Inquiries about the men's romantic and sexual lives tend to be brief, albeit invasive and focused on the relevance of these preferences to their dangerousness. For example, in 1980, Bruce Davis was asked whether he was married or considered marriage, and he briefly replied that he had not yet found the right person. The Board left it at that.[30] A similar brief inquiry at Bobby Beausoleil's 1979 hearing shows some curiosity about the nature of his family visits, asking him whether he received "a trailer visit," code for a conjugal visit.[31]

Intimacy comes up again at Beausoleil's 1980 hearing, when the Board discusses a 115 he received for hugging and kissing with a "female visitor." Coronado asks, "Did they have this kind of problem with you in the visiting room?" Beausoleil responds:

> The visiting rule states that there are two kisses allowed per visit at the beginning and at the end. A third kiss and you're out. This rule has not been enforced for many years at this institution. It's been enforced only when someone is taking it to the point where it would be embarrassing to other particular individuals in the visiting room. I've never conducted myself or been accused of conducting myself in any way that would be offensive to others. As the write-up says, I kissed and hugged my visitor. However, certain staff people recently have tried to enforce the rule verbatim. And this has created a great deal of conflict and what I feel is harassment, especially toward the visitors.[32]

Beausoleil's private life reemerges in 1985, when the Board and the prosecutor address his discipline for a private enterprise without authorization. Among the materials against him are drawings he had made of "mothers spanking children, . . . reputed to be with a sexual connotation attached to the, to the activity"[33] and a classification received for possessing "photography of children in the nude."[34] The disciplinary write-up associated with this was, at that time, under appeal, and Beausoleil does not respond to the panel's questions about it, following his attorney's advice. But the prosecutor states that Beausoleil's enterprise was "a front for a newsletter disseminating what I would refer to as, if not sexually explicit material, at least material that exploits, uh, what I would call abnormal interest in bare-bottom spanking of children." He continues:

> In the very first series of photographs appears to be what I would call a satyr—half man, half goat—it appears to be a devil's head with goat ears. My understanding, that is a symbol in connection with Satanism. I also read from the prison documents that Mr. Beausoleil has a tattoo on his left leg, I believe that's similar to that. . . . I'm wondering if there is any connection between the articles, the photographs, the tattoos, and the, uh, uh, movie that Mr. Beausoleil appeared in, and cultism, Satanism, and the Manson Family.[35]

Beausoleil responds only with regard to the photography: "It was based upon photographs of my daughter, who was a newborn child, and it was, you know, like in the bathtub, or something like that, that my wife had sent."[36]

Concerns about Beausoleil's art are raised again in 2005, when the commissioners ask him about the appropriateness of his drawings. Beausoleil responds: "I realize that they are erotic and they are things that I did with my wife early in our relationship."[37] But there is another problem with Beausoleil's art: The commissioners are concerned that public displays of his work exploit the notoriety of the crime.

> FARMER: You had an opening with your paintings in connection
> with an album. . . . It included a showing of your paintings, which
> included the paintings which are—I'm not going to describe them
> as obscene because I'm not a prude and they don't offend me—on the
> other hand, given your position, you're a cult figure. People look to
> you solely to the fact that you were involved with Charlie Manson.
> As you indicate you have a responsibility to the public, and are aware
> of that, how could you be connected with the display of these pictures
> in 2005? I think that speaks to your judgment. Can you respond to that?
>
> BEAUSOLEIL: It was the only recent work I've done that was included in
> that series. . . . I had no idea that anyone was going to put up any sort of
> retrospective work. There are some pieces that I have done, as I said, way
> back when, shortly after my wife and I were married and they were done
> for her. They were done for our own—they weren't done for publication
> or publishing or whatever. I realize that things get out of control and
> things got out of control in that situation and they should not have been
> put up on any internet site. I had no idea that they would be.

Farmer proceeds to criticize Beausoleil's wife for exposing the pictures to others. When Beausoleil reiterates the mistake and that he had written to the gallery to take the website down, Board member Garner-Easter responds, "I understand that you may not have given that authorization, but even if your wife is your agent—in the past Board hearings the investigation has gone into her association with your business as well. Again, it does show very poor judgment."[38] The parole rejection decision explicitly relies on the gallery incident as evidence of

> extraordinary exhibition of terrible judgment. . . . You can talk about you
> didn't do it, or your wife did it, or your contractor did it, but these are people
> that you choose to be in contractual relationships with. . . . It's not just Robert
> Beausoleil, the great guitar player, a musician. It's not just Robert Beausoleil,
> the great artist. There's always in there "and former associate, or friend, of
> Charles Manson." So, if you realize, as you say you do, your obligation to
> disassociate yourself and to demonstrate to the public as part of your suitabil-
> ity, your disassociation, well, then you have to do it.[39]

This critique of Beausoleil's vocational interests as capitalizing on his own crime contrast with earlier encouragement of his skills, and with the early interest of the Board in Patricia Krenwinkel's marketable skills as an artist. The Board seems to praise Krenwinkel for having created an embroidery piece with Leslie Van Houten "that you sold or were going to sell or was valued at $1,500."[40] They do not scold her for the sale, nor do they suggest that the price is related to the notoriety of the artists.

The art gallery incident highlights the risk that behavior of others—family members, friends, employers, and the like (in terms of glorifying a convicted murderer's art by sensationalizing his crimes)—might be imputed to the inmate. Also, it is an example of a personal association regarded as a microcosm of poor judgment, echoing the inmate's poor decision to associate with the Manson Family.

By contrast, the inquiries into the women's romantic partners seem more invasive and moralistic and less connected to dangerousness. At Patricia Krenwinkel's 1980 hearing, the Board inquired about her efforts to exit the PTU (security housing, which offered fewer educational and vocational opportunities) for the education building. Krenwinkel explains that she wanted to "go to a unit where I had a few friends, a few women that are involved in my educational program, a counselor which I felt would be of assistance to me." Board member Crow responds: "There were some prior indications of homosexual relationships. And I wondered if there was any connection between where you wish to live and any relationship that you had going on campus." Krenwinkel denies the allegation.[41]

Susan Atkins's hearings reveal a schoolmarmish approach. During her first marriage, the Board asked her repeated questions about her husband and their plans together. By 1985, the marriage had unraveled, and the prosecutor, Kay, responds like a concerned father:

> She says, "Oh now, I've got my act together and I'm not going to let men do anything to me anymore." Well, as recently as about the time of the last Board hearing she'd taken up with this ne'er-do-well who was going to pay off the—the Governor and get her out. And just looking at that situation, I mean it's obvious to anybody that he's a flake, and yet she took up with him and went right along with the program 'cause he was going to get her out. Who's she going to take up with if we let her out? Who? We don't know. But generally I can guarantee you that it won't be someone that we'll be proud to have her with.[42]

An even more extreme example can be found in Leslie Van Houten's 1982 hearing, where the Board discussed her marriage to Bill Cywin. Cywin, a jail inmate in Virginia, had written to Van Houten while in custody and came to California to visit her after his parole. Board member Lopez warns Van Houten:

LOPEZ: Do you know he's in jail now?

VAN HOUTEN: Yes, I do.

LOPEZ: Do you know why he's in jail?

VAN HOUTEN: From what I understand, he's charged with receiving stolen property.

LOPEZ: And do you know that he was in possession of a uniform that is used by female members of the staff when they are pregnant?

VAN HOUTEN: They told me that here.... All of a sudden there were things that I hadn't really had the foresight to see that I have addressed with him and I'm hurt, I'm disappointed. I'm questioning his ability to get his life in order. I'm questioning the way he chooses to take care of problems when the pressure is on, and if Bill can't come to conclusions to change his behavior, then I've written him and told him that our marriage will be in very big trouble because I don't live my life like that.[43]

In answering the Board's questions, Van Houten discusses her need of a relationship: "When I met Bill, there were parts of me that in the years in here have laid dormant and I think they are reflected in my psychiatric reports continuously, too, my little girl nature, my—there was a sense of immaturity, and I myself needed to have some form of relationship, other than the ones that are sparked or created in this environment."[44] This soliloquy makes it seem as if the need for romantic and sexual attachment is pathological or immature, and of course evokes memories of the crime of commitment. Lopez scolds her for her naïveté:

LOPEZ: You were cautious?

VAN HOUTEN: Yeah, sure, and still am, more than ever.

LOPEZ: How many times did he visit you during this period?

VAN HOUTEN: Once a week and then we had two FLU visits.

LOPEZ: At that time did it occur to you that perhaps you should delve into his background because knowing—

VAN HOUTEN: Well, I knew he had a record for embezzling and that he did time for embezzlement, but—

. . .

LOPEZ: Now that we have set this up where you can take a look at it and we have shared it with you because we feel, as a panel, it's only fair to share with you what we know about this marriage.[45]

This exchange yielded the following verbiage in the rejection decision: "Prisoner's recent marriage to a parolee who is currently incarcerated as a parole violator, is consistent with her past history of selecting male companions who are lacking in stability."[46]

Like disciplinary write-ups, personal and romantic choices are constructed as microcosms of personality flaws. Krenwinkel's choice to move to a different dormitory could reflect pathological lack of femininity or manipulation. Atkins's and Van Houten's poor choices in partners could reflect their lack of judgment in other areas of their lives.

GOING WITH THE PROGRAM

At his "lifer school," Wattley discusses the Board's requirements to "program." He uses the word *program* as a verb, leaving me unclear on whether this means that the inmate is constantly in a state of enrichment and activity scheduling, or that the inmate is being programmed, transformed from the inside, so as to match the insights deduced from the crime. Then, Wattley says, matter-of-factly, "When the Board requires that you attend programs that do not exist, here's a list of self-help books that we assign the inmates when necessary."

I am not sure I heard well. The Board requires inmates to attend programs that do not exist? That rehabilitation and programming has become scarce in California prisons is well known to me. Colleagues who lead programs in San Quentin have to interview and pick appropriate candidates; demand always exceeds supply. And more programs are available in San Quentin, where scores of do-gooders from the Bay Area volunteer, than in more remote prisons in rural areas.[47] Joan Petersilia, familiar with the operation of California prisons from years of quantitative and qualitative research, observes:

Increased dollars have funded operating costs for more prisons, but not more rehabilitation programs. Fewer programs, and a lack of incentives for inmates to participate in them, mean that fewer inmates leave prison having participated in programs to address work, education, and substance use deficiencies. In-prison substance abuse programs are expanding, but programs are often minimal and many inmates do little more than serve time before they are released. The Office of National Drug Control Policy reported that 70–85 percent of state prison inmates need substance abuse treatment; however, just 13 percent receive any kind of treatment in prison.[48]

Wattley explains that panel attorneys regularly recommend books in lieu of nonexistent anger management programs. He also explains that twelve-step programs, which people on the outside attend at least several times a week, are available for inmates only once every few weeks, diluting their possible utility. Padding the inmate's record with self-help books and informal self-education in order to check a box required by the Board at a previous hearing is quite common.

In the transcripts, I saw frequent evidence of programs that had ceased to exist or became unavailable to inmates, even though the Board thought them suitable and beneficial for the inmates. In 1981, the Board was pleased with Krenwinkel's participation in a "creative dynamics" class:

COLLIER: Are you still involved in that?

KRENWINKEL: No. That program has stopped in the institution.

COLLIER: Okay. I think there was also some discussion that you had been involved in what's called a long termer's group, the lifer's group?

KRENWINKEL: Initially, in '76 I did, and then the organization went defunct. Right now the organization has tried to get back on its feet again.[49]

Moreover, existing programs are not necessarily available or open to the inmates whom the Board required to attend. Migrating between institutions and being assigned to security housing, which limit the inmates' mobility within the prison, can put the kibosh on a program plan, or in the case of solitary confinement, on attending any program at all. At the end of his 1982 hearing, Bobby Beausoleil is told by the Board to continue his "positive programming" and to attend a psychiatric evaluation at Vacaville. He resists this requirement: "You request that I maintain a positive program and that I continue in my program endeavors. And I will not be able to do that if I— from this point forward, if I transfer to Vacaville, because I will have to go there as a protective custody case [on account of his enmity with the Aryan

Brotherhood], which will—you know, once you get that on, you cannot get that off."[50] Board member Patterson responds: "We are not a classification Board. I don't know what your security problems are. I don't even know if Mr. Manson is on the Main Line or if there are Aryan Brotherhood running wild at C.M.F. So I don't know these things."[51]

A similar issue with regard to Manson himself emerges in 1979, at a hearing from which he is absent. It becomes clear that "he has never been involved in an educational program because most of the time he had been in lockup status. . . . Vocational instruction, none, again because of his confinement status."[52] That the limitations on his participation in programs was due to being housed in a solitary confinement unit did not stop the Board from giving lack of participation as one of the reasons for Manson's denial of parole: "The prisoner has not participated in any institutional program which could very well enhance his ability to successfully complete a period of parole. . . . Panel does note that the prisoner has been in a highly restrictive housing confinement since his inception in the Department of Corrections. However, this should not have completely prohibited the prisoner from making attempts to participate in constructive programs."[53]

What such programs would consist of, in solitary confinement, is an open question, and it is plausible to argue that Manson would not participate in standard prison programs regardless of where he was housed. But in Patricia Krenwinkel's 1982 hearing, a similar issue emerges despite the fact that the correctional counselor (Landry) explains to the Board member (Roos) that her secure housing is not a consequence of her own behavior: "We do have more secure housing for individuals who may need to protect their own safety." Roos replies: "Okay, so it's not just because the person has a problem, it may be that other inmates may have a problem with them."[54]

Another problematic aspect of programs is datedness. As early as the 1980s, technology-based programs would become obsolete soon after inmates completed them, and the nature of prison programs would prevent the inmates from updating their experience. The Board nonetheless blamed inmates for not pursuing these opportunities. Board member McReynolds asks Patricia Krenwinkel, "When you were able to enter [certified programs], can you speak to why you have not availed?" Krenwinkel replies, "Especially like right now when I'm in data processing, it's like in most vocations are being constantly updated. . . . Any computer technology is moving at such a fast rate that what you learn in that program will basically be outdated probably within maybe three years."[55] This problem has been exacerbated in the internet era, when inmates learn how to go online through printouts and stenciled materials, without access to the internet itself.[56]

Again, these contradictions between the Board's requirement of "programming" and the programs' actual availability and value are pervasive and transcend the context of the Manson cases. Victor Shammas provides one outrageous example in which an inmate who spent more than two decades in a Security Housing Unit (SHU) is penalized for not having participated in sufficient programs. When the inmate explains the unavailability of programs, his response is "met with resounding disapproval in the deputy commissioner's closing statement and was made the object of savage scorn":

> "You really don't have a relapse prevention awareness. You are in many ways not a grownup man," said the deputy commissioner. "You lack self-sufficiency. Your plans include just being parasitic as soon as you get out, [by] living with somebody." The inmate was minimizing because the right type of "programming hasn't been done yet." And yet the panel recognized that this was due to circumstances beyond the inmate's control: "In fairness to you, you've been in SHU for 26 years and without a lot of access to programming," said the commissioner. Even this admission, however, was tempered by the commissioner's suggestion that "one of the benefits" of residing in a SHU—where individuals are isolated from almost all human contact in a state of mind-numbing monotony likened to torture (Amnesty International 2012)—was that "you don't have an opportunity to interact with anybody" and the inmate could therefore remain free from "violent interactions with anyone."[57]

These misattributions of blame remind me of my interview with Karlene Faith, who in the mid-1970s tutored Krenwinkel, Atkins, and Van Houten in prison. At Faith's home, I saw an illustration inspired by her social justice work, which depicts three fish of different sizes: The little one says, "There is no justice in the world." The middle fish, who is chasing the little fish and is chased by the big fish, says, "There is some justice in the world." The big fish, who is chasing the middle fish, says, "The world is just."

The hearings suggest that the commissioners are well aware that programs cannot be accessed from solitary confinement and that the program repertoire is either very difficult to access or ill-suited for the inmate's individual needs. What these records evince is breathtaking indifference to the inapplicability of the programming requirement.

DOING YOUR STEPS: THE PREVALENCE OF TWELVE-STEP
SUBSTANCE ABUSE PROGRAMS

There is, however, one type of program that tends to be both available and highly valued by the Board: the twelve-step-style substance abuse self-help group. Young, Mukamal, and Favre-Bulle's study of parole suitability factors, which controlled for participation in programs, found a strong correlation between participation in such programs and odds of release. The authors found this result somewhat difficult to interpret: perhaps the Board holds these programs in high regard, or perhaps the overall prevalence of substance abuse among prison inmates makes these programs relevant to a large subsection of the prison population.[58] One peculiar finding was that the commissioners frequently quizzed inmates about the steps (e.g., "What is Step Eight?"). Correctly answering these questions did not correlate with higher odds of release. However, failing this "quiz" (inaccurately reciting the verbiage for each step or confounding different steps) was negatively correlated with a parole grant.

The Board's enchantment with twelve-step programs contrasts with the increasing doubts as to their value.[59] Since most addicts never recover from their addiction, it is hard to assess success or to causally attribute it to participation in the program.[60] Recent trends in addiction treatment compare addiction to learning disorders[61] or adopt a harm-reduction approach, which relies on the realistic assumption that, for most addicts, complete cessation of use is impossible.[62] Another criticism of twelve-step programs is related to their reliance on submission to a higher power, which despite its vagueness, adds a religious flavor to the meetings.[63]

Despite these concerns about twelve-step programs, the Board seems to favor them over many other forms of programming. It is not difficult to guess why. First, in a prison environment, it is hard to imagine drug use constructed as a public health concern rather than a grave moral failure.[64] And second, against a backdrop of budgetary shortages and few programs, a self-help program that can be run by the inmates themselves and does not require expertise is easier and more convenient to maintain than evidence-based programs. In the transcripts, the Board repeatedly criticizes inmates for not attending drug programs, even when doing so would be difficult given time and space constraints. For example, in 1980, Patricia Krenwinkel is asked why she is not attending any drug programs:

KRENWINKEL: Programs like AA and NA are offered are only at night. And I am close custody. So, I am unable to participate in any of the programs which deal directly with abuse. They are all evening programs.

BROWN: Do you have any interest in that area?

KRENWINKEL: Yes, I do.

BROWN: I'm going to ask you the $64 [sic] question. We are all aware of the crimes that led to your confinement in prison. We are looking at an institutional record thus far . . . that indicates a clear disciplinary record. It indicates a very heavy emphasis on education. There is nothing in the drug area. The work area has been kind of consumed by the education and the custody status you have been in.[65]

Krenwinkel is held accountable for the fallacies in her own rehabilitation record—particularly, the absence of drug programs—which she cannot attend because of her classification.

The programming debacle continues in 1982, when Krenwinkel has been drug-free for more than a decade, and her psychiatric evaluation reveals no need for therapy. The Board recommends twelve-step programs even as the correctional counselor explains that "Alcoholics Anonymous is available, but would not be available to her because that's an evening activity and she's not allowed out at night" and "we do not have a daytime Narcotics Anonymous or Alcoholics Anonymous." Notably, Board member Roos admits that Krenwinkel "doesn't have any specific need for psychotherapeutic assistance, but that it could possibly benefit her with feelings of frustration and depression."[66]

Like Krenwinkel, Bobby Beausoleil repeatedly resists the Board's requirement to join AA, explaining that he does not have alcohol or drug programs. When he finally relents, his explanation to the Board evinces his effort to find usefulness and meaning in a program that does not really address his particular needs:

KOENIG: Since the panel did request it, I got into the program. I was dubious about the program, because I have never had a alcohol program—I mean alcohol problem. But now that I've been in the program, I actually like it very much. I'm—it's—there are guys there that are going there that are really concerned about improving themselves and understanding what has motivated them in coming to terms with the problems in their lives. And it's rare, it's hard to find in here and I've really enjoyed.

KOENIG: Why do you think the psychiatrists, psychologists in every report, the last three reports, state that conditions of parole should include routine drug and alcohol monitoring?

BEAUSOLEIL: Well, I think that that's probably wise. I have no problem with that. I mean I don't—I have never really had a real serious drug problem. I never put a needle in my arm. I never used cocaine. I've never used heroin. I've never used barbiturates. I have smoked pot. I have experimented with LSD. And that's been the full extent of my drug involvement. I don't say that to say that this isn't some sort of a problem relating to drugs. And it has, it is a problem if it's caused me two disciplinary reports in the past. So I do recognize that it is a problem that I should address and I'm addressing it in AA.[67]

After this exchange, Board member Koenig presses Beausoleil to admit that he has a drug problem. In this hearing, and in several others, Beausoleil is asked to recite the Twelve Steps and is scolded for inaccuracies.

Two inmates—Leslie Van Houten and Susan Atkins—express, as part of their "insight," the opinion that the crime they committed was drug related. Both participate in drug programs, though their actual substance abuse was limited to the context of their hippie commune milieu in the 1960s. Both are also quizzed by the Board about the steps.

The Board has particular interest in Step Eight: "Made a list of all persons we had harmed, and became willing to make amends to them all." Discussing the list of people to make amends to and the inmate's difficulty in making such amends often returns the conversation to the past and to the inmate's insight and remorse.

SUSPICIONS ABOUT RELIGION: INSINCERE OR TOO SINCERE?

The Board's fondness for twelve-step programs would suggest a favorable attitude toward religion-based programs, which, like the twelve steps, could support the insight inquiry. Indeed, finding religion in prison is a well-documented cultural phenomenon, often associated with spiritual and moral awakening.[68] It arguably assists in adjusting to the prison experience,[69] helps inmates find social peers,[70] and offers a transformational, often interracial community.[71] Moreover, Evangelical Christianity does not carry the racial and political undertones associated with prisoners' conversion to Islam, which fueled much of the institutional animosity and rioting of the 1960s and 1970s.[72] By contrast, white Christianity enjoys a relatively noncontroversial mainstream position in American political and cultural life.

Fairly early in their incarceration, three Manson Family members—Susan Atkins, Bruce Davis, and Tex Watson—became born-again Christians and remained devoutly so throughout the decades of their incarceration. Davis obtained a PhD in divinity;[73] Susan Atkins and Tex Watson both wrote books in which they credited religion as the most important force in their postconviction lives.[74]

The act of testifying before the Board, in itself, can be layered with religious meaning for adherents to a charismatic, proselytizing religion, characterized by the consistent responsibility to offer ministry to others and draw them closer to a personal relationship with their Savior.[75] Offering testimony in this religious context is remarkably similar to expressing and performing "insight" before the Board. Moreover, the Christian practice of "witnessing" often refers to one's previous life, and maximizing one's bad acts prior to conversion plays an important rhetorical role in highlighting the magnitude of the transformative experience.[76] As Tanya Erzen argues, carceral and religious reliances on "witnessing" share stylistic and symbolic elements to the point that she calls them "testimonial politics."[77] Nevertheless, the Board is suspicious of religious conversions. The hearing transcripts of Davis, Watson, and Atkins demonstrate the Board's discomfort with the role of religion in the inmates' lives: it is outside the Board's scripted plan for the inmate, it is insincere, or, it is too sincere for the prison environment.

As early as Davis's 1978 hearing, the prison's protestant chaplain, McGee, comes to testify on his behalf, arguing that Davis had undergone spiritual transformation and was no longer a danger. The Board is suspicious of this change:

BAKES: Do you think that this could be a mask, that this is a cover-up, that behind this pleasant appearance is a—

MCGEE: No. I've seen him day-in and day-out. I don't believe that in any way that it's phony or a shuck or anything like that. He's real.

WAY: I want to make this comment, and maybe I'll put it to you. You might be able to shed some light on the problem that occurs to me, and I think it occurs to some of the other members of our Board and our Hearing Representatives.

In this Manson case, we have Mr. Davis's born-again experience as a clerk to the Protestant. Tex Watson is a clerk to the Protestant at CMC. That's San Luis Obispo. Susan Atkins is born again and has been baptized and has embraced Christianity. Do you have any explanation for this?

MCGEE: I can't say anything about Tex Watson or Susan Atkins. I don't know them.

WAY: I wondered if you had a theological feeling that maybe there's something about the experience that they went through that affected their lives to a degree that they make this change. But you feel it's for real.

MCGEE: I do.

BAKES: Can I suggest an answer to that?

WAY: Yes.

BAKES: Saul of Tarsus had the same experience. St. Paul in other words.[78]

In 1981, Davis seems to have furthered his focus on Christian ministry. At the hearing, he argues that "in my biblical studies and that—I consider that vocational training, studies for the ministry. That may be a small point, but I'd just like to add that, that I consider that vocational training."[79] He also defines his activity in a therapy Christian group as an alternative to secular self-help groups: "Instead of the solutions to the problem coming from secular humanism or philosophy, psychology, it comes from the Bible as much as can be applied, which is practically most of it."[80]

It then emerges that Davis has a leadership position with the Christian counseling groups as a Yoke Fellow who moderates his own group. This raises a concern in Davis's psychological evaluation, which states that "he becomes rather agitated when it is suggested that he has switched his loyalties from one god-like figure to another."[81] Davis is asked for his take on this:

DAVIS: Well, my interpretation is that the things I was doing before I came to prison, the subsequent acts for my conviction, are in no way harmonious or should be construed as acceptable in light of what I do now. In other words, I'm not doing the same thing, nor do I see parallel action like I was doing and that I'm still doing it. I'm not.

BROWN: Do you see any parallel actions as far as loyalties are concerned?

DAVIS: Well, okay. The discussion came about when we—they said, "Well now, you were with Charlie and you and everybody else did essentially what he said." Then the man went on to say, "Now you're a Christian and you do what Jesus says." Well, the implication is "that's just as bad as doing what Charlie said. You haven't changed a bit. You're still doing the same old thing, doing what somebody said." So, that was kind of the input I got, or the feeling, so in that I do see a similarity, okay. I see a parallel that at one time I was—when I was in the Family, part of the Family, that's essentially true. And now I'm a Christian, and I do what the Lord says in the Bible, okay, to the best of my ability. Now, I guess that is a parallel. On that level.[82]

This exchange is remarkable. According to both the Helter Skelter and the cult narratives, Manson fashioned himself, to some extent, after Jesus. But it is a surprisingly bold, even jarring, exchange when taken in the sociocultural context of a country that regularly exhibits great deference to religion and religious claims. To a true believer, as Davis claimed to be, the comparison between Manson and Jesus must have sounded incredibly offensive: the two ideologies would be, to him, as day and night. As an added insult, the Board then draws a parallel between these involvements and his involvement with an American Nazi group in his early days at Folsom.

The Board is also suspicious of religious programs because they constitute a self-initiated, unscripted avenue of personal growth, as opposed to the Board-endorsed programs charted at the end of each parole denial. At this point in time, Davis is deeply involved in his religious program several times a week. But the Board wants him to attend secular therapeutic programs, which he resists. What he interprets as religious adherence, they interpret as insubordination:

> CHADERJIAN: Were you putting something on for the Psychiatric Council? Were you giving them a reply which you felt they wanted to hear? Were you insincere when you told them you would be agreeable to get into a formal therapy program?
>
> DAVIS: Well, no.
>
> CHADERJIAN: Well, then, why is Dadisman [the psychiatrist] after his—
>
> DAVIS: Well, okay. I hear your question. And the Yoke Fellow program is a formal program, but okay, that's okay. There seems to be two ways, two programs, PCP [the psychiatric counseling program] and Yoke Fellows, to my way of looking at it. So, one of them is based on a Christian point of view and morality and ethics, and the other is based on other things. So, I chose the one that is close to my presuppositions and my philosophical outlook.
>
> CHADERJIAN: Very well. I see what you're saying, but I don't feel that that's what the Psychiatric Council had in mind when they were talking about a formalized therapy program. But I understand where you're coming from.[83]

Chaderjian again explains that the Psychiatric Council's recommendation may have something to do with a concern that, yet again, Davis has become "a firm follower when there's a stronger will before you." Expectedly, this riles Davis up and leads to a contentious exchange:

> CHADERJIAN: Christian philosophy is very comforting and, you know, expiates one's sins and gives you forgiveness, and all other attendant benefits . . .
>
> DAVIS: I think that we could safely draw a qualitative difference between a firm follower of Charlie Manson or a firm follower of the Nazi Party or a firm follower of Jesus Christ.[84]
>
> CHADERJIAN: Yes.
>
> DAVIS: I believe, and I believe that energy directed in those areas can be seen to have very different results.
>
> CHADERJIAN: Okay.
>
> DAVIS: All right. So to say, "Well, just because you are a Christian, you're doing the same thing as you did—"
>
> CHADERJIAN: No, I don't think anybody said that. But if you know anything about Christian theology, historically there have been wars with thousands and thousands of persons killed in defense of Christianity.

We're talking about human behavior and conduct. That's what we're talking about.

DAVIS: Like the Apostle Paul.

CHADERJIAN: That's an example that could be given, I guess.

DAVIS: Okay.

BROWN: Young man, we don't usually get into a lengthy discussion with you about whether you are right or whether you are wrong. We listen to your statements and we make up our minds what's important as to what we hear. We are not going to knock your saying that religion is your life. If that's a vocation to you, that's fine. If that's psychiatric therapy for you, that's fine. But I think that you should reevaluate.[85]

Another aspect of the Board's concern about Davis's religion involves suspicion that the Christian ministry is a cover for Manson-type activities. This is evident at Davis's 1982 hearing, where the Board is concerned because fellow Manson Family member Tex Watson works in the same ministry:

CORONADO: You're working with Tex Watson in this chapel at this time?

DAVIS: Um-hmm.

CORONADO: And they make a statement that they should break up you and Tex Watson being in the same place or working the same area. Do you recall who made that statement? . . . Have there been any problems between you and Tex Watson working in the chapel?

DAVIS: No.

CORONADO: He's also some sort of minister. Does he hold some type of services in there?

DAVIS: (nods head up and down)

CORONADO: What do you do: hold joint services?

DAVIS: No. No, in fact we don't. We don't have any services that are together, both of us in the same group.[86]

Similar doubts are voiced at Charles Watson's hearings. As early as 1978, the prosecutor, Stephen Kay, prefaces the interview of the inmate by declaring that he finds Watson's faith "not at all unusual" and that religion is "not something new on the part of these people. This was something that they had in the beginning. A lot of them thought that Manson was Jesus Christ and that whatever he said was the word of God. And they quote the Bible and twist it to mean what they wanted it to mean."[87]

Board member Del Pesco expresses similar doubts to the ones expressed to Bruce Davis: "Now, this total commitment [to Manson] took you to the offenses that we have discussed in great detail. And now you are into this other total commitment.... What assurance do you feel that this commitment will maintain 'normal' direction and not give way to another total commitment and God knows what that might be, the third one?"[88]

Watson responds:

> Today my life is controlled not by evil, but it is controlled by goodness; and that goodness comes from God, and that goodness comes from the Holy Spirit. And my life each day is growing toward God and toward living a more holy and complete life. And I do not see in my whole life over ever turning to go back in the other direction. There is no possibility . . . and this is about the only assurance that I can give you. And I can understand your question because I have no pat answer for it, and I have no way to prove it. I have nothing you can see, in other words, to say that I won't.[89]

A third concern about religion is overzealousness. Susan Atkins's early hearings occur only a few years after her conversion, and her enthusiasm for her new path is evident when she says that "when the death penalty was abolished in 1972, for the first time in maybe 12 years I got on my knees and I thanked God, a God I didn't even know existed.... I realized I had a whole new life."[90] The Board, by contrast, is preoccupied the impact of Atkins's religious fervor on her disciplinary write-ups, one of which is an unauthorized phone call. Atkins explains, "I called a brother in Christ in Charlotte, North Carolina, to share with him what Jesus Christ has meant to me in the last few years and what he has done for me in my life in the last four years."[91] Similarly, the Board warns her, "You have become overzealous to the point of creating an institutional problem with your religious activities."[92] The Board refers to language Atkins had used with regard to her bible group: "Susan was cautioned against placing herself in a position of religious leadership in violation of the Director's Rule 3211: Ministry. She denies the statement as quoted and requests the opportunity to talk to the student chaplain." Worse, Atkins received a 115 for proselytizing to another inmate. The Board quotes from an evaluation: "Susan was confronted about pushing her religion on others and was told she was setting herself up as a minister of religion . . . and there was some concern about Yvonne not taking her medication, that she felt she would be healed through her religious beliefs."[93]

Atkins explains:

Being a fairly new Christian, only a year old into Christ, so to speak, when I was moved to the Psychiatric Treatment Unit, I was very zealous. I had found peace, forgiveness, love and acceptance in God's sight. I found something I wanted to share. It's like—I don't mean to belittle God or put him in a box or anything, but if you get a bargain-basement deal, you want to go tell your neighbors, "Hey, there's a sale down there, and you can get anything almost for free that you want to buy." And that's the type of attitude that I had. As a new Christian, I had to learn how to present my faith in God in an acceptable way to my peers so that it would not be rejected, so that it would not be thought that I was pushing. And granted, there have been times when I have pushed.[94]

It is important to understand Atkins's ministry in the context of the Christian mandate to proselytize, which originates in St. Matthew's Gospel.[95] Moreover, the Evangelical witnessing style, in which people often talk up their bad behavior before being saved, dovetails with the expectations from inmates at parole hearings and at rehabilitation programs.[96] In the late 1970s, this style of testimony was heavily influenced by Billy Graham and Jerry Falwell, both of whom frequently described themselves as aimless sinners before their salvation.[97] But such personal testimony, while perhaps appropriate at a hearing or a program, is problematic when addressing other inmates, who are literally a captive audience and might not share the speaker's religious enthusiasm. But to address such efforts as a disciplinary offense in the context of an apparently sincere conversion is to put a new convert in a difficult spiritual position.

This complex perspective of religion is not endemic to the Manson Family. Though the concern about replacing Manson with Jesus is unique to my case study, my interviewees found various instances in which the Board suspected people of insincere conversions or chastised them for their overzealousness. Victor Shammas comments that religion is "often viewed by the Board as a proxy of pacification and introspection" but tells of an incident in which

the panel discovered that the inmate had switched between different religious denominations while in prison and had engaged in an activity considered incompatible with the tenets of the latest religious affiliation.... "I see you had a hamburger in 2009," the deputy commissioner said. "It's not the crime of the century, but I want to see where you're at in terms of your faith." Such minor acts—far from criminal—are construed as indicators of insincerity, which could be used as a proxy for an inmate's continued dangerousness.[98]

Another way to understand the Board's concern about religion might be to frame it as part of a broader concern with unscripted programs, to which we turn next.

THE BOARD KNOWS BEST: SUSPICION ABOUT
INDEPENDENT PERSONAL GROWTH

Sometimes, an inmate's personal interests collide with the Board's official recommendations. Some Manson Family inmates sought atypical, independent paths toward personal growth. Most specifically, Patricia Krenwinkel and Leslie Van Houten sought numerous academic and vocational certifications that were not on the prison's regular programmatic menu, and Bobby Beausoleil, already an accomplished and respected artist and musician at the time of his incarceration, continued to make efforts to advance in his profession. The Board's approach toward these ambitious undertakings has been lukewarm at best. Seeking academic certification was seen as presumptuous; assuming that one would find work in the area of one's academic expertise, unrealistic. The Board repeatedly confronts the inmates with the fact that they might have to work tedious, menial jobs on the outside and their personal growth efforts are a pipe dream. This approach is especially evident in Beausoleil's case.

The first thing I noticed was the Board's efforts, in various hearings, to push inmates to monetize their art or degrees. Patricia Krenwinkel, who sells her needlework, is asked to "give us an idea of what one of your paintings would go for."[99] Leslie Van Houten attends correspondence college courses with Antioch College as an effort to get around her restricted housing status, and the Board interrogates her as to the validity of her degree, leading her to explain that "it's not like a send-in-a-matchbook-cover."[100]

The deepest conflicts were provoked by Bobby Beausoleil's vocational choices. For several years, despite the Board's strong encouragement to take his GED certificate, Beausoleil opted instead to further his musical career behind bars. Here, Board member Brown expresses doubt about the viability of Beausoleil's career:

BROWN: What did you have when you were on the outside?

BEAUSOLEIL: I'm a professional musician.

BROWN: Just a musician.

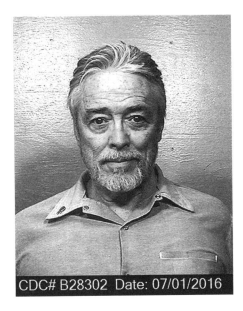

CDC# B28302 Date: 07/01/2016

PHOTO 7. Robert "Bobby" Beausoleil in 2016. (California Department of Corrections and Rehabilitation via Associated Press)

BEAUSOLEIL: I've been playing professionally since I was 17.

BROWN: Other than that. I'm saying you have nothing other than the musician trade.

BEAUSOLEIL: Well, I have made a considerable sum since I have been in through my art work.

BROWN: Art work.

BEAUSOLEIL: Graphic arts.

BROWN: Painting?

BEAUSOLEIL: Not necessarily, no. Things like graphic arts, commercial art. I made most of my money in here doing book covers and things like that, stationery design.

BROWN: Have you been able to sell them on the outside?

BEAUSOLEIL: Oh, yeah.

BROWN: How much money have you been able to earn in that area?

BEAUSOLEIL: If I really apply myself—I don't need that much money in here. I'm not trying to make a whole bundle or anything. But I usually make about seventy-five to a hundred a book cover, maybe forty, fifty dollars for a stationery design.

BROWN: How much have you been able to earn since you've been in the institution doing this kind of work?[101]

Recall that, at the time of his incarceration, Beausoleil was an influential figure in the countercultural music and film scene. Behind bars he continued this work by working on a soundtrack for the film *Lucifer Rises,* directed by Kenneth Anger, in which he had starred before his arrest.[102] Beausoleil tries to frame his musical work as self-directed programming, explaining how his expertise and professional skills contribute to the prison as a whole. He says that he is "pretty much the one solely responsible, if anyone is, for putting the music program at DVI [Deuel Vocational Institution] together. I mean, there wasn't any music when I came."

> BROWN: What is the music program?
>
> BEAUSOLEIL: The music program now consists of about five different, five or six different bands, different groups representing different, mainly different ethnic groups. There is a Black soul group, Mexican group, country western. We are trying to, you know, represent everyone. We have a music room; we have about, oh, maybe five, six, seven thousand dollars' worth of music equipment that we didn't have before I started.[103]

The Board again presses Beausoleil to obtain his GED: "I am relatively sure," says Board member Smith, "you feel you do not need it because you are in the music trade, where it is not an emphasis."

> BEAUSOLEIL: It's not that. If there were subjects that would be applicable, you know, to my vocation.
>
> SMITH: Okay. We would suggest that you check with the educational staff to see if you can take the GED test. And you may be able to qualify simply by taking that test to get your high school diploma. But we think it's important enough to mention that and to list it as something you should work on for your next hearing.[104]

The following year, this conflict escalates, as the Board admonishes Beausoleil for not participating in "formalized training." He replies: "There was no provisions for the type of program that I have been involved in. . . . I have been involved in a lot of programs that I would assume would be self-help programs."[105] The lack of documentation for his efforts frustrates him: "I've tried to come up with something that I could show the Board to account for myself for the past number of years, and it's very difficult, because the programs that I'm involved in are not really formal, classified as self-help programs, even though they are."[106]

By 1980 Beausoleil gives up, takes the GED as per the Board's require-ment, and enrolls in college courses.[107] He is frustrated by the lack of "a GED for what you can do with your hands or whatever, for other types of skills other than basic high school knowledge."[108] His frustration with the parole board requirements continues:

> The self-help groups that are available here at DI are very few to begin with. Dr. Macomber, who handles the group therapy, feels that I don't belong in group therapy and I don't require it. Alcoholics Anonymous, I've never in my life had a drinking problem.... Narcotics—I've never had a narcotic prob-lem; apart from smoking marijuana occasionally and few LSD hits in the sixties, I'm not now inclined toward a narcotic problem.... Gavel Club, this is for speaking. I don't have trouble speaking. So there's really, as far as this type of self-help group, there's really nothing that is necessarily applicable to me. So, what I've done is I've tried to create my own self-help program. I don't know if anybody would give you official credit for this or not, but I'm in col-lege. I'm integral to the TV studio now. We are currently programming a lot of educational programs, entertainment. And I'm very much involved in that.[109]

In response, the Board requires that he participate in Category D evaluation to affirm the stated decreased violence potential.[110]

Part of the problem is the fact that the self-directed nature of Beausoleil's vocational advancement does not provide the sort of documentation that the Board recognizes; there is no one to put a laudatory chrono in his file. By 1983, his C-file documentation finally lists him as "music program coordina-tor" at DVI.[111] At that time he is taking college courses in music production, an area he is already familiar with, and getting good grades.

In 1985, Beausoleil is listed as a high school student despite having passed his GED and earned numerous college credits, because

> I have run out of things to do within, that are applied to my intended occupa-tion on the outside, and the closest thing I could find to something I could apply in terms of gaining additional knowledge is in the band room, in the music room, inasmuch as my hope is to, is to make a living for myself in the design of musical instruments. I teach—even though I'm classified as a stu-dent, I'm assigned to maintain the equipment and to perform some limited teaching functions, and also just sort of keep the peace down there.[112]

The issue of inappropriate programs recurs throughout his incarceration, though Beausoleil handles it with increasing grace and humility: "Well, there hasn't been any vocational, although working in multimedia is a constant learning process. There is software to learn constantly to stay up to date. So, I have continued to upgrade in my vocation in that respect, but not formally because there is no one here that can teach me anymore."[113]

Beausoleil's journey confirms that the prison programming machine cannot easily accommodate people of exceptional skills and abilities, or people whose lives prior to confinement involved professional or educational achievement. There is strong pressure, even on overqualified inmates to conform to the existing programming even when unsuitable. Moreover, obtaining proper documentation of programs is as important as actually participating in the programs. Finally, the transcripts suggest that the conflict stems not just from the content but also from the undertone of the debate: Beausoleil comes off as arrogant and defiant, which the Board does not suffer gladly. We move on to discussing the inmates' demeanor at the hearing.

DEMEANOR DURING THE HEARING: PERFORMING INSIGHT WITH "REHEARSED AUTHENTICITY"

Just like insight, rehabilitation and transformation are not just *experienced;* they are *performed.* The transcripts show that the inmate's demeanor is mined by the Board for evidence of his or her sincerity, remorse, and genuine transformation. The audience is wider than just the commissioners; in the room are not only the prosecutor and victims but also representatives of the media and cameras. As early as 1979, Leslie Van Houten's attorney observed that it was "peculiar, if not downright unfair and unreasonable, that the media should be present and the defendant's own family can't be present, nor can sophisticated, knowledgeable psychiatric observers be present."[114]

Efforts to object to media coverage invariably fail. In 1985, Patricia Krenwinkel's attorney argued that the camera and lights were "extremely distracting. . . . We make this objection also on the basis that such television and radio coverage is obstructing the hearing process—and that it is also prejudicial to the proceedings that are before us at this time." The objection was immediately overruled: Board member Aceto stated, "We have been through this, at least three years that I am aware of. . . . I don't find (an exact) distraction for the panel, as long as we are able to see and view the prisoner and counsel and the rest of the people in the room."[115]

The media presence and recording lend the hearing an artificial quality. Inmates speak into a microphone and are often asked to enunciate clearly for the transcriber. The Board requires that they explain their nonverbal gestures, such as nodding, shaking their heads, or smiling. Eloquence is rewarded only insofar as it comes off as authentic. These features are not unique to the Manson cases. Victor Shammas, who attended several parole hearings, observes that the ability to convey rehabilitation—to be "verified" as rehabilitated—hinges "on a personal capacity to (i) verbally express thoughts and feelings, (ii) speak in a reflective manner, and (iii) produce linguistic utterances in a socially legitimate form"—capacities that "are unevenly distributed in social space. It is the expectations of participation and verification that forms the basis of the notion of 'insight.'"[116]

The focus on demeanor developed gradually. The early hearings see the Board members focusing more on the content of the inmates' presentation and debating them on their attendance in programs or disciplinary records. Even when such records are close to pristine—minimal write-ups and extensive program participation—the Board can always deny parole on the grounds of the heinousness of the crime. The post-*Lawrence* era, by contrast, is characterized by a retreat away from objective assessment of the prisoners' programming records and toward a more subjective, vague assessment of their performance. The words "poor performance" appear in at least half of the post-*Lawrence* Manson Family hearings as justification of parole denial.

The examination of demeanor is especially rough on the women in the study, all of whom were criticized by Stephen Kay, to their faces, as being cold and unemotional, from which he deduced a lack of remorse. The Board openly agrees with this characterization, and as argued in chapter 4, the expectation-laden encounter with the victims in the hearing room adds to this impression. The lack of crying or emotional outbursts is treated poorly, though even when the inmates cry, it is seen as excessive or manipulative.

Even an inmate's presence or absence is part of the performance. After several hearings in which the factual details of the crime yielded a heated discussion, Charles Watson decided, in his 2006 hearing, to waive his presence at the hearing. The Board discusses his sincerity and remorse on the basis of file documentation in the absence of direct questioning.[117] At his 2011 hearing, Watson is present, but on advice of his attorney he refuses to answer direct questions. Board member Prizmich explains that this decision has a price:

> And I want to make sure you understand that if you do speak with us that it's important, it's one of the components that we use to help us reach a decision regarding suitability, is one's honesty. So I'm advising you, it's very important for you to be honest with us. And if there is a point during the hearing that you wish to make something, some commentary on something we've said, I'm going to swear you in now so that you're sworn in prior to the hearing. So if you could raise your right hand, I'll give you the oath.[118]

But even being present in the room can be interpreted as effrontery. In the documentary *Life after Manson,* Debra Tate is seen confronting Krenwinkel. Tate, as explained above, provides an accusatory account of her position, speaking directly to Krenwinkel, who does not reply, and accusing her of indifference and lack of remorse. The prosecutor, Patrick Sequeira, argues that Krenwinkel's very presence at the hearing, which suggests hope for parole, is proof of her lack of remorse:

> I think if she had true remorse and she truly understood her crimes and the horrific nature of it, she wouldn't be here at a parole hearing. She would just accept a punishment and not come to her parole hearings, that she would just say, "I deserve to spend the rest of my life in prison for what I've done." But yet, she is here telling us that she's done everything the Board has told her to do and so she should be released, that she somehow is worthy because she's taken a few classes here and there, because she has a job outside or a place to live.[119]

Sequeira's understanding of remorse seems to suggest that true remorse cannot exist side by side with a sense of redeemability. Anyone who believes in their capacity for change cannot be truly remorseful. This obviously puts the inmates in a performative bind. As explained above, Krenwinkel's absence from her 1982 hearing was interpreted by the prosecutor present at the time, Kay, as inability to handle stress and thus lack of readiness for release. In the highly artificial atmosphere of the hearing, no behavior will satisfy the authenticity test.

Juxtaposing the meanings imputed to Krenwinkel's presence and to Watson's absence (or silence) suggests that any act, verbal or nonverbal, can be interpreted as lack of insight or remorse. To expect authenticity or sincerity under these circumstances is, to say the least, challenging.

Only at Charles Manson's hearings does the Board's appetite for scrutinizing the inmate's performance remain unsatisfied, because, against the backdrop of the other inmates' attempts to convince the Board of their insight and rehabilitation, Manson refuses to follow along. His demeanor is reminiscent of the defiant death row inmates described by Meredith Rountree as courting their own executions.[120] At his first hearing, Manson launches into a lengthy tirade against the establishment, in support of his own innocence, and in exultation of his special powers:

> And all that mental thing that you put in your televisions and you put in your books, and then you sell hack off of your children's minds—then your children wises up and they take knives and go off and kill a whole bunch of people, and then you come back and say, "Well, Charlie has got all them kids doing all of that." No, Charlie hasn't got those kids doing anything. Your system is failing because you're not being honest with yourself. . . . Now, I will accept responsibility for reflecting onto those children, and here's what I reflected onto those children: Faith in yourself, confidence in your own ability to be your own self. Stand on your own two feet and do what you think is right, and don't let no news media brainwash you into thinking that somebody is on your side, because you have got to stand by yourself when the chips come down. You have to stand alone, just like I have had to stand alone against all you people.[121]
>
> . . . I know what everyone is thinking. I know what they're thinking before they are thinking it. I have already went through everybody's minds. I have already went through what I call the mind. From Jesus Christ to the cross, all the way down, I see what makes people go. . . . You see in me what you see in yourself.[122]

Manson refused to attend his 1979 hearing. His attorney, Glen DeRonde, challenges the Board members on the basis of bias:

> I understand that no member of this Board has been able to escape the notoriety that Mr. Manson has received. But I suppose you would have to ask yourselves whether or not you constitute an unbiased panel in this matter by virtue of all the publicity associated with this man with regard to movies, books, news broadcasts, etc. And if each member of the panel would be inclined to give me an answer whether or not they can disregard these extraneous items, learned outside Mr. Manson's Central File, and can decide this matter impartially, then we can proceed.[123]

In 1980, Manson is present at his hearing, again ranting and raving against the system: "Yeah, I'm a danger. I'm a danger to lies. I'm a danger to confusion. I'm a danger to things that aren't in the proper perspective. There's a lot of things I'm a danger to. I might even get convicted next time for promoting a little harmony. And then maybe I'll get a doing somebody some good prior with a feeling of honor and truth within my own existence. Maybe that would be a felony by then. Of course, the way you're going you'll outlaw everything until you've outlawed yourself."[124]

And in 1981, Manson argues that his ten years in solitary confinement have clouded his mind to the point that he cannot understand the proceedings: "I ain't got no mind. It's gone, man. I don't understand half the things you are saying."[125] The hearing proceeds as before, including lengthy tirades by Manson.

In 1986, Manson begins the hearing with a contentious refusal to accept his lawyer. He then argues against the legality of the Board:

MANSON: You take my life for fifteen years illegally and—

COLLIER: Are you going to be—

MANSON: Now we're going to get legal?

COLLIER: Are you going to be answering questions? If you are, why don't you—

MANSON: I'm just sitting here. I—I don't—I—

COLLIER: Are you going to be saying anything at all?

MANSON: —I wrote a statement that I wanted to make for the record. What you people do—that's your confusion.[126]

The remainder of the hearing is characterized by tirades and discussions of Manson's activities inside his cell.[127]

The last year Manson attends his parole hearing is 1997. His 2002 hearing is held in the presence of his state-appointed attorney, Patrick Sparks. The commissioner addresses Sparks as follows: "Mr. Patrick Sparks has been appointed by the State to represent Mr. Manson. Mr. Manson refused to meet with Mr. Sparks. Therefore, Mr. Sparks is at a substantial disadvantage and has indicated that he would like to be removed or dismissed from this case. Mr. Sparks, would you like to?" Sparks responds: "That's an accurate statement, and I'll confirm that. That, in fact, Mr. Manson did not interview and I don't believe that my participation at this hearing would facilitate his parole at this time."[128]

The Board officially allows Sparks to withdraw and declares a recess,[129] after which the commissioner makes a statement about the way in which the committee would have respected Manson's rights had he been present: "Were Mr. Manson to appear today, he would not have been required to discuss the commitment offense with the Panel. He would not have been required to

Charles Manson at his 1986 parole hearing. (Associated Press)

speak to the Panel. Nor would he be required to actually discuss any aspects at all with the Panel. Again, he has chosen not to appear at all. And had he—because he's refused to attend, and had he decided not to speak to us, we would not and will not hold that against him."[130]

The panel then proceeds to read the verbatim description of Manson's crime, as they had done at the hearings at which he was present. They then quote Manson as refusing to express remorse at his 1997 appearance (what he actually said was that he had not given an order to kill the victims).[131] The Board tries to make sense of Manson's file in his absence, without much success:

> In a previous report, Mr. Manson stated that in terms of parole plans, he had none. He's had a variety of responses to that question or that issue. At one point in 1992, he stated he wasn't interested in paroling. He would be lost in our society, and his main concern was to be released to a general population setting in order to program. There are a number of letters in the file. There are a total of 80 signatures on a petition. The signatures all appear to come from people in England. There are 15 different form letters or individual letters in the file, all of these supporting release for Mr. Manson. And the letters are signed by people who seem to be scattered all over the United States, the 15 letters.[132]

For counterbalance, the police department has provided a letter as well, which cites the original crime and the "risk to the community" posed by

Manson, but does not elucidate whether said risk is current or stems from anything beyond the crimes themselves: "[The Commanding Officer of the Robbery/Homicide Division] writes that Mr. Manson was an active participant in the mutilation and murders of several persons in the Los Angeles area. Crimes committed by Mr. Manson were of such brutality and complete lack of humanity that it is clear Mr. Manson has no concern for human life. It is the opinion of the Los Angeles Police Department that the release of Mr. Manson will create considerable risk to the community and that his release is unequivocally contrary to the interests of society." Commissioner Mackenberg recites Manson's unhappy and unproductive prison experience and his disciplinary violations, concluding that "by and large he has not had a very happy time of it in the last five years. If it sounds like a woeful tale, it's not because I'm trying to simply disrespect Mr. Manson; it appears that he has serious mental health issues. That they're causing him some very real problems."[133]

Mackenberg's summary is as much about a failure of the California prison system as it is Manson's:

> The long and short of it is, is that it's difficult to say a whole lot about the last five years other than that he seems to go back and forth between the Protective Housing Unit, Administrative Segregation, Security Housing, back to Protective Housing Unit. So that's kind of like a sad circle of rounds in this institution. He doesn't seem to benefit a whole lot from treatment inasmuch as he resists it so that he often refuses apparently to see the psychologist and doesn't want to see psychiatrists and that it's difficult to get him to do the things that they think he should do in order to forward his programs to be able to come to the Board at some point and say really, I ought to be able to go home.

The prosecutor, Kay, discusses Manson's manipulations, and again inaccurately characterizes Manson's legal position: "He has never understood why he was convicted for these murders because he always thought that if he got other people to commit the murders, then they could be convicted of the murders. But if he didn't physically do it, then he couldn't be convicted."[134]

As mentioned before, Manson's claim was not that he could not be convicted without physical participation in the crime. His factual contention was that he had not ordered the others to kill the victims. But Kay hits the nail on the head with the following observation: "He knows that he's never going to get paroled, and he's just not going to go along with the program."[135]

Last to speak before Manson's expected denial of parole is Debra Tate, who evinces enough familiarity with the parole board to say:

> I'm a little disappointed that Mr. Manson chose not to show up today. However, in order not to waste any time, I also believe that Mr. Manson, for obvious reasons, should be denied parole for five years. I implore you to please give him the five years so that I don't have to come and see you folks again so soon, although I love you dearly. He is totally unsuitable for release into society in my opinion, and I implore you to please keep him in so that society can have peace for at least five more years.[136]

At his subsequent parole hearing in 2007, not only does Manson not show up, but he is unrepresented before the committee, and the commissioner states for the record the Board's intention to "do everything we can to ensure that his rights have not been violated." She then theatrically recites Manson's rights, as if narrating a hypothetical play in which Manson had showed up for his hearing, which makes his absence even more glaring:

> At this point I would have asked him did he review his Central File, did he get a timely notice of the hearing. It appeared that he did. He declined and refused to sign whether or not he was going to review his C-File, and that was done on January the 23rd, 2007. And also there were no relevant documents that he had to produce. We would always ask that at this time as well. I would also ask him if he had—let him know that he had an additional right to be heard by an impartial Panel, and again, since he's not here, I would assume he does not object to the Panel. I would also—the next item that I would ask him is—and let him know that he would not be required to either discuss his offense if he desires not to do so and we cannot hold that against him, but however, we do accept the finding of the court to be true.[137]

The absurdity of this play with not only Manson but a representing attorney in absentia as well is an illustration of Kay's insight from the 2002 hearing: Manson, who had no hope of being granted parole, forced the Board into playing a role they did not intend. They find themselves analyzing his psychiatric diagnosis, also obtained in his absence (antisocial personality disorder and psychopathy[138]) and reading for the record a letter of support from a thirteen-year-old girl.[139]

The prosecutor, Sequeira, provides a standard narrative closely following the Helter Skelter narrative. Notably, Debra Tate actually provides an argument for current risk posed by the inmate: "I would like it to go on the record that I disagree with some of the things read in the Central File. I believe that

Mr. Manson has one very prolific talent and that talent is to pick sociopaths. That is the same reason in which he should never be granted any kind of a release. There are still people that are influenced by him. They grow in numbers every day via the internet, and in regard to that, any one of these people being released poses a great public safety issue."[140]

The Board's frustration with having had to play Manson's game is evident in their decision as well: "We'd like to also go on record to state that we feel that Mr. Manson should be attending these hearings, these suitability hearings, in order for the Panel to be able to discuss and clarify any discrepancies that may be in his record, that he constantly said that this or that is not here, and we could also question him on some of the various conflicting versions that he's given in relationship to the crimes."[141]

Manson's last parole hearing, which he also did not attend, was held in 2012. However, this time Manson is represented by a new attorney, Dejon Lewis, who, in contrast to Sparks, tries to provide representation for the client, who did not cooperate with him,[142] by making both legal and factual points. Notably, Board member Peck, perhaps frustrated with Manson's absence, chooses to address him in the second person throughout the hearing, as if to force engagement on him: "And Mr. Manson, I'm speaking to you through the record now. We have reviewed your Central File. We've reviewed your prior transcripts, and nothing that happens here today is going to change the court findings. We're not here to retry your case. We're going to accept as true the findings of the court. We're here for the sole purpose of determining your suitability for parole."[143]

As the hearing begins, Lewis presents a legal objection to the timing of the parole hearings. As mentioned above, Marsy's Law, an ostensibly pro-victim legislative initiative, increased the time between parole hearings to an initial fifteen years, and it was applied to people serving current prison terms even if they had originally been incarcerated long before its enactment. Lewis makes the argument that the law should not apply retroactively, and Peck summarily dismisses his argument.[144]

Lewis's legal commentary merited, arguably, a lengthier and more serious discussion. In *Gilman v. Davis,* the federal district court in Sacramento had ordered the Board to stop applying Proposition 9 (Marsy's Law) to plaintiffs, holding that Marsy's Law, which drastically increased the period between parole hearings, is probably unconstitutional when applied to prisoners whose crimes were committed before the law passed.[145] The court will conduct further hearings to determine whether it is unconstitutional. If it is, the

Board can no longer deny prisoners parole for up to fifteen years. Peck's summary dismissal of Lewis's argument leaves open the question whether he was even aware of the decision in *Gilman*.

Peck proceeds to quote Manson's interview with the prison psychiatrist: "I am special. I am not like the average inmate. I have put five people in the grave. I have been in prison most of my life. I am a very dangerous man." Further in the psychological assessment, he stated, "I don't care about the Board's opinion. I don't care about your opinion."[146] As Peck reviews the psychiatrist's diagnosis, he reads this observation: "Clinically, while limited, this indicates some degree of improved insight into his violent and anti-social behavior, considering his previous pattern of denial of wrongdoing."[147]

Once more, a solitary support letter is presented on Manson's behalf, which Peck leans toward dismissing as vague:

> There is a letter by an individual named John E. Ashcraft that says he's Mr. Manson's best friend and there's—I really don't know if this is even a legitimate letter or not a legitimate letter. But it basically says that he says that Mr. Manson told him that he, that once he did not want to get out on parole, but now he wants to. And if he can, then he wants to live—then Mr. Ashcraft is offering residence in Fullerton. But so that, frankly, is the only support letter that I have, unless you have—do you have any other support letters?[148]

But Lewis refuses to go along with this dismissal and actually argues to the point:

> I will say, though, Mr. Manson is 77 years old. He doesn't need to have a job at this time. He can draw Social Security at this point if he was to get a parole date, and him living with Mr. Ashcraft would cover those parole plans, I think. I'm not going to say they're viable, because we haven't or the Board hasn't backed that letter up by, you know, investigating Mr. Ashcraft and what not, but it seems to me if he is genuine in offering him a place to live that that would be an adequate parole plan for a gentleman who is 77 years old.[149]

As in previous hearings, the police department sent a letter opposing the release, and the prosecutor, Sequeira, expresses similar sentiments, echoing, as before, Bugliosi's demonic narrative. Quoting Manson's words to his psychiatrist, Sequeira essentially asks the Board to give Manson what he asked for: "In his own words, Manson is telling this Board and essentially the public as well, that he is dangerous and he is completely unsuitable for parole."[150]

At this point, Lewis embarks on the thankless job of doing the most with what he has, which is practically nothing. He recounts Manson's absolute lack of collaboration with prison authorities and failure to achieve any educational or vocational milestones.

> My client has not accomplished any of these milestones. Why is the question? Why? Yesterday, while watching CNN, I listened to Mark Geragos, Henry Byers, and Alan Dershowitz just destroy the two former attorneys for George Zimmerman in the Trayvon Martin case for commenting on Mr. Zimmerman's mental state. They were of the opinion that this was unprofessional behavior for attorneys to do so. Well, my client has been tried and convicted and has served over 30 years in prison, and I think that's the difference between the two cases from what I'm about to say. Mr. Manson has not even remotely accomplished any minimal milestones that the Board would like to see an inmate who they are considering parole to do. I cannot purport to you that Mr. Manson has a mental disorder causing his utter failure in the rehabilitation process. I'm not a mental health professional, and I have never met him, and several psychologists say that he has no Axis-I severe mental disorder. But one thing is clear to me is that corrections or rehabilitation has not taken place here for Mr. Manson. It is my belief that Mr. Manson could benefit from hospitalization, given his age and his need for more geriatric care as he increases in age. He would also receive excellent psychosocial support in that type of environment. Mr. Manson needs hospitalization, not further incarceration in a state prison of this type.[151]

This is a remarkably generous and therapeutic observation on Lewis's part, but it receives little attention or sympathy from the Board. Peck reads the decision to deny parole, again by addressing Manson in the second person through the record. He mentions that "you chose not to be with us today," and continues:

> We have not yet, in any of our documents, seen any indication of remorse. We have no indication that you have any kind of insight into the causative factors of the life crime. You have absolutely no parole plans. You had a significant drug problem while you were in society, and this drug problem is still unresolved. You've been involved in absolutely no rehabilitative programs or self-help to address your substance abuse history. I think the statement that you made to the psychologist or the psychiatrist in the Comprehensive Risk Assessment told us a lot of what we needed to know, and I want to make sure I get this right so I'm just going to read what it, what you told Dr. Reed, and you said, "I am special. I am not like the average inmate. I have put five people in the grave. I've been in prison most of my life. I am a very dangerous man." And this Panel agrees with that statement.[152]

What can we learn from these last three hearings? Against the backdrop of the Board's usual modus operandi, which involves an adjudication of the value of the inmate's institutional record as well as of the rehearsed authenticity and sincerity of the inmate's presentation, the hearings with Manson in absentia reveal some of the embarrassment and frustration of an institutional engagement with someone who flat out rejects the rules of engagement. For the most part, these hearings stand in stark contrast to the vast majority of inmates—not just the remaining inmates in this case—who make a valiant effort to play the game. It would be easy (and likely correct) to conclude that the Board made the right call, that Manson was unsuitable for parole, and that the system "won." But in denying him parole, the Board merely came to the predetermined conclusion that Manson set up for it: remaining in control of others till the end of his life.

SIX

Reimagining the Future

THE PAST CASTS ITS SHADOW ON THE
INMATE'S POSTRELEASE PLANS

Whatever thou desirest will come to pass. . . . The boundary line
between going upwards or going downwards is here now. If thou
givest way to indecision for even a second, thou wilt have to suffer misery for a long, long time. This is the moment. Hold fast to
one single purpose. Persistently join up the chain of good acts.

The Tibetan Book of the Dead

Shortly after undergoing open-heart surgery, Buddhist publisher Sam
Bercholz collapsed in the hospital, and for a brief time experienced intense
and dramatic visions of human suffering, guided through the hell of human-
inflicted suffering by the Buddha of Hell. Years later, he discussed his experience with renowned Tibetan American artist Pema Namdol Thaye. Thaye
contributed his artistic vision to Bercholz's powerful narrative and brought
his visions to life in a series of powerful and evocative paintings. The outcome
of the collaboration was the book *A Guided Tour of Hell,* as well as an epony-
mous art exhibition based on Bercholz's narrative and Thaye's art.[1]

Bercholz's experiences evoke the Buddhist concept of Bardo, a purgatorial
in-between realm in which beings realize their suffering and reexperience it
from various perspectives before being reborn into the wheel of samsara
(more on the Bardo at the beginning of chapter 7). In his intense spiritual
journey, Bercholz meets beings who, in past lives, were focused on their greed
and desire of money, sensual experiences, romantic attachments, or fame;
their fates in the Bardo reflect poetic retribution for their greed, aversion, and
ignorance.

As I examine Thaye's art with wide-open eyes and an astonished heart, I
realize something important about the Bardo: the future of the beings in
purgatory is marked by their past. Indeed, the concept of karma drives the
nature and particulars of rebirth,[2] which is seen as a "necessary corollary," a

"derivative" of karma.[3] I am struck by how well this Buddhist principle reflects the parole hearing experience.

The general theme found in the Board's discussion of the inmate's risk, promise, and postparole plans is the extent to which the past—primarily the crime of commitment—overshadows and guides the inmate's future. More specifically, I found the following themes:

1. The Board invariably relies on psychiatric reports to assess risk, but inmates' files contain numerous reports and tests of various kinds, which makes the psychiatric information at the hearing a panacea. Since the Board tends to err on the side of risk and public safety, it can always find *something* in the inmate's psychiatric assessment to rely on. When the evaluation includes a clinical diagnosis of a personality disorder or an assessment that the inmate might pose risk due to past history, the Board tends to accept that assessment wholesale. By contrast, positive assessments, predicting little or no risk to public safety, tend to be downplayed, either by discrediting their authors (as nonpsychiatrists or private, independent clinicians) or by recurring to less optimistic risk assessments from previous years.

2. The Board tends to be pessimistic about the inmate's postrelease plans for employment and finances, especially when such plans involve intellectual or creative work; these are regarded as overambitious and unrealistic. While the skepticism seems overall warranted, it often penalizes inmates for the institution's failure to offer them programs that actually prepare them for outside life.

3. As the parole process has become more politicized and involves more engagement from the public and victims' rights organizations, the hearings evince an inconsistent treatment of support and opposition letters. The Board tends to harbor suspicion about supportive letters from family and friends, distinguishing between people who truly know the inmates well and people who might be supporting them because of the notoriety of the case. However, opposition letters, even in the form of petitions signed by people clearly unfamiliar with the case, tend to be treated as pertinent.

4. When inmates raise issues involving health and aging, the Board evinces a clear preference for looking back and discussing the past than for the future, sometimes astonishingly ignoring terminal illness and old age when discussing future risk.

RISK ASSESSMENT: THE PSYCHIATRIC REPORT
AS A PANACEA

A considerable portion of every hearing is devoted to parsing out the psychological and/or psychiatric evaluations of the inmate in an effort to assess the risk of release. This is consistent throughout the decades covered by this study. The Board's attention to these evaluations is consistent throughout the research period and understandable; prior to the politicization of the parole process, the emphasis at parole hearings was on future risk and the claim to professionalism and expertise required deference to clinical professionals.

This deference did not change much over time, and as Young, Mukamal, and Favre-Bulle found in their quantitative study of suitability findings, there is correlation between the content of the psychiatric reports and the decision to grant or deny parole. However, Young and her colleagues found it challenging to operationalize the different psychiatric tests: in their sample, which covered hearings between 2007 and 2010, "any given inmate had taken between one and four different tests: Historical, Clinical, and Risk Management Scales (HCR-20), Clinician Generic Risk assessment, Axis V Global Assessment of Functioning (GAF), and/or the Hare Psychopathy Checklist–Revised (PCLR-Hare)." Given this variation, the study could operationalize the tests only by using a binary variable: whether or not the inmate received only "low-risk" scores (regardless of how many tests were taken). The results indicated that inmates who received only low-risk scores were twice as likely to be granted parole as inmates who received at least one score that was not "low."[4]

My qualitative analysis of the hearing transcripts lends context to this finding and explains the difficulty in assessing the impact of the psychiatric and psychological evaluations on the Board's decision-making process. Since my study reached back into the late 1970s, I found a plethora of risk assessment reports and methods. Generally, the older transcripts featured clinical assessments, whose content largely overlapped with the Board's discussion of the crime of commitment, remorse, and insight. Some of these reports were composed by psychiatrists and some by psychologists or other correctional counselors; the later transcripts included more actuarial, statistical test results. Moreover, in newer transcripts (after multiple parole denials over decades of incarceration), the inmate's C-file includes archaeological layers of psychiatric evaluations from previous hearings, covering the inmate's entire incarceration experience, and is inconsistent in nature.

Consequently, the psychiatric documentation in the inmate's file is a panacea in which one can find evidence of dangerousness as well as lack thereof. While all inmates in this study, with the exception of Charles Manson (who did not cooperate with prison clinicians), were evaluated at their last few hearings as possessing a lower-than-average risk of violence (sometimes a negligible risk), their initial clinical assessments from the early- to mid-seventies were less conclusive. In some cases, clinical assessments included risk of violence; in other cases, the psychiatric reports indicated the clinicians' confusion about the contrast between an inmate's demeanor in prison and the heinous crimes in the past.

One possible conclusion is that the Board's decision to keep the Manson Family inmates behind bars is merely political, and its reliance on whatever psychiatric evidence supports this decision is pretextual. But it is worth keeping in mind that, in the late 1970s, it would still have been conceivable for at least some the inmates to have been released (as explained in chapter 2). At Bruce Davis's 1978 hearing, the prosecutor, Compton, objected to his release, and his rhetoric indicates that he was truly concerned that the Board might actually release Davis:

> If the Board desires to set a date—and very strongly, the evidence in this case behooves setting a date for Mr. Davis at this time. If that is your view, though, let me discuss briefly what date would appear to be appropriate. As far as the matrix is concerned, it would appear that at least III D would be appropriate and possibly get into the area of IV F. At the time there was great public concern about what was happening, the bizarre killings of individuals for no real reason, makes one—the public was concerned at the time due to these killings. . . . There are numerous reasons why the highest term, if a date is set, should be taken. . . . There was a second crime, of course, murder. That should be considered as far as a separate time, a separate period of time, and that was the maximum, I believe, because it was committed at the same time, and that would be 84 months, as I can interpret the matrix as far as other offenses are concerned. There was a firearm used during the Hinman case. There was evidence that the Defendant pointed it at Mr. Hinman while Manson slashed Mr. Hinman on the side of his face all the way down. That would be use of the firearm by the defendant.[5]

By 1985, however, the political landscape had dramatically changed. Life without parole was born, life with parole had been extended; and the power of the Board was diminished and limited. The gubernatorial veto power would become law in 1988. The victims' rights movement could already boast legislative successes in California and nationwide. This punitive turn permeated the hearings through public petitions against the inmates' release, as well as through the victims' increased presence at hearings. Against this backdrop, Davis's belief that his release (earnestly discussed in previous hearings) was still a possibility reads as surprisingly naïve: "But the law, the law at one time said that in seven years I could be eligible for parole. Whether we still go by what other people said, well, that's yet to be determined, I suppose. I don't really know. I don't know the thinking of how you all really think about what that used to be like. But I think we're at a point to where my parole would not be an unthinkable thing. I don't think it's—I don't think it's a great leap beyond a reasonable, a reasonable assumption."[6]

Davis was in for a rude awakening. After being recommended for release by the Board in 2010, 2012, 2015, and 2017, he received gubernatorial reversals and is still incarcerated in 2019. But even as early as 1978, it was not entirely clear how an inmate could positively demonstrate lack of risk. Patricia Krenwinkel expresses this frustration at her 1978 hearing: "I don't know what I can say to say that I know it would never happen again, that I would not take somebody's life. I don't know. You know, I know that inside myself, but there's no way that I can impart that to you through any words that I may use."[7]

As demonstrated earlier, the Board readily draws conclusions about insight, remorse, and dangerousness from the inmate's demeanor at the hearing. But it is on safer ground when relying on professional opinions regarding the validity and sincerity of the inmate's sentiments about the crime. Indeed, a comprehensive psychological profile addresses all aspects of the inmate's behavior, crime of commitment, and so on, rather than just clinically assessing his or her mental health. In a newsletter for parolee hopefuls, prisoner rights attorney Charles Carbone offers recommendations to the parolees undergoing an assessment:[8]

> Don't try to run the show. It's a psych interview conducted by the psychologist, not conducted by you. Let the psychologist run the show. Trying to dominate the interview just pisses off the interviewer.... Don't be passive either: It's a difficult balancing act, but without running the show, be engaged.... Show emotion without being fake. Talk about your remorse, your acceptance of what occurred in addition to the crime's impact. Have an outline IN ADVANCE about what you want to say on EACH of these topics. Be specific in your list of what you accept responsibility for including both your actions and inactions which led to the crime.... Don't ask how you did.

Unless the examiner decides to answer that question and divulge that information without prompting, it's best not to fish for how you did.

Carbone, as well as my interviewees, seems to regard the evaluation as a dress rehearsal of sorts for the hearing itself. As explained above, over time, the clinical interview is supplemented by various psychiatric tests, but the body of information provided by mental health professionals is comprehensive and covers everything the Board might be interested in—including the "nexus" between the crime and the inmate's future dangerousness.

Because the files typically contain so many reports, opinions, and tests, risk assessment becomes a contested ground: the Board, the prosecutor, and the inmate and his or her lawyer all chime in, in an effort to credit some parts of the body of information and discredit others. There is always ready support for any opinion. The early years for all inmates reflect multiple, and changing, diagnostic categories. Even people diagnosed with "passive aggressive personality with dissocial personality features" do not really require treatment.[9] "Antisocial personality" appears every few years for everyone.

The contention often revolves around the professional credentials of the evaluators, especially the appropriateness of psychologists versus psychiatrists. This kind of struggle can be seen over several years of Bobby Beausoleil's hearings. At his 1980 hearing, Beausoleil complains that his earlier assessment, on which the Board relies, was conducted and written by correctional counselors and merely signed by a psychiatrist—a practice that he claims was no longer allowed in 1980. Board member Coronado responds, "I don't know where your information comes from."[10] Board member Pizarro makes Beausoleil an expert on his own condition:

> There is no sign as far as I can determine that you are mentally ill or that you are brain damaged. There are signs, and you are described as alert, verbal, articulate, and with the ability to express yourself. Now, the question in my mind, and maybe in the mind of a lot of people here and outside—is this hostility that you had still remaining but not openly expressed now? In other words, you know now to express it? . . . In other words, your first hurdle is this suitability or—putting it rather bluntly—are you dangerous?[11]

Subsequently, at his 1982 hearing, Beausoleil provides an opinion from a private psychologist, who writes: "It is my feeling that the inmate probably has no more violence potential currently than the average person, and after fourteen years, may, in fact, be ready for trial of further freedom in a graded fashion."[12] The Board balks at this external opinion because its author, an outsider to the correctional system, did not subscribe to the prison classification system or use the usual vernacular: "He is not saying 'is ready for parole' or 'is ready to be released' or statements to that effect." Beausoleil responds: "I don't think that it is his place to do that. He—I am certain—feels that's your job."[13]

On the other side of the debate is the institutional psychologist, who recommended moving Beausoleil into segregated housing, because, according to Beausoleil, he thought that "there are too many of you Manson guys out here" (including Watson and Davis). Board member Coronado explains how the psych council came to ascribe an antisocial personality disorder to Beausoleil: "Regardless of the subjects under discussion, he seemed to be invariably arrived at a position where he was presenting himself as a victim of injustice. His sustained belief that he can defy authority and assign himself to the institution of his choice indicates that there is a great deal of compensatory grandiosity as a reaction to the low self-esteem."[14]

At the 1983 hearing, Board member Patterson explains the aftermath: because of concerns about conflicts with Manson and the Aryan Brotherhood, "the alternative was for you to go to a lock-up unit [for evaluation], a unit where you'd have very little freedom for a 90-day period, . . . which, according to what we read, you refused to do."

Beausoleil explains that he refused this classification because it would mean that he "would be in protective custody, which would negate the possibility of my being able to go back to the main line here or possibly another institution."[15] As an alternative to the evaluation that could not be carried out, Beausoleil explains he had undergone individual psychotherapy: "I've done everything conceivably possible to—."

Board member Patterson discounts its value: "Your individual psychotherapy, as I understand it, is an hour every three weeks, for about a six-month period, which we have no—evaluation following that."[16]

Beausoleil directly critiques prisons' mental health services: "I've seen what, at least in one institution, what the Category D program is, and I think that you have expectations beyond what you should have for that program . . . just speaking frankly."

Patterson responds: "Well, maybe that's because you got such a poor recommendation."

Beausoleil resists: "It isn't. . . . I went and saw this guy one hour every three weeks."[17]

In 1984, Beausoleil explains that his therapist "didn't seem to think I needed [therapy], but he did it because there was some question by the Board as to, you know, they wanted some clarification."[18] His attorney, Helbert, challenges part of the institutional psychiatric report, which explains Beausoleil's prison conduct as motivated by an effort to be granted parole. Helbert interprets this as a statement that his client is being manipulative, and he highlights the artificial aspect of the entire process: "The comment by [the psychiatrist] that [Beausoleil] . . . is very determined in his effort to justify earning favorable release consideration by the Board of Prison Terms . . . I think we'd be foolish to think that anybody would not go into that program coming out or trying to meet that expectation for the Board of Prison Terms."[19]

And at Beausoleil's 1985 hearing, the opinion states that "his ability to maintain appropriate controls . . . [is] primarily contingent upon the supportive structure that the institution provides. . . . He is presently viewed as an individual who will likely remain somewhat defensive, a non-conformist personality, and quite energetic and active in idealistic or creative thinking."[20] In other words, not violent or dangerous within prison, but unpredictable postrelease.

An even more contentious conversation about clinical health care erupts at Bruce Davis's 1982 hearing, where he criticizes secular mental health professionals: "They have a lot to say about what's wrong. But as far as their solutions, they never seem to present a solution that's, you know, an answer."[21] Board member Coronado's response reveals that the Board finds formal psychiatric therapy useful because it yields an assessment of dangerousness: "How are they going to be able to probe the personality of Mr. Davis in order to determine whether in fact there have been those gains in terms of insight and how you deal with certain stressful situations that may develop and how you're going to react to them when you're released to the streets . . . if there is not that opportunity to do it?"[22]

The clinical assessment of the female inmates presents special difficulties, the first of which is that risk assessment tools were designed for *male* inmates. At Susan Atkins's 2005, hearing, the Board cites a psychiatric opinion, according to which "Doctor Smith offers a diagnosis on Axis I of ply [sic] substance dependence in remission and Axis II, a personality disorder not otherwise specified with antisocial and passive aggressive features."[23] The Board continues: "And he notes that it isn't possible to apply [the dangerousness scheme] directly to women prisoners. That it, in fact, was designed for men to give some ideas of the dangerousness after release."[24]

The overall unsuitability of risk assessment for women manifests itself in some peculiar exchanges. Overall, the assessments find little to no pathology, and the Board struggles to make sense of the lack of "nexus" between the crime of the past and the projection for a low-risk future. For example, at Patricia Krenwinkel's 1982 hearing, the Board cites a psychological opinion that concludes that Krenwinkel is not in need of therapy, except to assist with frustration and depression. The prosecutor, Kay, argues against the opinion, discrediting the author as a "psychologist, not a medical doctor, not a psychiatrist,"[25] and asks the Board to rely instead on an earlier psychiatric evaluation ascribing antisocial personality.

In general, the assessment of the women's violent potential relies almost entirely on the crime of commitment, even though by the late 1970s they were no longer adolescents and had been in prison for approximately a decade. Krenwinkel's assessment takes a peculiar turn when the clinician asks her "why Germans were autocrats. We discussed why Germany, by the way that it's seated in the European continent, is surrounded by other countries. We proceeded to talk at great length about the German people."[26] It could be that this conversation aimed to gauge Krenwinkel's opinions regarding obedience to authority because of her history; as Melnick notes in *Creepy Crawling*, the comparison between Manson and Hitler has been a permanent fixture in public consciousness.[27] But even so, this focus would suggest that the psychologist was assessing Krenwinkel's dangerousness from the perspective of her past crimes rather than from her present condition.

Leslie Van Houten's 1979 hearing also reflects the Board's discomfort with her lack of dangerousness. The Board launches into a lengthy retrospective of Van Houten's psychiatric evaluations since 1971. The first evaluations reveal drug dependency and close alliance with the members and values of the Manson Family. The psychiatrists suspect schizophrenia. As the years go by, a psychiatrist comments, "These conditions have ebbed and paled with the passage of time." He finds that Van Houten "has disassociated herself from that situation" and that "from a psychiatric point of view, there are no contraindications for parole consideration."[28] This reads as a retrospective of recovery from cult influence. But there is always a foothold for risk and dangerousness, and Board member DeLeon finds it in one of the psychiatric evaluations that referred to Van Houten's drug dependency back in the 1960s: "From the time you were 14 years old, you were involved in the use of drugs. And then, you now, in Spahn Ranch, involved in the use of drugs, and then, coming to the institution and involved in the use of acid. And then, years later, you know, stopped in possession of marijuana, which is an extremely serious offense ... and then, the diagnosis of drug dependence that indicates, you know, the history, really. How do you see that?"[29] The Board concludes: "She has now had eight years of good behavior up and down, but in a rather restricted setting. What we are saying is that, because she has gone in and out of these phases, we want a longer period of time of successes before we project a parole date."[30]

The following hearing, in 1980, includes an almost identical retrospective. The Board again denies Van Houten parole, this time with a refreshingly honest explanation: "In spite of the numerous psychiatric and psychological reports which indicate a diagnosis of no mental illness, the panel at this time cannot correlate such findings with the elements and the bizarre conduct which transpired during the commission of the crimes. Consequently, this panel requires a longer period of psychiatric observation prior to reaching the question of suitability."[31]

When inmates challenge the Board's selective reliance on psychiatric opinions, they are sometimes successful in court, especially when the denial decision relies on old evaluations while ignoring newer, more favorable ones. For example, in *In re Gaul,* the court reversed the governor's decision to deny parole, which was based on Gaul's crime, his record before the commission of the crime, and a ten-year-old negative psychological evaluation. As the court explained, the file contained two more recent, more positive evaluations, and there was no evidence to establish that Gaul currently posed an unreasonable risk.[32]

By contrast, relying on a recent evaluation of dangerousness, even to justify a poorly reasoned denial decision, is a strategy that the courts support. In *In re Criscione,* the court upheld a Board decision to deny parole to an inmate whose crime of commitment was the murder of his girlfriend and who had a history of abusing female partners. The court found that Criscione's record of programming and rehabilitation failed to address his abusive and violent behavioral patterns. While the decision acknowledged that the Board had failed to explain the nexus between Criscione's history and his current dangerousness, the court filled in the blanks by looking directly at the evidence. It was enough, the court held, that the Board had relied on a recent psychological evaluation that noted his potential for violence in future relationships with women.[33]

It might be an exaggeration to argue that that Board uses the psychiatric opinion as a rhetorical crutch for its political decision to deny parole. It is clear from the hearings that the Board greatly respects clinical evaluations. But the ever-changing nature of these evaluations suggests that the Board reads and interprets them through a lens of overall concern about public safety.

PESSIMISM ABOUT THE FUTURE:
RESIDENCE, VOCATION, AND FINANCES

Recall from chapter 1 Yael Hassin's experiment contrasting parole decisions made by computer and by committee.[34] The computer's greater reluctance to grant parole highlighted the mistakes human decision-makers made in releasing people who recidivated. But the study could not identify false positives—situations in which people who were kept behind bars but would not recidivate if released.[35]

The Board's assessment of the inmates' postrelease plans reveals a pessimistic bias against desistance similar to that of Hassin's computer, which is understandable in light of the political consequences of releasing someone who might seriously recidivate. There are virtually no public consequences stemming from incarcerating someone who would *not* recidivate. Granted, the Board's suspicion is understandable and sometimes laudable; postrelease plans are not always realistic or feasible. Unsurprisingly, Young, Mukamal, and Favre-Bulle found that the odds of a parole grant are significantly higher for people whose files include actual letters from family members offering them housing, as well as ones from prospective employers.[36] Accordingly, the Board's reactions reveal pessimism about residence offers, critiques of inmates' personal choices and associations, and concerns about chosen vocations. When Susan Atkins, at her 1985 hearing, presents letters from three relatives offering her a home, Board member Jauregui expresses doubt: "Three? Three of your relatives have said, hey, when you get out, you need a place to stay, come to us. Is that in the county of commitment?"[37] Her change in circumstances is mentioned: "Now, you did get married; however, you got—you're—that's—that's done with. You have no children out of that marriage."[38] But this change indicates a disconcerting lack of consistency: "You have stated that primarily you were thinking of owning a boutique. You were then interested in a foundation program. And then you thought about out-of-state job. And then, presumably when you got married, you figured you'd be a housewife. Now all of that is behind you? . . . None of those—none of those appeal to you anymore, or have no meaning?"[39]

When considering this exchange, it is important to remember that the inmates in the study, like many others, come up for parole repeatedly over the course of decades, in which familial relationships, vocational interests and skill sets, and market opportunities tend to ebb and flow. But the lack of consistency is imputed to the inmate. For example, at Atkins's hearing in 1988, the Board is again troubled by her change of plans (and recent marriage): "We know that you have, ahh . . . recently married, and you stated to the counselor that your plans are simply to live with your husband and settle into that, that type of environment. But at one time you indicated that you really were not going to be satisfied just being a quote 'housewife,' that there were a lot of other things necessary." Atkins explains: "In 1985 my counselor at the time gave a confidential packet containing my parole plans to the board . . . stating where I would work and who I would work for. For privacy reasons for that particular individual because this is a high notoriety case, I wanted to keep that information confidential. Those parole plans, with the exception of where I would reside, remain the same. I will reside with my husband."[40]

Atkins' changed circumstances are emblematic of a person serving a lengthy sentence. Throughout the years, connections become looser, aging family members and health changes affect the ability to stay in touch, and plans invariably change.

Also notable here is Board member McReynold's tone when explaining to Atkins that, as a parole hopeful, her life will be extremely curtailed and closely supervised:

> It's kinda been laid out to you that when, when you are, are paroled, you'll have special restrictions, ahh . . . due to your history and the fact that you're a parolee, ahh . . . particularly you would be expected to participate in ongoing ahh . . . parole outpatient clinic psychotherapy. You would be tested routinely for substance abuse. You would be required to abstain from use of alcohol. That's particular to you because of your background. . . . The restriction in the community, related to alcohol, is extremely restrictive. It means if you go to a cocktail party and everybody else is having that one social drink, you don't have that option. You can't have one bottle of beer you can't do any . . .[41]

By 2005, Atkins, who by now has been married to James Whitehouse for seventeen years, has a different parole plan: she would work as a paralegal in her husband's law office.[42] Board member Castro had expressed concern about the soundness of this plan, as well as Atkins's overall stability, when she married Whitehouse ("Is he willing to wait, ahh . . . for a life crime?").[43]

Whitehouse, who represents Atkins before the Board, complains that the psychiatrist assesses Atkins as unstable based on her past rather than her present: "And then he goes on to say that inmate Atkins was living in a non— in a violent drug-using anti-social communal group at the time the crime was committed. It isn't mentioned that you've been married for 17 1/2 years, and nowhere did that pop out of the equation here."[44] There is a gendered aspect to this component. As Atkins's relationship stability comes to the forefront of the conversation, in Bobby Beausoleil's case the concern seems to be his financial reliance on his wife, Barbara: "And this house. Did you own this house before the marriage? . . . She owned it. Oh." Beausoleil explains: "Now it's joint. I've made some of the payments."[45]

One permanent issue plaguing Beausoleil's parole plans involves a mismatch between his plans to reside in San Luis Obispo and, subsequently, for a residence in Oregon or his county of commitment, Los Angeles. In 1992, the commissioners explain that some counties have complained about the abundance of parolees, and even an out-of-state parolee is expected to plan to reside in the county of commitment. These, of course, require the cooperation of Beausoleil's wife, who moves for him from Sacramento to Arroyo Grande and subsequently to Oregon.[46]

The Board is also pessimistic about future occupations that involve academic education; it regards menial occupations as more realistic ventures for the formerly incarcerated. At his hearings throughout the 1980s and 1990s, Bruce Davis, who eventually goes on to earn a PhD in religion, is continuously asked about his practical skills (he responds by explaining that he can weld).

Similarly, Patricia Krenwinkel, who takes an interest in sociology and goes on to earn dozens of college credits, is scolded in 1978 for the lack of practicality of her plans: "Maybe you'll find that, as you get out on the outside, you cannot get a position as you have planned in recreation or forestry or whatever. And you may have to do something very menial and very difficult that is not in keeping with your obvious talents."[47] At her 1979 hearing, the Board again observes that she is overly focused on her academics and should seek vocational training for menial jobs instead.[48] In 1980, the Board is concerned with another aspect of Krenwinkel's interest in counseling: the extent to which she would have any moral legitimacy in the eyes of potential clients ("How would you answer [a client] who says, 'why should I listen to you?'"). Krenwinkel's answer reflects the kind of humility and maturity that makes one think she could be an excellent counselor:

Well, I think it would be a matter of there doesn't need to be the need, unless I guess it would be felt by the counselor himself, to say, "Because I have been there." Sometimes I don't think that is an accurate answer. I think if someone feels that you cannot help them, if people are completely rebuffed against you, then there is no help you could give them anyway.... I mean, just because, you know, I have committed a crime and someone else has committed the crime doesn't mean that we are, you know, that we automatically understand each other entirely, because I may not know the way that this person mentally or emotionally came to this crime or what they felt inside of them ... so, I wouldn't find it would be a pat answer that you could give someone to say, "Well, because I have been there with you I should understand," or get those kinds of ridiculous inner notions.[49]

The Board's suspicion of academic and artistic endeavors is reasonable and well taken. But blaming the inmates for unrealistic postrelease plans is not. Until the 1990s, programs in prison tended to be academic rather than vocational—Eric Cummins mentions the era of "bibliotherapy" in California prisons[50]—and, as Michelle Phelps explains, they were not proven to be effective.[51] When Robert Martinson and others conducted metaresearch to evaluate prison rehabilitation programming, they famously found no significant reduction in recidivism; their study is colloquially remembered as concluding that "nothing works" in prison reform.[52] Later critics, such as Francis Cullen, noted that beyond the methodological flaws in Martinson's meta-analysis, he was critiquing programs that were not evidence-based and unsuitable for recidivism reduction.[53] The Board's expectations of rehabilitation should be taken in conjunction with the paucity of rehabilitation programming: not only are programs scarce and out of reach for many inmates, but for many years they also did not provide realistic vocational skills. Faulting the inmates for their own unpreparedness for release seems unfair.

This is also the case for the Board's pessimism about the inmates' projected finances; again, the realities of prison life, which make earning and saving money a virtual impossibility, are imputed to the inmates. At Susan Atkins's 1988 hearing, the Board inquires after her savings. Atkins explains: "It is impossible to save money and survive in prison."[54]

The prosecutor, Kay, chimes in, turning a suspicion that Atkins was making money in prison to her detriment: "It was discussed that Ms. Atkins had a thriving manicure business here at the prison where she manicured the other prisoners' nails, and made quite a bit of money at that."

Atkins replies: "Mr. Kay, it was never documented.... It was a false accusation. I do not now, nor have I ever had a thriving manicure business. It's impossible because I have to work six hours a day and to program. I do not have the time to do other people's fingernails and profit from them. I just don't have the time."[55]

The Board's doubts seem justified when dealing with inmates with few skills and meager savings, but less so regarding Bobby Beausoleil's profitable art and music career. In 1978, while Beausoleil was composing a film soundtrack behind bars, Board member Burton characterizes his postrelease plans as "very grandiose ideas, you know. . . . Recording studios and band for a guy that's been out of circulation for a long time? I'm not saying they are impossible dreams. I'm talking about the immediate. The immediate is to eat."[56] In 1980, the Board confronts Beausoleil with his obligations to support two or three children from previous relationships, as well as his new wife. He responds: "I think I am capable of doing that today or any day. I have enough skills and enough drive and enough interest in what I'm doing that I'm sure I can manage this. I have enough offers from people that do require the type of talents I have that I have no doubts that I'm capable of making it financially."[57]

In 1982, Beausoleil and his new wife, Barbara, plan on starting a business manufacturing synthesizers. Board member Pizarro's discussion of his plans seems jocular and dismissive: "I don't mean to sound ignorant. But I don't even know what a synthesizer is. And, you know, I have always contended that, if a human being walked up on the bandstand, he is going to get electrocuted nowadays."[58] Beausoleil protests, and Pizarro explains that he said that "tongue in cheek." In a further exchange, Pizarro reveals that he is unfamiliar with BFA degrees.[59]

Even Beausoleil's proficiency, solid prospects, and detailed future plans can be seen through a negative lens. In 1983, Board member Aceto remarks, "You have a lot of potential, in which your manipulative capabilities are . . ." Beausoleil retorts: "That's a bad choice of words."[60]

And even when his plans are viewed through a positive lens, in 1985, Beausoleil and Board member Jauregui disagree on who should be credited with his success:

JAUREGUI: Well, I've already drawn a conclusion that you have excellent parole plans. There's no doubt that you had a wild hair up your butt when you came to prison, and you certainly were, you were in the wrong environment and you weren't doing very well. Prison has sure helped you.

BEAUSOLEIL: It has, sir. Well, I've helped myself in prison. Prison doesn't do it for you. You have to do it yourself.

JAUREGUI: Well, a lot of people come in here and never do anything.

BEAUSOLEIL: That's what I mean.[61]

This exchange is emblematic of the general perspective on postrelease plans: the inmates' successes are attributed to the prison, whereas any flaws in their preparedness for the outside world are imputed to their own failings.

LETTERS OF SUPPORT AND OPPOSITION

An important aspect of the lawyer's work is to solicit letters of support for the inmate's file. Often, these letters are written by people who are personally familiar with the inmate. In the Manson Family cases, however, the files are rife with letters of support and opposition not only from people related to the case and/or familiar with the inmate, but also from the general public. The transcripts reveal a preference for support letters that are heartfelt and sentimental, particularly from family members. However, letters that minimize the inmate's culpability—even when not endorsed by the inmate—tend to be imputed to the inmate and viewed negatively by the Board. This is visible in Beausoleil's 1985 hearing[62] and also in the Board's displeasure in 2003 with the publication of Karlene Faith's book, which argues against Leslie Van Houten's culpability.[63] The Board sometimes reads the letters verbatim into the transcripts, such as this letter written by Susan Atkins's fourteen-year-old niece for her 2005 hearing:

> I know that some people would say let her rot, but that's because these people don't know her. They don't know who she really is; how sweet, how kind she is. They don't know her like I do.... When I visit my aunt, one of the biggest things that bothers me is that she can't even touch me or touch money ... as if they don't trust her.... They act as if she's going to steal money from us. Only she's not a thief and she's not a murderer. She's simply a woman living in the worst place she could live, even though she has so much love for God and everyone else in the world. It would knock them and all of us off of our feet.... I know as well as you that God has forgiven her. Now she's waiting for your forgiveness and now it's your turn to forgive.[64]

At Bobby Beausoleil's 2005 hearing, Board member Farmer draws a distinction between support letters by relatives and friends on one hand and "fan mail" from unknown people on the other: "What I'm trying to do is separate from these letters those that may have just been sent in because of support by reputation from those that you are personally connected with, okay?"[65] Farmer then proceeds to describe each author and ask Beausoleil about them, which enables Beausoleil to paint a heartwarming picture of extended family, friends, and professional acquaintances. The prosecutor, Patrick Sequeira, interjects to resist:

> SEQUEIRA: Excuse me, I just want to interrupt for just a second. Is it necessary to go into an explanation of who every single person was who wrote a letter. I mean, I think the letters speak for themselves and I think that we really should move on. The letters are very detailed as to who the people are and to what they have to say in favor of the inmate. I just think we need to move on with the hearing rather than to go into a long explanation about how long the inmate has known all these people and—
>
> FARMER: Well, I'll take part of the responsibility for that because I keep asking. So, I think—
>
> SEQUEIRA: I think that if he just acknowledges—
>
> FARMER: The concern is well taken. The letters are self-explanatory; however, Mr. Beausoleil, if there are particular ones that go beyond that, feel free to bring that to my attention without getting into everyone.[66]

Sequeira's interjection succeeds in halting an optimistic moment at the hearing and reflects his role as the "moral memory" of the Board, focusing the hearing back to what he deems most relevant: the inmate's past crimes.

The Board does not make a similar effort to separate the wheat from the chaff in letters of opposition, perhaps because of the hearings' media coverage and perhaps because of a sense that that the Board owes it to the public to at least take public views into consideration. The first time that opposition letters are mentioned is at Patricia Krenwinkel's 1979 hearing, where Board member Roos mentions that "the Board of Prison Terms has received in its office approximately 3,500 signatures opposing parole release."[67] By 1982, multiple petitions against the release are circulated and placed in all files. At Bruce Davis's 1984 hearing, Board member Lander mentions being in receipt of several such petitions, with 1,553, "between 700 and 1,745," 3,500, and 1,250 signatures respectively.[68]

The emergence of these petitions dovetails with the birth of the victims' rights movement and is a harbinger of the emotional-political turn in parole that would come to characterize the 1980s. The use of petition-form opposition letters in particular reflects the shift from the professional to the political. The emergence of these petitions is especially notable because it precedes the gubernatorial veto, which further politicized the process (as I explain in chapter 2 under "Solidifying 'Life de Facto'").

At Leslie Van Houten's 1981 hearing, the Board tallies the letters and finds that the support letters were "closer to 100 who at least knew you at one time . . . as you were a child and your church." The opposition comes from "some friends and relatives, apparently, of the victims who have written. And then, of course, the publicity that was received in Southern California generated by the Manson Family in total generated the response."[69] Prosecutor Kay puts a negative spin on the tally: "This group, Friends of Leslie, has had a concerted effort to get letters in for her. I know that people who have known her—and, I mean, I think it's great that people support her that way." He goes on: "However, there has been no effort on my part to solicit letters from a society of people who don't think that she should be granted parole. Believe me, if I did that, this room would be sky high with letters. I have made no effort to solicit any—I mean, I didn't even know about the petition with 650 signatures. I think this is—as I'll get into in my argument—is a very significant case from society's point of view, very important one."[70]

It appears that, in 1981, the Board regarded letters from people with personal connection to the crime as more relevant than letters stemming from the mere notoriety of the crime. Interestingly, Kay proposes the opposite logic: to him, letters and petitions from complete strangers suggest the political and emotional impact of the case and argue strongly against release. He repeats the same argument in 1985, spinning the opposition from strangers as a strength of his case: "These letters and petitions were not just from California. They were from throughout the United States."[71]

By 1993, the political-emotional aspect of opposition letters has prevailed. Van Houten is surprised to hear that opposition letters for her release can be cut out of the newspaper and filled in:

> GIAQUINTO: Also, we did receive a number of what appears to be petitions that were in a national magazine. And the—there's about—what's been represented to be 42,000 of these and they say, "I'm outraged that Susan Atkins, Charles Tex Watson, Patricia Krenwinkle [sic], and Leslie Van Houten are being considered for parole. I don't want to see this savage gang of killers set free to commit crimes again against other innocent citizens." Andthentheysaythattheybasicallywantyoutostayinprison. Okay, And there's—
>
> VAN HOUTEN: What are they, like coupons?
>
> GIAQUINTO: Well, they're—they're apparently a portion of the national magazine that you could cut out. It already had the verbiage on there—

VAN HOUTEN: Oh.

GIAQUINTO:—and then you would—

VAN HOUTEN: Like an ad.

GIAQUINTO:—fill in your name.[72]

These developments exemplify the longitudinal turn in the public's approach to parole. Parole is no longer a quiet, private, clinical inquiry that prioritizes relevant voices of professionals and of people intimately connected with the inmate and the case. It has become a public scene for airing strong emotions, where voices of strangers, especially when organized by victims and their advocates, are amplified through mass-production methods.

THE PAST OVERSHADOWING THE FUTURE:
PAROLE AND THE PASSAGE OF TIME

Finally, the transcripts reflect the powerful hold of the past—particularly the crime of commitment—over the future. At several points in the hearings, the Board expresses serious doubts that the inmates might ever manage to overcome the notoriety of their crimes. At Leslie Van Houten's 1979 hearing, Board member DeLeon worries that Van Houten will have "opportunities that would change your lifestyle, lecturing opportunities, writing opportunities, and things of that nature . . . because of your background and your position and your experience." Van Houten understands he worries about her "becoming, like kind of a sideshow. And, no, I wouldn't. Like I say, the only thing I will ever do would be talking to—well, where I feel I'm the most benefit, like is talking to girls that have the similar makeup that are at the turning point of 16 or 17 years old that are starting to experiment. And, like, I would rather do that on a very personal basis."[73]

As decades passed, the inmates tried to use the temporal distance from the crime in their favor. For example, in 1980, Patricia Krenwinkel explained: "At the time that the crime was committed and I was arrested, I was 21. When I left my home I was 18. Adolescence has its own—had its own substance. And now, definitely, I am an adult. I am 32 years old. And I have been—I've grown up inside this institution for nearly a decade. . . . I found that change is something which I find occurring continuously within myself."[74]

From a criminological standpoint, aging out of crime is a strong argument for parole; indeed, Young, Mukamal, and Favre-Bulle found that the odds of a parole grant increase significantly with the parolee's age at the time of the hearing, and inversely with the parolee's age at the time the crime was committed.[75] But in the Manson Family cases, ironically, the stronghold of the past intensifies as the inmates age—even in the undeniable presence of terminal illness.

At her 2009 hearing, Susan Atkins is wheeled into the room on a gurney. She has a brain tumor in advanced state of progression and is hardly responsive. But the commissioners observe, in her presence, that the file indicates "nothing in regards to disabilities." Still, her correctional counselor found that she "did have significant issues in regard to mobility and she also had hearing issues. . . . She would need help regarding her documents, understanding procedures and forms, would need a wheelchair, and would be taken to the board if required to be present on a bed or gurney. . . . She was unable to write at this time and she needed help for her hearing to hear or hear at her hearing and that she didn't have hearings aids." Whitehouse clarifies that the hearing aids make no difference, as Atkins "can't put them in and we can't put them in without hurting her and she can't communicate whether or not they're working or how they're adjusted." Board member O'Hara confirms that she is on "a mobile bed—gurney or bed. She is not awake at this time . . . today looks as though she's not going to be awake or she's not awake for this particular hearing."[76]

As the hearing enters its first stage—discussing the crime of commitment—Whitehouse points out the absurdity of doing so under the circumstances: after *Lawrence,* "the commitment offense is only relevant if it's predictive of future behavior, and concerning Susan hasn't moved out of her bed for 18 months I'm not sure how absolutely anything that's happened during the past bears any relevance to her current dangerousness or future dangerousness other than her medical condition." Board member O'Hara, however, is determined to go with the program: Atkins's "frailness at this time" is "a component." But everybody in this room is an a seat based on their past and the past is important to determine where—or the—I guess the low point that she has fallen and why she is here today."[77]

As Atkins lies in the room, nonresponsive, the Board proceeds describe her childhood, her association with Manson, and the crimes, and even mistakenly identifies her as a fitness instructor (in lieu of Patricia Krenwinkel).[78] The Board even ventures into a discussion of a disciplinary write-up from 1992. They continue to discuss her lack of cooperation with the clinical evaluation: the doctor, they say, "did conduct the clinical interview in Ms. Atkins's

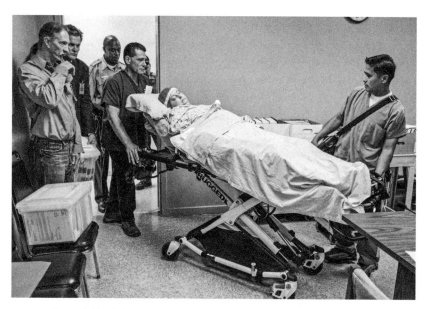

PHOTO 9. Susan Atkins being wheeled on a gurney into a parole hearing room at the Central California Women's Facility in Chowchilla, California, September 2, 2009, as James Whitehouse, her attorney and husband, *left,* watches. (Associated Press/Ben Margot)

hospital room" and "throughout the report there were some areas where— [quoting from the report] 'Inmate refused or was unable to discuss what if any behavioral problems she exhibited during the course of her youth when assessed by the undersigned examiner.'"[79] They quote the psychiatrist, who observed that "the inmate's negligible participation in the clinical interview precluded the undersigned examiner from assessing her degree of insight, self-awareness."[80]

The psychiatric review, incredibly, thought necessary to assess the terminally ill woman's potential for violence, discusses "some things that could increase Ms. Atkins's risk of violent recidivism—things such as exposure to charismatic, highly anti-social, violence-prone individuals, substance relapse, infrequent participation in substance-related self-help groups such as NA, AA, manifestation of anti-social and/or dependent personality features, weapon possession, inability to maintain a permanent residence, decreased pro-social support and/or financial difficulties." The factors on the other side include "authoring a comprehensive relapse-prevention program, expanded pro-social support in the free community, attending her bachelor's degree, and/or further deterioration of her medical condition."[81]

Whitehouse, painfully aware that his wife will never be able to complete her bachelor's degree or participate in any sort of program or in any sort of mayhem in the "free community," balks:

> And as [the psychologist] sat in her hospital room looking at a woman who literally can't sit herself up in bed he never got around to mentioning that. You know, I'm going to just, you know, take a shot in the dark but I'm guessing that absolutely nothing you expose her to is going to make her jump up out of this bed and do anything. And just—I'm sorry, it just kind of bugged me that nowhere did he come around to mentioning her physical condition prevents her from doing anything including feeding herself, and the constant comments that she refused to participate just riled me a little bit.[82]

Board member O'Hara responds in a way that seems particularly tone-deaf: "In regards to psych reports we have seen—there's sort of a spectrum and we do see low—we've seen very low. I have actually seen very low. But still low is, you know, where you want it."[83]

Whitehouse presents hospice programs, saying that he will cover the finances.

O'Hara responds, "You can cover it. Okay. Makes me a little more uncomfortable. If you're really well off, that's wonderful. The rest of us, we have to make sure our insurance covers it."[84] It is doubtful that at that moment Whitehouse, about to lose his spouse to a brain tumor, feels "wonderful" about his resources.

O'Hara then proceeds to read a letter from Barbara Hoyt, which recounts the horrors of the murders, saying, "She claims now that she was frozen in fear but how could she have written the word 'pig' on the victim's front door with the victim's own blood? Even on her deathbed about to meet her maker she still isn't telling the truth."[85]

The prosecutor, Sequeira, goes on at length about the crimes, this time referring to the Manson Family as a "criminal terrorist organization."[86] He also argues that Atkins was manipulative in the late 1970s. He even ventures into a lengthy monologue about Atkins's choice to name her son Zezo Ze Zadfrack and then change his name to Paul. This is relevant, Sequeira explains, because "to me this is just an example of the revisionist history because it's quite clear that Ms. Atkins over the years not only has gone from denying the murders but she clearly has minimized her involvement in the crime."[87]

Whitehouse explodes again:

For the record, she's lying in her gurney here. She is paralyzed over 85 percent of her body. She can move her head up and down. She can move it to the side. She used to have partial use of her left arm, partial limited use, meaning she can't wave to you. She can't give you a thumbs up. She no longer can point at you, I believe. She can't snap her fingers. And this is the evidence.... We haven't been able to get her in a wheelchair for well over a year. Permanent speech impairment—"does not communicate, speaking or writing"—complex medical needs, assistance needed eating, bathing, grooming, moving, cleaning, permanent speech and comprehension impairment due to underlying medical problems.... That's the only evidence regarding her medical condition. And all those things have to do with what we are supposed to be looking for the future of behavior. In light of that, is there anything that her commitment offense has to do that's probative to what she's going to be doing in the future as far as you know? That's a question.[88]

Atkins then gives her final statement:

WHITEHOUSE: Do you know where you are? You're at your parole hearing and hopefully you're rested and you have a chance to make a statement. Would you like to hear what we talked about?

ATKINS: No.

WHITEHOUSE: If I say the Lord is my—

ATKINS: Shepherd.

WHITEHOUSE: I shall not—

ATKINS: Want.

WHITEHOUSE: He makes me to lie down in—

ATKINS: In green pastures.

WHITEHOUSE: He leadeth me beside the—

ATKINS: Still waters.

WHITEHOUSE: He restoreth my—

ATKINS: Soul.

WHITEHOUSE: He leadeth me on the paths of righteousness for his name's sake. Lo though I walk through the valley of the Shadow of—

ATKINS: Death.

WHITEHOUSE: —I shall fear no—

ATKINS: Evil.

WHITEHOUSE: —for thou art with me. Thy rod and thy staff they—

ATKINS: Comfort me.

WHITEHOUSE: I'll prepare us a table before me in the presence of my—

ATKINS: Enemies.

WHITEHOUSE: Now anointeth my head with—

ATKINS: Oil.

WHITEHOUSE: My cup runneth—my cup runneth—

ATKINS: Over.

Whitehouse; Surely goodness and kindness will follow me—goodness and mercy will follow me all the—

ATKINS: Days of my life.

WHITEHOUSE: And I shall dwell in the—

ATKINS: House of the Lord forever.

WHITEHOUSE: Amen. Our God is what? Our God is an—

ATKINS: Awesome God.

WHITEHOUSE: Yeah. I'm extremely proud of you. And that's it. We were practicing that for over a year.[89]

In the theater of the parole hearing, the dying inmate's words are not the last scene. That place is reserved for the victim's statement, and Debra Tate delivers hers:

> I feel heartfelt compassion for the process that Ms. Atkins is suffering now as I'm very familiar. I was my mother's sole caretaker until the end of her life. I will pray for her soul when she draws her last breath. Up to that point I think that she needs to be in these controlled environments. I cannot say that she could not influence others even if not by direct contact by the message that goes out. I have to be responsible to society. You, I would like to think, need to be responsible to society. . . . This can cause a ripple effect that is unbelievable. . . . Once you start compromising the law there's no going back.[90]

Anthony Dimaria adds: "I feel genuine compassion for Ms. Atkins as she deals with this disease. But in no way should an illness dealt by fate mitigate punishment for crimes of this magnitude for which she was originally sentenced to death."[91]

The Board denies parole due to the risk that Atkins poses to society:

> In this particular case this is one of the most atrocious undertakings in criminality in California history. We do note that this weighed very heavily in the Panel's decision here today in the reasons for denial. . . . By clear and convincing evidence we have no substantial doubt for the reasons cited before Ms. Atkins does not require a more lengthy period of incarceration in the next threshold of seven years. . . . After weighing all the evidence presented today,

Ms. Atkins is unsuitable for parole because she poses an unreasonable risk if released and requires at least an additional three years of incarceration.[92]

A straightforward interpretation of *Lawrence,* decided only a year earlier, would be that the nonresponsive, dying woman poses no risk and should therefore not be held incarcerated merely for the heinousness of the crime. But the Board's reasoning spins *Lawrence* and the Helter Skelter narrative to legitimize its decision: "This Panel feels that these Manson killings and the rampage that went on is almost iconic and they have the ability to influence many other people, and she still has that ability as part of that group."[93]

The dangerousness of Atkins's fans and admirers—whom she rebuked in her books and at her hearings—is imputed to the dying woman. The past casts a long shadow on the little prison room where an immobile body lies on a gurney, unable to participate in the hearings, save for reciting the prayer that characterized the last three and a half decades of her life.

SEVEN

In Bardo

> Those of heavy evil karma cannot possibly fail to be liberated by
> hearing this Doctrine [and recognizing] . . . at whatever distance
> one may be wandering in the Bardo, one heareth and cometh, for
> one possesseth the slender sense of supernormal perception and
> foreknowledge; and, recollecting and apprehending instanta-
> neously, the mind is capable of being changed [or influenced].
>
> *The Tibetan Book of the Dead*

Bobby Beausoleil's painting *The Ride Out of Bardo* depicts a skeletal motor-
cyclist atop a shiny cruiser, explosively riding away from a foggy horizon
toward the viewer.[1]

"Bardo" (བར་དོ), literally translated as "liminal state," refers to the state of
existence between death and rebirth.[2] *The Tibetan Book of the Dead* instructs
how to guide a recently deceased person through several Bardos, bracketing
the last moments of the person's life, the process of dying, and the voyage
toward reincarnation or, for the enlightened, toward liberation from the
cycle of birth and rebirth. The first Bardo offers the clearest experience of
reality; the following Bardos involve hallucinations and apparitions that arise
from the impulses of one's previous unskillful actions. For prepared and
appropriately trained individuals, the Bardo offers an opportunity for liberation, while others could be impelled into an undesirable rebirth by karmi-
cally created hallucinations.[3]

The concept of Bardo is also used figuratively to describe other liminal
states within life that offer opportunities for clear sight and liberation, such
as a prolonged illness or a meditation retreat. Indeed, some meditation tech-
niques are crafted to simulate Bardo.[4] But life offers plenty of opportunities
for deep and profound self-assessment. As Sogyal Rinpoche writes: "Bardos
are occurring continuously throughout both life and death, and are junctures
when the possibility of liberation, or enlightenment, is heightened. . . . [They]
are particularly powerful opportunities for liberation because there are, the

teachings show us, certain moments that are much more powerful than others and much more charged with potential, when whatever you do has a crucial and far-reaching effect."[5]

The parole hearing cycle—the preparation, the hearing itself, and the recovery from a negative decision—can be seen as a Bardo. In an explanatory note accompanying his painting, Beausoleil writes: "Some souls are said to become disoriented upon death of the body and may become stalled in the Bardo for a while; others want to get the hell out of there as fast as they can!" Parole as Bardo is a cycle between hope and disappointment, preparation and hibernation, action and inaction, self-improvement and self-assessment, in which inmates have to participate and their lawyers act as "hope managers."[6]

What keeps the Manson Family inmates, and many other lifers, in Bardo? Leaving the Bardo, as we have seen, requires walking a performative tightrope. When discussing their pasts, inmates must conform to the court record; at consecutive hearings, they must demonstrate fresher, deeper insights of the personal flaws that produced the crime and simultaneously maintain some consistency so as to not appear manipulative. They must shed the social context and confine their explanations to their personal flaws. Their remorse has to be read as authentic, even though they are not allowed to express it directly to the victims in the room. Their programming journey must be presented as a karmic antidote to the personal flaws that landed them in prison, even when it is limited by institutional inadequacies and scarce opportunities. And they must show change and transformation, even though the most physically obvious (and criminologically relevant) transformation—by old age and disease—can be overlooked. These performative guidelines match what I saw in prison rehabilitative programs, the Lifer School (see beginning of chapter 4), and the PPRN Research Network (see the beginning of chapter 5) and reflect Alessandro de Giorgi's observations about self-attribution among recently released people.[7] This is not a coincidence: the process of prisonization, which Donald Clemmer described as social acclimation to incarceration,[8] includes an acclimation to prison argot and to the philosophies that inform it.[9] For long-term inmates who participate in programs and have come up for parole multiple times, this learned language includes the therapeutic, transformative terminology that is required and expected at these settings.

This is not to say, of course, that expressing "insight" is fake or manipulative. Quite the contrary: whether a successful performance of insight comes from within or as a response to the requirements of program leaders and parole commissioners, it becomes natural to those who experience it, which explains why long-term inmates who have been repeatedly denied parole, despite sustained and earnest efforts, can marshal new hope as they prepare for a new hearing.

But is this hope realistic? Nearly forty years of denials would suggest that the political pressures against releasing the Manson Family inmates should discourage them from the effort. (Steve Grogan's 1985 release was an idiosyncratic incident with distinguishing particulars and is briefly discussed in chapter 2, under "Solidifying 'Life de Facto.'") But recent developments are grounds for hope.

It is important to preface these developments by saying that, as Philip Goodman, Joshua Page, and Michelle Phelps remind us in *Breaking the Pendulum,* identifying turns toward and away from punitivism can yield overgeneralizations.[10] This is especially true with regard to recent academic efforts to account for the decline in incarceration.[11] In the case of parole, Rita Shah reminds us that, even as parole became politicized, the rehabilitative ideal persisted as a bone of contention between those who sought to focus on controlling and supervising parolees according to the risk they pose and those who continued to stress the importance of the social work aspects of parole.[12] Similarly, efforts to reorganize the parole system in the early 2000s led to conflicts among administrators and parole agents; for many of them, at this point, supervision had become a tool of rehabilitation, and rehabilitation a tool of supervision, forming a feedback loop. Efforts to swing the system back toward rehabilitation were thwarted by massive prison overcrowding and bad conditions. Only in the late 2000s, when legislative efforts reduced incarceration rates, could parole be somewhat transformed. The 2009 corrections bill created nonrevocable parole and some intermediate steps before revocation, and the 2011 Public Safety Realignment shifted the lion's share of parole supervision to the counties, making the services more localized and, in some cases, divorcing parole supervision from incarceration. Judicial discretion regarding incarceration sentences would now enable even people who were not physically incarcerated to benefit from rehabilitative and reentry services in their counties.

Shah's analysis reflects the debate in parole literature over actuarial risk-assessment. Malcolm Feeley and Jonathan Simon suggest that, in a correctional system focused on herding and warehousing people to meet modest managerial goals, parole officers have become no more than "waste managers" who measure the success of parole with technical parameters, such as drug testing and other forms of mass surveillance.[13] But Mona Lynch, who interviewed parole officers about their adherence to this philosophy, found many of them resisted the top-down "waste management" model advocated by the administration and, instead, continued to try to offer individual social assistance to the parolees in their caseload.[14]

The general parole trend that Shah identifies—to punitivism and back again—is present in the parole hearings as well. The earlier hearings in the late 1970s and early 1980s reflect a blend of the traditional approach toward parole—release from prison once the inmate has shown rehabilitative transformation—and of the emerging approaches at the time, which emphasized risk and fear. The gradual solidification of the "extreme-punishment trifecta" from the late 1970s onward reverberates through the hearings, and the conversation evinces frustration with the fact that the inmates in question, who had originally been sentenced to death, would now fit better in the new category of life without parole (or in the new-and-improved death penalty, which in itself is a form of life without parole) than in the category to which they technically belonged, that of people who have some hope for release. This frustration is evident, as we have seen, in the way the committee rehashes the facts of the crimes, as well as in the victims' concern in those early days that the inmates might actually be released after ten or fifteen years, a not-unreasonable sentence for "ordinary" homicides at the time.

The later 1980s and 1990s reflect a calcification of punitiveness. The hearings during these years make unrealistic and contradictory demands on the inmates, view their rehabilitative activities and endeavors with suspicion and cynicism, and pathologize minute behavioral incidents. Simultaneously, we see the solidification of the victims' status, particularly under the leadership of the Tate family.

The more recent hearings, even though most of them still result in parole denials, take a more hopeful tone. They reflect a more direct and personal relationship between the commissioners and the inmates; three of the inmates in the study are recommended for parole (even though the decision has so far been reversed by the governor); and the Board seems more open to mitigating discourses, which matters because it suggests that a discursively closed system[15] can, nonetheless, have some openness to external ideas. It is also important because a parole recommendation could be attributed not to some grand mechanistic change, but to subtle changes in the correctional equilibrium. Here are several factors that might favor release and some that might hinder it.

CONDITIONS AND FACTORS SUPPORTING RELEASE

Judicial Review of Parole Boards

Throughout the 2000s, the California Supreme Court has become more active in critiquing the Board's decisions. Beginning with *Lawrence* and *Shaputis,* the court has required that parole decisions genuinely assess risk and rehabilitation, rather than be merely retributive.

Similar trends are reflected in federal litigation. In *Gilman v. Brown,*[16] inmates argued that that the gubernatorial veto and Marsy's Law should not apply retroactively, because they inflicted "a greater punishment than the law annexed to the crime, when committed" and therefore could apply only to inmates sentenced after their respective dates of passage. The district court found in Gilman's favor, but the Ninth Circuit reversed, arguing that the inmates had not proven that the new procedures under Marsy's Law worsened inmates' legal situation without providing them relief.

This victory for Marsy's Law's proponents was, however, dampened by the settlement in *Johnson v. Shaffer.*[17] This class action on behalf of 10,000 inmates focused on the Board's reliance on unscientific predictions of future risk in unfalsifiable psychological reports, and consequently its regular denials of parole. In October 2015, the District Court required the Board to establish, based on the circumstances of the crime, the minimum time that should be served before an inmate is released. For inmates to be held beyond that minimum, the Board must demonstrate their danger to the public. The settlement offered hope to lifers, because until *Johnson* their minimum sentence was calculated only after they were found suitable for parole (many of them had overstayed that minimum by the time the Board recommended their release). In addition, the settlement required reforms in the psychological risk assessment process (including consulting with experts and making the information available to inmates and their counsel), enabling inmates to challenge factual errors in their risk assessments.[18] As of October 2017, the court found that the Board had not fully complied with the settlement terms and retained control over the case for an additional year.[19]

Changes in the Parole Board

As the Board's practices were being challenged in courts, the Board itself underwent considerable administrative changes, some on its own accord and some in response to the litigation outcomes. Many of my interlocutors mentioned the appointment of Jennifer Shaffer as the executive officer of the Board as a watershed moment. Under Shaffer's leadership, the Board implemented more rigorous training on topics relevant to parole, including mental health and substance abuse. This change is reflected not only in the tenor of the newer transcripts, as reflected in chapters 4, 5, and 6, but also in the perceptions of the inmates and their attorneys. All the lawyers I interviewed expressed hope about the administration's newfound openness.

Another welcome development is the professional diversification of the Board's members. As discussed above, appointees of Governors Davis and Schwarzenegger, albeit diverse in terms of gender, race, and ethnicity, invariably had law enforcement or correctional backgrounds. While some of Governor Brown's appointees shared such backgrounds, Commissioner Rosalio Castro, appointed in 2015, had been a public defender and a private attorney; and Commissioner Dianne Dobbs, appointed in 2017, had been in private practice and in child advocacy. Professional diversification matters because of the strong effects of organizational cultures and conditioning; studies on police and prosecutorial culture repeatedly attribute miscarriages of justice to confirmation bias and "tunnel vision."[20]

Finally, it is significant that self-organized support groups for formerly incarcerated people are attended by parole agents and correctional psychologists who work with the Board. At the Peer Reentry Navigation Network (PRNN), which I discussed at the beginning of chapter 5, parole agents spoke up about their positive impressions of the attendees and stated that they shared these positive impressions with parole commissioners to strengthen their belief in the rehabilitation, desistance, and resilience of the successful parolees. The agents were well aware of the overall law-abiding profile of the group; one agent stated that lifers were his favorite category of parolees because of their maturity and readiness for life on the outside. Such positive feedback should encourage the Board to trust its own judgment to release and, it is to be hoped, dispel political concerns about recidivist "false negatives."

Without overstating these benign developments, it is worthwhile noticing that they reflect somewhat of a return to the ideas of rehabilitation and professionalism that characterized California corrections before the punitive turn. Professional enrichment of the ranks could add depth and value to risk assessment and would temper the existing cynicism about inmates' sincerity about insight and remorse. The continuing education program, as well as the court mandate to reform psychological evaluations, would contribute to the Board's understanding of the inmates' lives and challenges. Admittedly, the correctional model of the 1970s was not without serious problems. But its heart was in the right place, and a pull away from politics and toward professionalism will be beneficial.

Permeability to Outside Changes: Youth and Brainwashing

Another aspect of the return of professionalism to the decision-making process is the increased receptiveness of the Board to contextual issues, such as the dynamics of cults and the relevance of offenders' youth.

As explained above, the Manson Family trials were characterized by the prosecutor's effort to achieve two somewhat incompatible goals: painting Manson himself as the ringleader and mastermind behind all the murders, which required portraying him as a very powerful and influential figure and, at the same time, portraying the members of the cult, particularly the women, as free agents fully responsible for their part in the crimes (recall that, at the time, cults were not widely known or understood). In Leslie Van Houten's second and third trials,[21] the defense made an unsuccessful attempt to introduce the cult narrative.

Since Van Houten's trials, our understanding of cults and domination has deepened, with particular attention to the gendered aspect. The last decades have seen countless examples of sexual exploitation in hierarchical "new" religions, such as those of Mormon leader Warren Jeffs, guru Sri Chinmoy, and Bikram Choudhury, founder of Bikram yoga.[22] What early 1970s jurors might have seen as promiscuity and "free love," decision-makers of the #MeToo era might interpret as sexual exploitation. In anticipation of her 2017 parole hearing, Leslie Van Houten was seeking access to Tex Watson's recordings to support her claim of brainwashing and coercion in the hope that the Board would be receptive to such argument.[23]

More importantly, courts and parole boards have become much more receptive to the offender's age at the time of the crime. Since the early 2000s, our understanding of childhood and its implications as to accountability has undergone a dramatic scientific, legal, and social transformation. Recall the miscarriage of justice depicted in Ken Burns's documentary *The Central Park Five*,[24] in which five teenagers were accused and wrongly convicted of assaulting Trisha Meili in New York's Central Park in 1985 and leaving her for dead. Current audiences bristle at the tough prosecutorial interrogation of children, but the newspaper headlines of the day (as well as rabid ads and media appearances by a younger Donald Trump) depict the youngsters as a "wolf pack" of "superpredators." This case was no outlier: prompted by the media frenzy over the crack epidemic,[25] young criminal offenders, particularly African Americans, were regularly dehumanized, their age denoting danger rather than mitigation or rehabilitative potential.[26]

However, the early 2000s, new brain-imaging technologies enabled neuroscientists discover that the prefrontal cortex, which is responsible for the ability to delay gratification, exercise emotional regulation, and resist pressure, continuously grows well into our mid-twenties which explains impatience and rash decisions by teenagers and adolescents.[27]

These developments first permeated the legal field in *Roper v. Simmons*, where the Supreme Court struck down the death penalty for minors as unconstitutional.[28] The court found juveniles to be immature and irresponsible, more vulnerable to peer pressure, and possessing a "more transitory, less fixed" character. These differences "render suspect any conclusion that a juvenile falls among the worst offenders," and therefore, from a moral standpoint it would be misguided to equate the failings of a minor with those of an adult, for a greater possibility exists that a minor's character deficiencies will be reformed."

The decision in *Roper* energized petitioners serving lengthy sentences for crimes committed when they were minors, and other landmark decisions followed. In *Graham v. Florida,* the Supreme Court struck down life without parole for nonhomicide offenses committed by juveniles, citing similar rationales and explaining that the aims of punishment do not support such a harsh sentence for crimes other than homicide.[29] Subsequently, in *Miller v. Alabama,* the court invalidated, for juvenile offenders, sentencing schemes under which certain murder convictions yielded mandatory life-without-parole sentences, finding that such schemes "preclude a sentencer from taking account of an offender's ... chronological age and its hallmark features—among them, immaturity, impetuosity, and failure to appreciate risks and consequences ... And finally, this mandatory punishment disregards the possibility of rehabilitation even when the circumstances most suggest it."[30]

Miller did not explicitly state that it would apply retroactively to the many inmates already serving lengthy sentences under sentencing schemes that violated *Miller.* One such inmate was Henry Montgomery, convicted of the murder of a police officer when he was sixteen years old; at the time *Miller* was decided he was already in his late fifties, still serving time in Louisiana's notorious Angola prison. Montgomery appealed his sentence, arguing that *Miller* should apply retroactively.[31]

Under constitutional doctrine, as established in *Griffith v. Kentucky* and in *Teague v. Lane,* defendants whose cases are final face an uphill battle in reopening their cases in light of Supreme Court landmark decisions.[32] They must convince the court of one of the following three arguments: first, that the landmark decision does not announce a "new rule" but merely interprets prior precedent; second, that the new rule is substantive rather than procedural in nature; or third, that the new rule is a "watershed rule of criminal procedure" of such seminal importance that justice requires it to be retroactively applicable. In *Montgomery,* the Supreme Court was convinced of the second argument. It found that the *Miller* rule, according to which mandatory life-without-parole schemes could not apply to juveniles, was a substantive rule—a rule that "rendered life without parole an unconstitutional penalty for a class of defendants because of their status" and therefore should apply retroactively. The court was less decisive about the appropriate remedy, and Justice Kennedy opined that parole hearings might be a suitable forum for raising the age argument.

Before the Supreme Court announced its decision in *Miller,* a large California campaign waged by criminal justice nonprofits and human rights organizations yielded SB 9,[33] which required holding a judicial resentencing hearing for all juveniles serving life without parole. Along the same lines,

California lawmakers also adopted SB 260,[34] which expanded the access to resentencing hearings to juveniles serving other extreme sentences, short of life without parole. SB 260 was later amended by SB 261, further expanding the resentencing hearings to those who were under twenty-three years of age when committing the crime. This amendment better reflects neuroscience developments, according to which the prefrontal cortex continues to develop well into one's early twenties. In this respect and others, California is ahead of the rest of the nation in acknowledging the contribution of youth to crime.[35] A subsequent bill signed into law in 2017, SB 394, set the date for the first opportunity for a hearing by a person who was incarcerated as a minor at twenty-four years of incarceration.[36]

These developments finally found their way into the parole hearing room with the parole grant recommendation for Leslie Van Houten in 2016, in which the Board anchored its decision in the new understanding of youth:

> Your choices that you made in your life at an early age based on the belief system that the family was over when there was a dissolution led you to a lifestyle of drugs, running away, unplanned pregnancy, the abortion, anti-establishment philosophy of the times. You exhibited these hallmarks of youth at the time of the crime as compared to adults, lack of maturity, under-developed sense of responsibility, leading a reckless, impulsive lifestyle. So that was [SB] 261. That was what the Supreme Court has ruled on, and that is on point with the case factors we see before the Panel here today, so the great weight played a role. Your age played a role.[37]

It remains to be seen whether attention to youth significantly reforms the parole process. Recently, Beth Schwartzapfel observed that parole boards find ways to thwart the court's decision in *Montgomery*, arguing that long-term inmates who committed their crimes at a young age have not yet developed insight. The outcome is "a wave of lawsuits from those who claim parole officials are undermining their new constitutional obligations."[38]

This is especially true in California, where political considerations might lead the governor to reverse release recommendations, thus retaining political good will and protecting the gubernatorial office from public backlash. Notably, Governor Brown reversed the Board's recommendation and denied Van Houten's parole in 2017 and 2018, and Governor Newsom did the same in 2019.[39]

Nevertheless, it is telling that the Board—albeit more politically insulated than the governor—felt comfortable recommending the release of a high-profile inmate on the basis of age, a fact widely known from the time the crime was committed but only recently considered. This development bodes well for other inmates, and specifically for members of the Manson Family, whose young age was a deciding factor in their involvement with Manson in the first place.

Inmate-Related Changes

While external factors and policy changes may lead to changes in parole release policies, it would be overly cynical to completely discount the possibility that the Board can and does observe, in good faith, changes in the individual inmate's rehabilitation process.

Bobby Beausoleil experienced such good faith after his 2017 parole hearing, the last one in which he was denied parole. He reports that, after the hearing, he received a phone call from one of the commissioners hearing his case.[40] Beausoleil's impression of the conversation was positive and optimistic. He reported that the commissioner had lauded his progress toward release, encouraged him to follow the Board's recommendations, and spoke in a warm and humane manner. Beausoleil described that hearing as "the most intelligent parole hearing I've had." At his subsequent hearing, in 2019, the Board recommended his parole.

Another issue that bodes well for members of the Family is Charles Manson's death. With the demise of the man who personified the Helter Skelter narrative, the subversive narratives, which are kinder to his followers, may be better received.

CONDITIONS AND FACTORS HINDERING RELEASE

There are, however, some factors that may weigh against parole, the first of which is the continuing symbolic importance of the Manson murders. The murders continue to titillate the public imagination through novels and films that keep the murders fresh in the collective memory. Notably, even as the Board recommended Leslie Van Houten's release, one commissioner explicitly referred to the notoriety of the crime as the "sole basis for denial," in spite of her youth at the time and her extraordinary rehabilitation: "The mere mention of the name Manson half a century later invokes the thought of evil, fear, and danger to the general public and the perception and that's not only delegated to people in this city or this country, but around the world as was demonstrated by all the support and opposition we've seen."[41]

Indeed, recently, a woman found dead in 1969 near the site of several Manson Family killings was identified as Reet Jurvetson, a Montreal native, only nineteen years old at the time of her death. The Los Angeles Police Department is searching for two suspected killers and denies any connection to the Manson Family.[42] But this incident and others continuously spark curiosity about a series of tapes made by Tex Watson in 1969, in which he recounts in detail his participation in the murders. The tapes are rumored to contain information on additional unsolved murders,[43] which would dovetail with some insinuations made in Bugliosi's *Helter Skelter* of such crimes, including the death of one of Manson's attorneys.[44] The periodic resurfacing of information about possible crimes connected with the Family revives the horror and mystique of the murders and could influence the governor, if not the Board.

Bifurcation: The Retrenchment of Severity toward Violent Offenders

The idea that the violence of the crime in itself could be "the sole basis of denial" corresponds to a general postrecession trend in criminal justice, both in California and nationwide. After the financial crisis of 2008, states and localities, as well as the federal government, started pruning their incarceration regimes.[45] In 2009, for the first time in thirty-seven years, the United States prison population began to decline, a trend that continues as of this writing.[46] Katherine Beckett found that a considerable portion of the decline can be attributed to California's Criminal Justice Realignment.[47] But the Realignment, like other postrecession reforms, targeted those convicted of nonserious, nonviolent, nonsexual offenses.[48] Christopher Seeds juxtaposes the increasingly forgiving approach toward nonviolent offenders, particularly those associated with the understandably unpopular War on Drugs, with a renewed resolve to treat violent offenders severely.[49]

As John Pfaff, James Forman, and others have explained, this tactic is unlikely to reverse mass incarceration.[50] Most American prison inmates have been convicted of violent offenses, a consequence of charging practices by county prosecutors. One recent commentator even found that, just as sentences for nonviolent offenders decreased, sentences for violent offenders increased, which might explain why, despite efforts, the reduction in incarceration has been modest so far.[51]

This trend explains why the emotional valence of violent crimes continues to hold sway among the public and the legislature. One pertinent case in point is the legislative effort on California parole boards, SB 1242, which was brought before the Senate Committee on Public Safety on April 24, 2018.[52] The bill purports to "codify existing regulations and practices which establish the criteria that demonstrate a life-term inmate's suitability for parole." These criteria include the following:

- The inmate has remorse and insight into the nature of the crime of which the inmate is convicted, unless the inmate asserts his or her factual innocence of the crime.

- The inmate has not minimized his or her role in the crime and is credible about his or her role in the crime.

- The inmate demonstrates the changes the inmate has made to illustrate his or her departure from prior criminality.

- The inmate has been free from disciplinary actions for a reasonable period of time prior to the hearing.

- The inmate demonstrates positive activities while in custody.

- The inmate has developed realistic postrelease plans to avoid relapse or other conduct that contributed to prior criminality.

Ostensibly, the bill merely writes into law what the Board has been doing on its own accord, but a closer look at the justification for the bill is telling. The author of the bill, Senator Josh Newman, carefully crafts into the justification a redball crime involving the release of a man who had murdered a police officer. "On multiple occasions," Newman argues, "the Board has made deeply flawed parole grants in which it arguably failed in its obligation to prioritize public safety above the rights of dangerous criminals. Governor Brown, under his authority to review such grants, has been meticulous and thorough, making decisions that reflect a sober and thoughtful analysis of the cases before him. . . . There is no assurance, however, that his successors will apply a similar rigor."[53]

Newman's reasoning is squarely in the camp of the emotional pleas for severity from the 1970s and 1980s (discussed in chapter 2 under *"Furman v. Georgia, People v. Anderson,* and the 'Class of '72'"). His explanation exalts the gubernatorial political intervention in the professional internal decisions to release. It is unsurprising that the ACLU, which objects to the bill, takes the opposite tack, relying on professional, evidence-based standards. It cites a California Supreme Court concurring opinion, according to which "'the social science literature does not support a generalization that an inmate's lack of insight into the causes of past criminal activity or failure to admit the official version of the commitment offense is itself a reliable predictor of future dangerousness.'" The quoted opinion expressed concern that "'lack of insight' become, impermissibly, a new talisman with the potential to render almost all life inmates unsuitable for parole."[54]

But even if legal clarity could actually guarantee more predictable parole outcomes, SB 1242 (which was in committee when this book was written) would not further that goal by clarifying parole standards; rather, it would enshrine into law the existing nebulous standards that are the basis for problems in the parole system, none of which is a proven predictor of risk. That these standards are considered desirable is an example of the unchanging public opinion (or the legislature's perception of it) about violent offenders as people who cannot realistically change and are best kept behind bars for the rest of their lives.

The retrenchment of extreme punishment for violent offenders has taken an intriguing turn with Governor Gavin Newsom's 2019 decision to place a moratorium on the death penalty in California.[55] This decision, which provoked relief and ire reminiscent of the public reaction to *Anderson*,[56] might bode well for the Manson Family inmates in that it signals Newsom's independence and willingness to take controversial steps. However, Newsom justified halting the death penalty by holding up the existence of life without parole as a viable alternative,[57] and it is therefore unclear whether the moratorium merely signals a retrenchment of his position on other forms of extreme punishment.

Persistent Risk

Finally, it is also important not to discount the possibility that some inmates, despite old age and declining health, might still be perceived as posing risk to society. To the extent that parole is not merely a reward system for virtue, but a holistic assessment of risk, the parole board may be worried about releasing inmates who have disciples glorifying their past violent acts (even if they have personally disavowed violence). Some might argue that the decision not to release Manson before his death, despite his declining health, was justified, because Manson posed danger through his many still-existing fans who claim that he was innocent of the crimes. The extent to which the behavior of outsiders—fans, participants, the public as a whole—can be imputed to the inmate is a characteristic of the Manson Family cases and has shadowed their development from the outset. Whether this is a legitimate consideration or a thinly veiled political issue is debatable.

WHAT IS TO BE DONE?

Whether or not you believe that the Manson Family inmates deserve their freedom, some general conclusions can be drawn from the hearings, in spite of the idiosyncrasies of these particular cases. First among these is a call for more humility in parole hearings—we must admit our limited ability to discern someone's sincerity in a high-stakes situation and an ambience saturated with artifice.

During my work on this manuscript, I attended a social gathering in which I met a CDCR employee and a formerly incarcerated journalist. Conversation turned to the question of sincerity, and when I described my findings, the CDCR employee said: "If you were actually in the room, you'd be able to see body language and other nonverbal cues. That's what the commissioners go on when they assess sincerity." The journalist chuckled softly and replied, "you know, we saw a lot of people coming up before the board, and we knew what they were about in prison—who was real and who was just putting on a show. And often we would shake our heads when someone we knew was faking it got his date."

In addition to reading the hearing transcripts, I watched some video footage of the hearings.[58] If there was a telling nonverbal dimension to the inmates' demeanor, I did not discern it. The footage left me unable to determine whether the remorse they expressed—often tearful and quiet—was genuine. Given the commissioners' backgrounds, it is hard to imagine what psychological tools or expertise they possess that would enable them to detect the sincerity of the inmates. This is especially worrisome given the universal tendency to overestimate our lie-detection abilities. In a recent experiment, police officers and ordinary citizens were presented with videotaped confessions—some true, some false. The officers expressed more confidence in their ability to detect false confessions. The study found that police officers did worse than the ordinary citizens in distinguishing between true and false confessions.[59]

As Lilliana Paratore explains, the empirical evidence for a correlation between expressions of shame and remorse and rehabilitation is mixed.[60] Some clinical psychiatrists see shame and guilt as a "critical stepping stone in the rehabilitation process."[61] In studies examining postrelease behavior and correlating it to emotions expressed prior to release, the authors found a difference between guilt and shame: the former was found to be constructive and motivate reparative action, whereas the latter "exacerbates feelings of diminishment, worthlessness, and exposure."[62] Even if the nebulous concept of insight encompasses some version of guilt or shame that is conducive to rehabilitation, and if the commissioners, in the highly choreographed setting of the parole hearing, can be trusted to assess its sincerity, "these emotions are continually brokered against those indicating psychopathy."[63]

Rather than relying on theatrics, the Board should accept the possibility that rehabilitation is as rehabilitation does. Realistic, evidence-based, widely available prison rehabilitative programming would enable inmates to showcase their ability to exhibit responsibility, maturity, and restraint in professional environments. These should certainly matter more than minute, ancient disciplinary offenses that have already been taken into account in previous hearings.[64] If prisons are unable to provide programming that adequately prepares inmates for postrelease life, parole expectations should reflect these institutional failings. The requirement that inmates attend nonexistent or inaccessible programs, the negative assessment of inmates' efforts to compensate for the meager institutional offerings, and the tendency to blame inmates for their unpreparedness for postrelease life are deeply unfair.

In their list of ten recommendations for parole reform, Edward Rhine, Joan Petersilia, and Kevin Reitz open with a call to reform the institutional structure of parole boards by requiring that commissioners be appointed in a nonpartisan process, following the recommendation of a professional committee. They also recommend that Board members be required to have a degree in law or a relevant social science field.[65] Adopting this recommendation, particularly if the Board is supplemented by commissioners from therapeutic backgrounds, would help reverse the political/emotional turn illustrated by the Manson Family cases and mitigate political considerations in high-profile cases, but such considerations would not be eliminated entirely unless the gubernatorial veto power were abolished.

A difficult and sensitive question involves the benefit of including the "moral memory bloc"—the prosecutor, victims, and their representatives—at the hearing. Kathryne Young, who interviewed commissioners about their reactions to victim impact statements, highlights the destructive effect of equating victims' rights automatically with punitiveness.[66] She recommends opening the parole hearing to more people, including the inmate's family and friends.[67] Rhine, Petersilia, and Reitz recommend that victim input toward release be limited to the issue of dangerousness to the particular victim and certainly not extend to the overall recommendation whether to grant or deny parole. They express concerns about victim-led efforts to "retry the case" on parole, which they believe violates "principles of procedural fairness."[68] I join these observations and add that victims' presence at hearings should not offer them, or the prosecutor, an unrestricted platform to unprofessionally opine on the inmates' dangerousness decades after the crime of confinement. Specifically, the legal provision that forbids inmates from speaking directly to victims is counterproductive and artificial and reinforces a level of adversarialism that in many cases is as harmful and destructive to the victim as it is to the offender. I would strongly advise reconceptualizing the victim-offender confrontation as a healing and cathartic encounter (through victim-offender mediation, a community circle, and the like), divorced from the parole grant/denial decision, which would also empower the many victims who do not conform to the stereotypical punitive perspective to seek closure in ways that are healthy for them.

The Board's expectations should also take into account what we know about the criminality of lifers after their release, or more accurately, the lack thereof. In a study of California lifers conducted in 2011, Robert Weisberg, Debbie Mukamal, and Jordan Segall found that age and type of offense are not significant determinants of release.[69] This counterintuitive finding flies in the face of consistent findings from the field of life-course criminology, according to which criminality, particularly violent criminality, decreases with age.[70] As Weisberg, Mukamal, and Segall state in their report, "the incidence of commission of serious crimes by recently released lifers has been miniscule, and as compared to the larger inmate population, recidivism risk—at least among those deemed suitable for release by both the Board and the governor—is minimal."[71]

A related issue is the need to streamline the Board's understanding of, and reliance on, risk assessment instruments. Rhine, Petersilia, and Reitz recommend that actuarial risk assessment be "fully examined but not eliminated."[72] They call on states to open their risk assessment software to vigorous public challenges of their statistical validity and application. The cases in this book also suggest that judicial review continue to carefully examine the specific ways in which the Board relies on risk assessment, monitoring against the prioritization of old assessments over newer ones.

Embedded in the risk assessment debacle is the question whether parole suitability is a stamp of approval from a public safety perspective or a value-laden expression of society's opinion about the crime. Given the abundance of clues for the latter, the question of parole denial as a form of punishment is real and poignant. In his work on determinate and indeterminate sentences, W. David Ball proposes taking parole decisions into account as part of the sentencing process for the purpose of deciding what counts as "punishment" and what does not.[73] If parole is really designed to protect society, the preoccupation with the symbolic meaning of the crime of confinement, especially decades after the fact, is inappropriate. In any case, the Board should not be the arbiter of moral goodness. The protection of public safety, as well as the wise and prudent expenditure of public funds, should lead the hearings to focus on whether inmates might commit future crimes, not on moral judgments about their virtues and flaws.

Most importantly, my research left me fervently wishing for real rehabilitation in California prisons. The notion that inmates are responsible for their own rehabilitation unacceptably absolves our massive correctional machine from its obligation to deliver on what it purports to be doing. Prisons should develop a strong and convincing postrelease program, independent of the good will of donors, volunteers, and other do-gooders, with strong liaisons on the outside that can offer a real continuum of care postrelease. Since most inmates will eventually be released, it is time to put our tax money where our mouth is and actively work to make successful reentry a feasible reality.

The professional rehabilitation ethos that governed California corrections until the mid-1970s was deeply flawed, but at least it claimed to treat the people subjected to its regime as whole human beings capable of change. Shedding the artifice and performance from the process and basing it on real, documented participation in programs might remove the mystical dimension of personal virtue that parole boards seek to find in the inmates. But it will keep us safe at the same time as it compels us to respect the humanity and authenticity of our fellow human beings. Regardless of your opinion about these particular cases, it is time for all of us to get the hell out of Bardo.

NOTES

INTRODUCTION

1. Eli Keinan, "History of the State in a Wax Museum," *Davar,* June 8, 1973, http://jpress.org.il/olive/apa/nli_heb/?href=DAV%2F1973%2F06%2F08&page=55 &entityId=Ar05500#panel=document. The museum closed in 1995.

2. Joan Didion, "On the Morning After the Sixties," *The White Album* (New York: Simon & Schuster, 1979), 205.

3. David Williams, *Searching for God in the Sixties* (Newark: University of Delaware Press, 2010), 215.

4. Katherine Beckett, *Making Crime Pay: Law and Order in Contemporary American Politics* (New York: Oxford University Press, 1999).

5. California Penal Code § 290.46.

6. 42 U.S.C. § 16911 et seq.

7. 42 U.S.C § 3711 et seq.

8. 18 U.S.C. § 249.

9. 2006 Cal. Legis. Serv. Prop. 83 (Westlaw 2014); *In re* E.J., 47 Cal. 4th 1258, 1263 (2010).

10. California Penal Code § 679.026.

11. Jonathan Simon, *Governing through Crime: How the War on Crime Transformed America and Created a Culture of Fear* (New York: Oxford University Press, 2007).

12. Hadar Aviram, *Cheap on Crime: Recession-Era Politics and the Transformation of American Punishment* (Oakland: University of California Press, 2015); Marie Gottschalk, *Caught: The Prison State and the Lockdown of American Politics* (Princeton, NJ: Princeton University Press, 2014.

13. Charles J. Ogletree and Austin Sarat, eds., *The Road to Abolition? The Future of Capital Punishment in the United States* (New York: NYU Press, 2009); Hadar Aviram and Ryan Newby, "Death Row Economics: The Rise of Fiscally Prudent Anti-Death Penalty Activism," *Criminal Justice* 28, no. 1 (Spring 2013): 33–40;

Daniel LaChance, "The Death Penalty in the 21st Century," in *Oxford Research Encyclopedia of Criminology and Criminal Justice* (Oxford University Press, article published February 2019), https://oxfordre.com/criminology/view/10.1093/acrefore/9780190264079.001.0001/acrefore-9780190264079-e-462.

14. Lawrence O. Gostin, James G. Hodge, and Sarah A. Wetter, "Enforcing Federal Drug Laws in States Where Medical Marijuana Is Lawful," Viewpoint, *JAMA* 319, no. 14 (2018): 1435–36.

15. The public is more likely to support reforms that benefit nonviolent offenders even though risk and recidivism do not necessarily correlate with offense severity. Julie Gerlinger and Susan F. Turner, "California's Public Safety Realignment: Correctional Policy Based on Stakes Rather Than Risk," *Criminal Justice Policy Review* 26, no. 8 (2014): 805–27; Susan Turner and Julie Gerlinger, "Risk Assessment and Realignment," *Santa Clara Law Review* 53 (2014): 1039–61.

16. Christopher Seeds, "Bifurcation Nation: American Penal Policy in Late Mass Incarceration," *Punishment and Society* 19, no. 5 (2017).

17. John Pfaff, *Locked In: The True Causes of Mass Incarceration—and How to Achieve Real Reform* (New York: Basic Books, 2017).

18. Aviram, *Cheap on Crime*.

19. Aviram, *Cheap on Crime;* Noah Redlich, "When Politics Turn Deadly: The Failure of California's Proposition 62," *Harvard Politics,* March 13, 2018, http://harvardpolitics.com/columns/when-politics-turn-deadly-the-failure-of-californias-proposition-62/.

20. Austin Sarat, John Malague, Lakeisha Arias de los Santos, Katherine Pedersen, Noor Qasim, Logan Seymour, and Sarah Wishloff, "When the Death Penalty Goes Public: Referendum, Initiative, and the Fate of Capital Punishment," *Law & Social Inquiry,* April 20, 2018. Gavin Newsom's gubernatorial moratorium on the death penalty was met with criticism from conservative lawmakers for not being sensitive enough, in their opinion, to the voters' consistent wish to retain the death penalty: Eileen Frere, "Newsom Criticized over Death Penalty Moratorium by Victims' Parents," *ABC7 News,* April 13, 2019, https://abc7.com/gov-newsom-criticized-over-death-penalty-moratorium-by-victims-parents-/5246188/.

21. Ashker v. Brown, Governor of California, N.D. (2013); Center for Constitutional Rights, *California Solitary Confinement Statistics: Year One after Landmark Settlement,* October 18, 2016, https://ccrjustice.org/california-solitary-confinement-statistics-year-one-after-landmark-settlement.

22. S.B. 260 (Hancock), Youth Offender Parole Hearings (Cal., approved by governor September 16, 2013); S.B. 9 (Yee), Sentencing (Cal., approved by governor September 30, 2012).

23. Joan Petersilia and Jessica Greenlick Snyder, "Looking Past the Hype: 10 Questions Everyone Should Ask about California's Prison Realignment," *California Journal of Politics and Policy* 5, no. 2 (2013): 266–306, https://law.stanford.edu/wp-content/uploads/sites/default/files/publication/406310/doc/slspublic/petersilia-snyder-5(2)%20cjpp-pp266–306–2013.pdf.

24. Cheryl Hurd, Samantha Tata, and Jason Kandel, "Prop. 36 Passes; Will Modify California Three Strikes Law," Decision 2012, *NBC Bay Area,* November 8, 2012, www.nbcbayarea.com/news/local/177871121.html.

25. Paige St. John, "Prop. 47 Passes, Reducing Some Crime Penalties," *Los Angeles Times,* November 4, 2014, www.latimes.com/local/political/la-me-ff-prop-47-drug-possession-20141103-story.html.

26. Vanessa Barker, *The Politics of Imprisonment: How the Democratic Process Shapes How America Punishes Offenders* (New York: Oxford University Press, 2009).

27. John Gastil, Jon Hecht, and Tyrone Reitman, "Getting to Yes (or No): Making Ballot Initiatives More Voter-Friendly and Deliberative" (panel discussion, moderated by Carmen Sirianni, Ash Center for Democratic Governance and Innovation, Harvard Kennedy School, April 21, 2015), audio and podcast at https://ash.harvard.edu/event/getting-to-yes-or-no-making-ballot-initiatives-more-voter-friendly-and-deliberative.

28. Joshua Page, *The Toughest Beat: Politics, Punishment, and the Prison Officers Union in California* (New York: Oxford University Press, 2011).

29. Jonathan Simon, *Mass Incarceration on Trial: A Remarkable Court Decision and the Future of Prisons in America* (New York: Free Press, 2014).

30. Craig Haney, *Reforming Punishment: Psychological Limits to the Pains of Imprisonment* (Washington, DC: American Psychological Association, 2006); Juan Méndez, "Solitary Confinement Should Be Banned in Most Cases, UN Expert Says," *UN News,* October 18, 2011, www.un.org/apps/news/story.asp?NewsID=40097.

31. Keramet Reiter, "A Brief History of Pelican Bay," *Prisoner Hunger Strike Solidarity* (blog), n.d., https://prisonerhungerstrikesolidarity.wordpress.com/pelican-bay/305-2/.

32. Chrysanthi Leon, *Sex Fiends, Perverts, and Pedophiles: Understanding Sex Crime Policy in America* (New York: NYU Press, 2011).

33. Joan Petersilia, *When Prisoners Come Home: Parole and Prisoner Reentry* (New York: Oxford University Press, 2003); Nancy Mullane, *Life After Murder: Five Men in Search of Redemption* (New York: Public Affairs, 2012); John Irwin, *Lifers: Seeking Redemption in Prison,* Criminology and Justice Studies (New York: Routledge, 2009).

34. Frederic G. Reamer, *On the Parole Board: Reflections on Crime, Punishment, Redemption, and Justice* (New York: Columbia University Press, 2017).

35. Hannah Laqueur and Ryan Copus, "Synthetic Crowdsourcing: A Machine-Learning Approach to Inconsistency in Adjudication," last revised December 6, 2017, SSRN, https://ssrn.com/abstract=2694326, or http://dx.doi.org/10.2139/ssrn.2694326; Michael Liberton, Mitchell Silverman, and William R. Blount, "Predicting Parole Success for the First-Time Offender," *International Journal of Offender Therapy and Comparative Criminology* 36, no. 4 (1992); Robert Weisberg, Debbie A. Mukamal, and Jordan Segall, *Life in Limbo: An Examination of Parole*

Release for Prisoners Serving Life Sentences with the Possibility of Parole in California (Stanford, CA: Stanford Criminal Justice Center, 2011), https://law.stanford.edu /publications/life-in-limbo-an-examination-of-parole-release-for-prisoners-serving-life-sentences-with-the-possibility-of-parole-in-california/; E. Rely Vîlcică, "Revisiting Parole Decision Making: Testing for the Punitive Hypothesis in a Large U.S. Jurisdiction," *International Journal of Offender Therapy and Cognitive Criminology* 62, no. 5 (2018); Kathryne Young, Debbie A. Mukamal, and Thomas Favre-Bulle, "Predicting Parole Grants: An Analysis of Suitability Hearings for California's Lifer Inmates," *Federal Sentencing Reporter* 28 (2016): 268–77. A notable exception is Victor Shammas, "The Perils of Parole Hearings: California Lifers, Performative Disadvantage, and the Ideology of Insight," *Political and Legal Anthropology Review* 42, no. 1 (2019): 142–60.

36. Ed Sanders, *The Family* (New York: Thunder's Mouth Press, 2002).

37. Vincent Bugliosi and Curt Gentry, *Helter Skelter: The True Story of the Manson Murders* (New York: W.W. Norton, 1974).

38. People v. Anderson, 6 Cal. 3d. 628 (1972).

39. Proposition 17 amended the California Constitution by including Article I, Section 27 (now Section 17), which read as follows:

> All statutes of this state in effect on February 17, 1972, requiring, authorizing, imposing, or relating to the death penalty are in full force and effect, subject to legislative amendment or repeal by statute, initiative, or referendum.
>
> The death penalty provided for under those statutes shall not be deemed to be, or to constitute, the infliction of cruel or unusual punishments within the meaning of Article I, Section 6 nor shall such punishment for such offenses be deemed to contravene any other provision of this constitution.

40. Anselm Strauss and Juliet Corbin, "Grounded Theory Methodology: An Overview," in *Handbook of Qualitative Research,* ed. Norman K. Denzin and Yvonna S. Lincoln (Thousand Oaks, CA: Sage, 1994); Barney G. Glaser and Anselm L. Strauss, *The Discovery of Grounded Theory: Strategies for Qualitative Research* (New Brunswick, NJ, and London: Aldine Transaction, 1967).

41. For some critical thinking on grounded theory and the process of interpretation, see Gary Thomas and David James, "Reinventing Grounded Theory: Some Questions about Theory, Ground and Discovery," *British Educational Research Journal* 32, no. 6 (2006): 767–95.

42. *Life After Manson,* directed by Olivia Klaus, featuring Patricia Krenwinkel, Quiet Little Place Productions, 2014, www.lifeaftermanson.com/.

43. Karlene Faith, *The Long Prison Journey of Leslie Van Houten: Life beyond the Cult* (Boston: Northeastern University Press, 2001).

44. J.L. Austin, "Performative Utterances," in *Philosophical Papers* (London: Oxford University Press, 1970), 233–52. Performativity theorists have found elements of such constitutive communication in various aspects of life, such as "doing" or "performing" gender (rather than "being" of a particular gender). Judith Butler, *Excitable Speech: A Politics of the Performative* (London and New York: Routledge,

1997); Judith Butler, "Performative Agency," *Journal of Cultural Economy* 3, no. 2 (2010): 147–61; Chris Brickell, "Masculinities, Performativity, and Subversion: A Sociological Reappraisal," *Men and Masculinities* 8, no. 1 (2005): 24–43.

45. Erving Goffman, *The Presentation of Self in Everyday Life* (New York: Doubleday, 1956).

46. Erving Goffman, "Characteristics of Total Institutions," in *Symposium of Preventive and Social Psychiatry* (Washington, DC: Walter Reed Army Institute of Research, U.S. Government Printing Office, 1958), reprinted in *Crime, Law, and Society*, edited by Abraham S. Goldstein and Joseph Goldstein (New York: Free Press, 1971); Erving Goffman, *Asylums: Essays on the Social Situation of Mental Patients and Other Inmates* (Garden City, NY: Anchor Books, 1961); Erving Goffman, "On the Characteristics of Total Institutions: The Inmate World," in *The Prison: Studies in Institutional Organization and Change*, edited by Donald R. Cressey (New York: Holt, Rinehart and Winston, 1961); Erving Goffman, "On the Characteristics of Total Institutions: Staff-Inmate Relations," in Cressey, *The Prison*.

47. Shadd Maruna, *Making Good: How Convicts Reform and Rebuild Their Lives* (Washington, DC: American Psychological Association, 2010).

48. Mullane, *Life after Murder;* John Irwin, *Lifers: Seeking Redemption in Prison* (New York: Routledge, 2009); Jeff Manza and Christopher Uggen, *Locked Out: Felon Disenfranchisement and American Democracy* (New York: Oxford University Press, 2006).

49. Clifford Shaw and Henry McKay, *The Jack Roller: A Delinquent Boy's Story* (Chicago: University of Chicago Press, 1974); Lois Presser and Sveinung Sandberg, eds., *Narrative Criminology: Understanding Stories of Crime* (New York: NYU Press, 2015).

50. Richard Weisman, *Showing Remorse: Law and the Social Control of Emotion* (Aldershot, UK: Ashgate, 2014; Abingdon, UK, and New York: Routledge, 2016).

1. THE CALIFORNIA PAROLE PROCESS

Epigraph: *The Tibetan Book of the Dead*, 3rd ed., ed. W.Y. Evans-Wentz, trans. Lama Kazi Dawa-Sawdup (New York: Oxford University Press, 2000), 180.

1. Kevin Newmark, "On Parole: Blanchot, Saussure, Paulhan," *Yale French Studies* 106 (2004): 87–106.

2. Joan Petersilia, "Parole and Prisoner Reentry in the United States," *Perspectives* 24, no. 3 (2000): 32–46; Paul F. Cromwell and Rolando del Carmen, *Community-Based Corrections* (Belmont, CA: West/Wadsworth, 1999).

3. Todd Clear and George Cole, *American Corrections* (Belmont, CA: Wadsworth, 1997).

4. Howard Abadinsky, *Probation and Parole* (Upper Saddle River, NJ: Simon & Schuster, 1997).

5. Edward Rhine, William Smith, Ronald Jackson, Peggy Burke, and Roger LaBelle, *Paroling Authorities: Recent History and Current Practice* (Laurel, MD: American Correctional Association, 1991).

6. Joan Petersilia, "Parole and Prisoner Reentry in the United States," *Crime and Justice* 26 (1999): 479–529.

7. *The Shawshank Redemption,* written and directed by Frank Darabont, featuring Tim Robbins, Morgan Freeman, Bob Gunton, and William Sadler, produced by Castle Rock Entertainment, 1994.

8. Frank Darabont, *The Shawshank Redemption* screenplay, 1994, http://www.imsdb.com/scripts/Shawshank-Redemption,-The.html.

9. Darabont, *Shawshank Redemption.*

10. Darabont, *Shawshank Redemption.*

11. Stephen King, "Rita Hayworth and the Shawshank Redemption," in *Different Seasons* (New York: Viking Press, 1982).

12. For more on the political alliances and coalitions for and against the shift to determinacy, see chapter 2, "Determinate Sentencing and the Politicization of Punishment."

13. American Friends Service Committee, *Struggle for Justice: A Report on Crime and Punishment in America* (New York: Farrar Strauss and Giroux, 1971).

14. Robert Martinson, "What Works? Questions and Answers about Prison Reform," *The Public Interest* (Spring 1974).

15. Andrew Von Hirsch, *Doing Justice* (New York: Hill & Wang, 1976).

16. Edward E. Rhine, Joan Petersilia, and Kevin R. Reitz, "The Future of Parole Release," in *Reinventing American Criminal Justice,* ed. Michael Tonry and Daniel S. Nagin, vol. 46 of *Crime and Justice: A Review of Research,* ed. Michael Tonry (Chicago: University of Chicago Press, 2017).

17. Paula A. Johnson, "Senate Bill 42: The End of the Indeterminate Sentence" *Santa Clara Law Review* 17, no. 1, art. 4 (1977), http://digitalcommons.law.scu.edu/lawreview/vol17/iss1/4.

18. Alison Lawrence, *Making Sense of Sentencing: State Systems and Policies,* National Conference of State Legislatures, June 2015, https://www.ncsl.org/documents/cj/sentencing.pdf.

19. Edward E. Rhine, Alexis Watts, and Kevin Reitz, "Parole Boards within Indeterminate and Determinate Sentencing Structures," blog post, Robina Institute of Criminal Law and Criminal Justice, University of Minnesota Law School, April 3, 2018, https://robinainstitute.umn.edu/news-views/parole-boards-within-indeterminate-and-determinate-sentencing-structures.

20. For more on sentencing commissions, see Barbara Tombs-Souvey, "The Role of Sentencing Commissions," Robina Institute of Criminal Law and Criminal Justice, University of Minnesota Law School, September 30, 2015, https://sentencing.umn.edu/content/role-sentencing-commissions.

21. Michael Tonry, "Sentencing Commissions and Their Guidelines," *Crime & Justice* 17 (1993): 137–195, http://scholarship.law.umn.edu/faculty_articles/481.

22. Joan Petersilia, "Parole and Prisoner Reentry," 32.

23. To better understand the failure to create a sentencing commission in California, see Kara Dansky, "Understanding California Sentencing," *University of San Francisco Law Review* 43 (2008): 45–86.

24. California Penal Code § 213 B(2).

25. California Penal Code § 12021.55–12022.55.

26. California Penal Code § 186.22.

27. Apprendi v. New Jersey, 530 U.S. 466 (2000); Blakely v. Washington, 542 U.S. 296 (2004); United States v. Booker, 543 U.S. 220 (2005).

28. Cunningham v. California, 549 U.S. 270 (2007).

29. S.B. 40 (amending California Penal Code § 1170) (Cal. 2007).

30. J. Richard Couzens and Tricia A. Bigelow, *Awarding Custody Credits,* Judicial Council of California, February 2013, http://www.courts.ca.gov/partners/documents/Credits_Memo.pdf.

31. For an empirical review of the application of this ideology, see Katherine J. Rosich and Kamala Mallik Kane, "Truth in Sentencing and State Sentencing Practices," *NIJ Journal* 252 (July 2005), https://www.nij.gov/journals/252/Pages/sentencing.aspx.

32. For background on the realignment, see Margo Schlanger, "*Plata v. Brown* and Realignment: Jails, Prisons, Courts, and Politics," *Harvard Civil Rights–Civil Liberties Law Review* 48, no. 1 (2013): 165–215.

33. Dylan Sullivan and David Hurd, "Parole Hearings," § 47.1A, *California Criminal Law Procedure and Practice,* 2nd ed. (Berkeley, CA: Continuing Education of the Bar—California, 2014).

34. Sullivan and Hurd, "Parole Hearings," § 47.10.

35. California Penal Code § 3000.08(a) (2014).

36. Jennifer Steinhauer, "The Loneliness of Governor Schwarzenegger," *New York Times,* July 10, 2010, https://www.nytimes.com/2010/07/11/weekinreview/11steinhauer.html.

37. Sullivan and Hurd, "Parole Hearings," § 47.1C.

38. W. David Ball, "Heinous, Atrocious, and Cruel: Apprendi, Indeterminate Sentencing, and the Meaning of Punishment," *Columbia Law Review* 109 (June 2009): 893–972, at Santa Clara Law Digital Commons, https://digitalcommons.law.scu.edu/facpubs/16/.

39. California Penal Code § 189.

40. California Penal Code § 190.

41. California Penal Code § 209(b)(1).

42. Paula Ditton, and Doris James Wilson, *Truth in Sentencing in State Prisons* (Washington, DC: Bureau of Justice Statistics, 1999).

43. California Penal Code § 3051(a); California Penal Code § 3041.5(d).

44. California Penal Code § 3003(a).

45. Sullivan and Hurd, "Parole Hearings," § 47.1C.

46. Yael Hassin, "Early Release Committee for Prisoners versus Computer: Which Is Preferable?," *Criminology* 18, no. 3 (1980): 385–97.

47. Shai Danziger, Jonathan Levav, and Liora Avnaim-Pesso, "Extraneous Factors in Judicial Decisions," *Proceedings of the National Academy of Sciences* 108, no. 17 (2011): 6889–92.

48. Tammy Meredith, John Speir, and Sharon Johnson, "Developing and Implementing Automated Risk Assessment in Parole," *Justice Research and Policy* 9, no. 1 (2007): 1–24.

49. California Constitution, Art. V, § 8(b).

50. Joan Petersilia, "Parole and Prisoner Reentry," 34; Peggy B. Burke, *Abolishing Parole: Why the Emperor Has No Clothes* (Lexington, KY: American Probation and Parole Association; California, MO: Association of Paroling Authorities, 1995). In fact, therapeutic professionals who treated Timmendequas were concerned about the prospect of his return to sex crimes upon release. William Glaberson, "Stranger on the Block—A Special Report: At Center of 'Megan's Law' Case, a Man No One Could Reach," *New York Times,* May 28, 1996, http://www.nytimes.com/1996/05/28/nyregion/stranger-block-special-report-center-megan-s-law-case-man-no-one-could-reach.html.

51. Board of Parole Hearings, California Department of Corrections and Rehabilitation, "Suitability Hearing Summary, CY 1978 though CY 2012," http://www.cdcr.ca.gov/BOPH/docs/BPH_Hearing_Results_CY_1978_to_2012.pdf.

52. *In re* Lawrence, 44 Cal. 4th 1181, 190 P.3d 535, 82 Cal. Rptr. 3d 169.

53. For the hopes engendered in Lawrence, see Joey Hipolito, "*In re* Lawrence: Preserving the Possibility of Parole for California Prisoners," *California Law Review* 97, no. 6 (2009): 1887–97; Nancy Mullane, *Life after Murder: Five Men in Search of Redemption* (New York: Public Affairs, 2012).

54. David R. Friedman and Jackie M. Robinson, "Rebutting the Presumption: An Empirical Analysis of Parole Deferrals Under Marsy's Law," *Stanford Law Review* 66, no. 1 (January 2014).

55. Ashley Nellis, *Still Life: America's Increasing Use of Life and Long-Term Sentences* (Washington, DC: The Sentencing Project, 2017), http://www.sentencingproject.org/wp-content/uploads/2017/05/Still-Life.pdf. Whether clear distinctions between these categories matter from a human rights perspective is debatable. Dirk van Zyl Smit and Catherine Appleton, *Life Imprisonment: A Global Human Rights Analysis* (Cambridge, MA: Harvard University Press, 2019).

56. Friedman and Robinson, "Rebutting the Presumption."

57. Kathryne M. Young, Debbie A. Mukamal, and Thomas Favre-Bulle, "Predicting Parole Grants: An Analysis of Suitability Hearings for California's Lifer Inmates," *Federal Sentencing Reporter* 28 (2016): 268–77.

58. California Penal Code § 3044 (2014).

59. Board of Parole Hearings, California Department of Corrections and Rehabilitation, https://www.cdcr.ca.gov/bph/commisioners/.

60. Dirk van Zyl Smit and Alessandro Corda, "American Exceptionalism in Parole Release and Supervision: A European Perspective," in *American Exceptionalism in Crime and Punishment,* ed. Kevin R. Reitz (New York: Oxford University Press, 2018), https://ssrn.com/abstract=2811828.

61. Young, Mukamal, and Favre-Bull, "Predicting Parole Grants."

62. Board of Parole Hearings, California Department of Corrections and Rehabilitation, Meeting Agendas, https://www.cdcr.ca.gov/BOPH/meeting_agenda.html.

63. Author's participant observation at the executive board meetings, open sessions.

64. Author's interview with Keith Wattley.

65. William H. Lindsley et al., "Penal and Correctional Institutions," § 277, vol. 49, *California Jurisprudence,* 3rd ed. (Thomson West, 2015).

66. California Penal Code § 3041.5(b)(3) (2014).

67. Christopher R. Mock, "Parole Suitability Determinations in California: Ambiguous, Arbitrary, and Illusory," *Southern California Review of Law and Social Justice* 17 (2008): 895.

68. "Sentencing, Incarceration, and Parole of Offenders," California Department of Corrections and Rehabilitation, https://www.cdcr.ca.gov/victim-services/sentencing/.

69. Friedman and Robinson, "Rebutting the Presumption"; Matt Levine, "Timeline: History of California Lifers Up for Parole," KQED News, May 15, 2014, https://www.kqed.org/news/136126/timeline-history-of-california-lifers-up-for-parole.

70. California Code of Regulations Title 15, § 2255 (2014).

71. California Penal Code § 3041.5(b) (2014).

72. Author's interviews with Jason Campbell and with Keith Wattley.

73. Friedman and Robinson, "Rebutting the Presumption."

74. Mock, "Parole Suitability Determinations in California."

75. Mock, "Parole Suitability Determinations in California," 3.

76. *In re* Powell, 45 Cal. 3d 894, 905 (1988).

77. *In re* Lawrence, 44 Cal. 4th 1181, 1191 (2008).

78. California Code Regs. Title 15, § 2402(c)(1)–(6).

79. California Code Regs. Title 15, § 2402(c)(1)–(6).

80. Hipolito, "*In re* Lawrence," 1890.

81. Ebony L. Ruhland, Edward R. Rhine, Jason P. Robey, and Kelly Lyn Mitchell, *The Continuing Leverage of Releasing Authorities: Findings from a National Survey* (Minneapolis: Robina Institute of Criminal Law and Criminal Justice, University of Minnesota Law School, 2016); Kaleena J. Burkes, Edward E. Rhine, Jason P. Robey, and Ebony L. Ruhland, *Releasing Authority Chairs: A Comparative Snapshot across Three Decades* (Minneapolis: Robina Institute of Criminal Law and Criminal Justice, University of Minnesota Law School, 2017).

82. People v. Rodriguez, 51 Cal. 3d 437, 441 (1990).

83. *In re* Martinez, 1 Cal. 3d 641, 650 (1970).

84. Sullivan and Hurd, "Parole Hearings," § 47.18.

85. California Code Regs. Title 15, §§ 2031–2032.

86. California Code Regs. Title 15, § 2029.1.

87. California Penal Code § 3043(a).

88. California Penal Code § 3041.7.

89. California Penal Code § 3043.5.

90. California Code Regs., Title 15, § 2246; California Penal Code § 3043(a)(1); California Penal Code § 3042.

91. *In re* Dannenberg, 34 Cal. 4th 1061, 1084 (2005).

92. California Code Regs. Title 15, § 2246.

93. Sullivan and Hurd, "Parole Hearings," § 47.24.

94. California Penal Code § 3041.5(a)(2).

95. California Code Regs. Title 15, § 2255; California Penal Code 3041.5(a)(4)

96. Hipolito, "*In re* Lawrence," 1890.

97. Hipolito, "*In re* Lawrence," 1890.

98. Gideon v. Wainwright, 372 U.S. 335 (1963); Smit and Corda, "American Exceptionalism in Parole Release and Supervision," 433–36.

99. Harbison v. Bell, 556 U.S. 180 (2009).

100. California Code Regs. Title 15, § 2256.

101. Board of Parole Hearings, Panel Attorney Appointment Program, January 1, 2018, https://www.cdcr.ca.gov/BOPH/docs/Orientation%20Materials_2017 /Panel-Attorney-Program-Guide-2018.pdf.

102. Author's interview with Keith Wattley.

103. California Penal Code §§ 3052–3053.5.

104. California Code Regs. Title 15, § 2512.

105. Sullivan and Hurd, "Parole Hearings," § 47.5C.

106. California Penal Code § 3003.5.

107. People v. Lent, 15 Cal. 3d 481, 486 (1975).

108. People v. Keller, 76 Cal. App. 3d 827, 835 (1978).

109. People v. Burgener, 41 Cal. 3d 505, 532 (1986).

110. Sullivan and Hurd, "Parole Hearings," § 47.5C.

111. California Penal Code § 3000(b)(2).

112. California Penal Code § 3000(b)(4)(A).

113. Sullivan and Hurd, "Parole Hearings," § 47.5.

114. Author's communication with Kimberly Richman, cofounder of Alliance for C.H.A.N.G.E., July 24, 2018.

115. Sullivan and Hurd, "Parole Hearings," § 47.43.

116. Sullivan and Hurd, "Parole Hearings," § 47.6.

117. Sullivan and Hurd, "Parole Hearings," § 47.6.

118. California Penal Code § 3001.

119. Sullivan and Hurd, "Parole Hearings," § 47.6.

120. California Code Regs. Title 15, § 3723.

121. Sullivan and Hurd, "Parole Hearings," § 47.6.

122. Sullivan and Hurd, "Parole Hearings," § 47.8.

123. Sullivan and Hurd, "Parole Hearings," § 47.9.

124. California Penal Code § 3056(a).

125. Sullivan and Hurd, "Parole Hearings," § 47.7.

126. California Penal Code § 3000.1(d).

127. Sullivan and Hurd, "Parole Hearings," § 47.12.

128. *In re* Rosenkrantz, 80 Cal. App. 4th 409 (2000).

129. *In re* Rosenkrantz, 29 Cal. 4th 616 (2002).

130. *In re* Dannenberg, 34 Cal. 4th 1061 (2005).

131. *In re* Lewis, 172 Cal. App. 4th 13 (2009).

132. *In re* Lawrence, 44 Cal. 4th 1181 (2008); *In re* Shaputis, 44 Cal. 4th 1241 (2008).

133. Hipolito, "*In re* Lawrence," 1889.

134. *In re* Lawrence, 44 Cal. App. 4th 1181 (2008).

135. Hipolito, "*In re* Lawrence," 1891.5.

136. *Lawrence,* 44 Cal. 4th 1181.

137. *Lawrence,* 44 Cal. 4th 1181.

138. Hipolito, "*In re* Lawrence," 1892.

139. Hipolito, "*In re* Lawrence," 1888.

140. Levine, "Timeline," 2015.

141. Mullane, *Life after Murder.*

142. *Shaputis,* 44 Cal. 4th 1241.

143. Alison Dundes Renteln, *The Cultural Defense* (Oxford, UK: Oxford University Press, 2004).

144. Author's interview with Keith Wattley.

145. Hipolito, "*In re* Lawrence," 1894.6

146. Hipolito, "*In re* Lawrence," 1895.

147. Dana Littlefield, "Life with Parole No Longer Means Life Term," *San Diego Union-Tribune,* August 17, 2014.

148. Board of Parole Hearings, "Suitability Hearing Summary."

149. Littlefield, "Life with Parole."

150. Levine, "Timeline,"

151. Levine, "Timeline."

152. Hipolito, "*In re* Lawrence."

153. *In re* Loresch, 183 Cal. App. 4th 150 (2010).

154. *In re* Calderon, 184 Cal. App. 4th 670 (2010).

155. *In re* Ross, 140 U.S. 453 (1891).

156. Hayward v. Marshall, 603 F.3d 546 (9th Cir. 2010).

157. Pearson v. Muntz, 606 F.3d 606 (9th Cir. 2010).

2. THE MANSON FAMILY CASES AND THE BIRTH OF THE "EXTREME-PUNISHMENT TRIFECTA"

Epigraph: *The Tibetan Book of the Dead,* 3rd ed., ed. W.Y. Evans-Wentz, trans. Lama Kazi Dawa-Sawdup (New York: Oxford University Press, 2000), 189.

1. Becky Little, "Charles Manson Was Sentenced to Death. Why Wasn't He Executed?," History Channel, November 20, 2017, www.history.com/news/charles-manson-was-sentenced-to-death-why-wasnt-he-executed; Lucinda Chen, "Keeping

Charles Manson in Prison for 46 Years Cost Taxpayers over $1 Million" *Fortune,* November 21, 2017, http://fortune.com/2017/11/21/charles-manson-prison-cost/. I found Chen's estimate surprisingly low given the length of Manson's incarceration, especially considering his ill health since the 1980s. Moreover, the implied message that the death penalty would reduce the price tag was misleading: the expense involved in the death penalty is significant, partly because of the unique confinement conditions, security, and staffing requirements but mostly because the California Constitution (Art. I) provides free representation in postconviction capital proceedings. In 2016, the Legislative Analyst's Office estimated that had California adopted Proposition 62 and replaced the death penalty with life without parole, the state would have saved at least $150 million annually. Legislative Analyst's Office, "Proposition 62," November 8, 2016, https://lao.ca.gov/BallotAnalysis/Proposition?number=62&year=2016. Assuming that Manson and his followers, like hundreds of death row inmates, would have raised postconviction challenges, their cases might have cost considerably more throughout the years.

2. In Steve Grogan's case, the jury recommended death, but the judge gave him life in prison, factoring in his intellectual disability and drug dependence at the time of the murders.

3. One category I do not explicitly include here but that belongs within this regime of universal life-without-parole de facto is known as "virtual life"—determinate sentences that a person is unlikely to survive, typically fifty years or more under current sentencing regimes. Ashley Nellis, *Still Life: America's Increasing Use of Life and Long-Term Sentences* (Washington, DC: The Sentencing Project, 2017), https://www.sentencingproject.org/wp-content/uploads/2017/05/Still-Life.pdf.

4. Cathy Locke, "Crime Q & A: How Many California Prison Inmates Are Sentenced to Life without Parole?" *Sacramento Bee,* June 8, 2017, https://www.sacbee.com/news/local/crime/article155229769.html.

5. A Living Chance/California Coalition for Women Prisoners, "Proposition 62 and the Other Death Penalty," https://womenprisoners.org/2016/10/proposition-62-and-the-other-death-penalty/.

6. Josh Meisel, "Why I Will Vote No on California's Death Penalty Initiatives," *Social Justice Journal,* October 31, 2016, www.socialjusticejournal.org/why-i-will-vote-no-on-californias-death-penalty-initiatives/.

7. Brandon Garrett, "The Moral Problem of Life-Without-Parole Sentences," *Time,* October 26, 2017, https://time.com/4998858/death-penalty-life-without-parole/.

8. Hadar Aviram, "Are You Against the Death Penalty? Good. Then Vote against the Death Penalty," *Social Justice Journal,* October 31, 2016, www.socialjusticejournal.org/are-you-against-the-death-penalty-good-then-vote-against-the-death-penalty/.

9. For an excellent analysis of this point, see Marc Mauer and Ashley Nellis, *The Meaning of Life: The Case for Abolishing Life Sentences* (New York: New Press, 2018).

10. Matt Levin, "Behind California's Dramatic Increase in Lifers Freed from Prisons," KQED News, May 15, 2014, https://www.kqed.org/news/135494/behind-californias-dramatic-increase-in-murderers-freed-from-prisons.

11. Michael Brodheim, "Long-Term Incarceration: The Men and Women Who Have Been Locked Away for More than a Quarter Century in California's Prison System," *Elephant Journal,* January 29, 2018, n9, https://www.elephantjournal.com/now/long-term-incareration-the-men-and-women-who-have-been-locked-away-for-more-than-a-quarter-century-in-californias-prison-system/.

12. Brodheim, "Long Term Incarceration," n10, n11.

13. Brodheim, "Long-Term Incarceration." What is also notable here is that the Board of Parole Hearings itself, as explained in chapter 1, does not subscribe to this idea of "default release" despite the explicit language in the law.

14. Vincent Bugliosi, with Curt Gentry, *Helter Skelter: The True Story of the Manson Murders* (New York: W. W. Norton, 1974).

15. People v. Anderson, 6 Cal. 3d. 628 (1972).

16. Furman v. Georgia, 408 U.S. 238 (1972); the two other cases were Jackson v. Georgia, 225 Ga. 790 (1971) and Branch v. Texas, 447 S.W.2nd 932 (1971).

17. *Anderson,* 6 Cal. 3d 628, 656.

18. *Anderson,* 6 Cal. 3d 628.

19. *Furman,* 408 U.S. 238, 253.

20. Aikens v. California, 406 U.S. 813 (1972).

21. Author's conversation with two former California Supreme Court clerks, August 26 and 29, 2018. Both my interlocutors remembered being terrified that they were going to be suspected of leaking the decision.

22. UPI, "Reagan Raps Death Row, Vows to Change Ruling," *Argus,* February 18, 1972, 2.

23. Associated Press, "State Supreme Court Rules Execution Unconstitutional" *Santa Cruz Sentinel* 117, no. 43 (February 20, 1972).

24. Associated Press, "State Supreme Court Rules Execution Unconstitutional."

25. Jeffrey M. Jones, "U.S. Death Penalty Support Lowest since 1972," Politics, Gallup, October 26, 2017, https://news.gallup.com/poll/221030/death-penalty-support-lowest-1972.aspx.

26. Doug Willis, "No Bloodbath Even If Death Penalty Upheld," *Press-Telegram* (Long Beach, CA), February 16, 2018.

27. Daniel LaChance, *Executing Freedom: The Cultural Life of Capital Punishment in the United States* (Chicago: University of Chicago Press, 2016) 2–3, 50.

28. "Death Penalty," California Proposition 17, 1972, https://repository.uchastings.edu/ca_ballot_props/768/.

29. People v. Frierson, 25 Cal. 3d 142, 189 (1978.)

30. *Manson,* dir. Robert Hendrickson and Laurence Merrick, Merrick International, 1973.

31. Jones, "U.S. Death Penalty Support Lowest since 1972."

32. Gregg v. Georgia, 428 U.S. 153 (1976).

33. *Gregg,* 428 U.S. 153, 197–98.

34. The Supreme Court would find the death penalty unconstitutional for non-homicide cases only much later, in Kennedy v. Louisiana, 554 U.S. 407 (2008).

35. Paul Kaplan, Kerry Dunn, and Nicole Sherman, "Localism and Capital Judicial Override in Jefferson County, Alabama," *Sage Journals* 6, no. 2 (July 26, 2015), http://journals.sagepub.com/doi/10.1177/2153368715595268.

36. "Murder Penalty," California Proposition 7, November 7, 1978, https://repository.uchastings.edu/ca_ballot_props/840/.

37. Robert P. Studer, "Proposition 7 Ask Wider Death Penalties," *Desert Sun* (Palm Springs and Coachella Valley), October 24, 1978.

38. "Murder Penalty," California Proposition 7, 1978.

39. California Uniform Determinate Sentencing Act, 1976, Ch. 1139, § 350 (1976) Cal Laws Reg. Sess.

40. Hadar Aviram, *Cheap on Crime: Recession-Era Politics and the Transformation of American Punishment* (Oakland: University of California Press, February 2015).

41. Naomi Murakawa, *The First Civil Right: How Liberals Built Prison America* (New York: Oxford University Press, 2014); Elizabeth Hinton, *From the War on Poverty to the War on Crime: The Making of Mass Incarceration in America* (Cambridge, MA: Harvard University Press, 2016).

42. California Attorneys for Criminal Justice, letter to Edmund G. Brown Jr., September 15, 1976 (California State Archives, Governor's Chapter Bill File).

43. ACLU of Northern California, letter to Edmund G. Brown Jr., August 30, 1976 (California State Archives, Governor's Chapter Bill File).

44. Harold Vogelin, telegram to Edmund Brown Jr., September 7, 1976 (California State Archives, Governor's Chapter Bill File).

45. California Probation, Parole, and Correctional Association (CPPCA), letter to Edmund G. Brown Jr., September 14, 1976, p. 2 (California State Archives, Governor's Chapter Bill File).

46. CPPCA, letter to Brown, p. 3.

47. Office of the Chief Legislative Analyst, City of Los Angeles, letter to Edmund G. Brown Jr., September 13, 1976.

48. Ashley Nellis, *Life Goes On: The Historic Rise in Life Sentences in America* (Washington, DC: The Sentencing Project, 2013), 6, https://sentencingproject.org/wp-content/uploads/2015/12/Life-Goes-On.pdf.

49. Nellis, *Life Goes On*, 3.

50. Nellis, *Life Goes On*, 13.

51. Alisa Statman, with Brie Tate, *Restless Souls: The Sharon Tate Family Account of Stardom, the Manson Murders, and a Crusade for Justice* (New York: HarperCollins, 2012), 147.

52. Statman, *Restless Souls*, 153.

53. Massie was executed in 2001. California Department of Corrections and Rehabilitation, "Executed Inmate Summary—Robert Lee Massie," https://sites.cdcr.ca.gov/capital-punishment/inmates-executed-1978-to-present/robert-lee-massie/.

54. Katherine Beckett, *Making Crime Pay: Law and Order in Contemporary American Politics* (New York: Oxford University Press, 1999).

55. For a discussion of some efforts to bridge these gaps, see Michael D. Maltz, *Bridging Gaps in Police Crime Data: A Discussion Paper from the BJS Fellows Program,* Bureau of Justice Statistics, September 1999, https://www.bjs.gov/content/pub/pdf/bgpcd.pdf.

56. National Organization of Parents of Murdered Children, "History of POMC," 2018, www.pomc.com/history.html.

57. Karen L. Kennard, "The Victim's Veto: A Way to Increase Victim Impact on Criminal Case Dispositions," *California Law Review* 77, no. 2, art. 5 (March 1989), https://scholarship.law.berkeley.edu/cgi/viewcontent.cgi?article=1876&context=californialawreview.

58. Edwin Villmaore and Virginia Neto, *Victim Appearances at Sentencing under the California Victims' Bill of Rights,* National Institute of Justice, March 1987, 11, https://www.ncjrs.gov/pdffiles1/Digitization/104915NCJRS.pdf.

59. Villmaore and Neto, *Victim Appearances,* 12.

60. Statman, *Restless Souls,* 149.

61. Statman, *Restless Souls,* 148.

62. Statman, *Restless Souls,* 149.

63. "June 12, 1981, Tom Snyder's Prison Interview with Charles Manson Aired on NBC," YouTube, February 2015, https://youtu.be/TrTWJncDnCM.

64. "Charles Manson Interview with Charlie Rose on *Nightwatch* (Complete)," YouTube, February 2015, https://youtu.be/H4uT6ou_ZGw.

65. Tom Shales, "Rivera's 'Devil Worship' Was TV at Its Worst," *San Jose Mercury News,* October 31, 1988.

66. *Charles Manson Superstar,* dir. Nikolas Schreck, prod. Video Werewolf, 1989.

67. Associated Press, "Paroled Manson Follower Working as House Painter," *San Francisco Chronicle,* May 9, 1986, 30.

68. *San Jose Mercury News,* "The Charles Manson Family: Where Are They Now?," *Marin Independent Journal,* February 19, 2015, www.marinij.com/general-news/20150219/the-charles-manson-family-where-are-they-now.

69. Matt Fountain/Associated Press, "Manson Family Member Bruce Davis Seeks Parole after 40 Years," *New York Daily News,* March 12, 2014, www.nydailynews.com/news/national/manson-family-member-bruce-davis-seeks-parole-40-years-article-1.1094755.

70. The two states requiring the additional layer of review were Oklahoma and Maryland. Dana Littlefield, "Life with Parole No Longer Means Life Term: Legal Ruling Causes Steady Rise in Parole for California's Lifers," August 17, 2014, https://www.sandiegouniontribune.com/sdut-parole-life-california-prison-inmates-crime-2014aug17-htmlstory.html. Notably, voices in Maryland, including that of former governor, call for the removal of the governor from the parole process. Angela Jacob, "Governor Should Be Removed from Parole Process, Former Md. Gov. Says," NBC News Washington, March 8, 2018, https://www.nbcwashington.com/news/local/Former-MD-Gov-Says-Should-be-Removed-from-Parole-Process-476271173.html.

71. California Constitution, Art. V, § 8.

72. California Secretary of State, Voter Information Guide for 1988, General Election (1988), https://repository.uchastings.edu/ca_ballot_props/988.

73. California Voter Information Guide, 1988.

74. Susan Atkins, *Child of Satan, Child of God* (San Juan Capistrano, CA: Menelorelin Dorenay's Publishing, 2005).

75. Susan Atkins-Whitehouse, *The Myth of Helter Skelter* (San Juan Capistrano, CA: Menelorelin Dorenay's Publishing, 2012).

76. Tex Watson, as told to Chaplain Ray, *Will You Die for Me?* (Atlanta, GA?: Cross Roads Publications, 1978).

77. Charles "Tex" Watson, *Manson's Right-Hand Man Speaks Out* (Jackson, CA: Abounding Love Ministries, 2003).

78. Ashley Broughton, "Aging Manson 'Family' Members Long for Freedom," CNN, March 30, 2009, www.cnn.com/2009/CRIME/03/30/manson.family.aging/.

79. David Lohr, "Charles 'Tex' Watson: No Parole 42 Years After Manson 'Family' Killings," *Huffington Post,* November 17, 2011, www.huffingtonpost.com/2011/11/17/charles-tex-watson-parole-manson-killings_n_1097760.html.

80. Lohr, "Charles 'Tex' Watson."

81. Frank Mickadeit, "On Victims' Day, Henry Nicholas Recalls Sister," *Orange County Register,* April 21, 2010, www.ocregister.com/articles/nicholas-245053-marsy-victims.html.

82. David Friedman and Jackie Robinson, "Rebutting the Presumption: An Empirical Analysis of Parole Deferrals Under Marsy's Law," *Stanford Law Review* 66, no. 183; Mickadeit, "On Victims' Day."

83. Mickadeit, "On Victims' Day."

84. Friedman and Robinson, "Rebutting the Presumption," 184.

85. Friedman and Robinson, "Rebutting the Presumption," 184.

86. California Penal Code § 3041.5(b)(2)(A)(2004), amended by id. § 3041.5(b)(3)(2008).

87. California Secretary of State, "Votes for and against November 4, 2008, State Ballot Measures," https://elections.cdn.sos.ca.gov/sov/2008-general/7_votes_for_against.pdf.

88. Shadia Merukeb spoke at a panel titled "Dangerousness, Risk, and Release" at the California Correctional Crisis Conference, March 21, 2009. Merukeb is cited in my summary of the panel: Hadar Aviram, "Dangerousness, Risk, and Release," *California Correctional Crisis* (blog), March 21, 2009, http://californiacorrectionscrisis.blogspot.com/2009/03/dangerousness-risk-and-release.html.

89. Laura L. Richardson, "Impact of Marsy's Law on Parole in California: An Empirical Study," July 7, 2011, SSRN, https://papers.ssrn.com/sol3/papers.cfm?abstract_id=1878594.

90. California Constitution Art. II, § 8 (d, f). Theoretically, under the California Constitution, all propositions are subject to the Single Subject Rule and can be challenged in court pre-election if their double focus might mislead voters to think

they are voting on one issue when they are in fact voting for more. However, the rule proves almost impossible to enforce: it turns out that whether something counts as one or more issues is subject to interpretation and often malleable to the judge's partisan views. See Mike Gilbert and Robert Cooter, "Constitutional Law and Economics," *Research Methods in Constitutional Law: A Handbook,* February 1, 2018, http://ssrn.com/abstract=3123253; John G. Matsusaka and Richard L. Hasen, "Aggressive Enforcement of the Single Subject Rule," *Election Law Journal* 9 (2010): 399, https://gould.usc.edu/assets/docs/Matsusaka_Aggressive_Enforcement.pdf.

91. Friedman and Robinson, "Rebutting the Presumption," 184.

92. Friedman and Robinson, "Rebutting the Presumption," 184–85.

93. California Penal Code. § 3041.5(b)(2)(A)(2004), amended by id. § 3041.5(b)(3)(2008); California Code Regs. Title 15, §2255 (2014); Kathryne M. Young, Debbie Mukamal and Thomas Fabre-Bulle, "Predicting Parole Grants: An Analysis of Suitability Hearings for California's Lifer Inmates," *Federal Sentencing Reporter* 28 (2016): 268–77.

94. Richardson, "Impact of Marsy's Law."

95. Richardson, "Impact of Marsy's Law."

96. "Charles Manson Family Member Susan Atkins' 23rd Psalm Death Bed Last Words, ABC News GMA," Daily Motion, September 13, 2011, https://www.dailymotion.com/video/x27em7r .

97. I discuss Atkins's last hearing in detail in chapter 6.

98. Statman, *Restless Souls,* 377.

99. Statman, *Restless Souls,* 380.

3. THE TRIUMPH OF HELTER SKELTER

Epigraph: *The Tibetan Book of the Dead,* 3rd ed., ed. W.Y. Evans-Wentz, trans. Lama Kazi Dawa-Sawdup (New York: Oxford University Press, 2000), 190.

1. I visited the museum on June 5, 2016. Visiting information is available at http://www.museumofdeath.net/nola.

2. Roland Barthes, "An Introduction to the Structural Analysis of Narrative," *New Literary History* 6, art. 2 (1975): 237.

3. William Labov, "Oral Narratives of Personal Experience" (written for *Cambridge Encyclopedia of the Language Sciences,* January 2011), https://www.ling.upenn.edu/~wlabov/Papers/FebOralNarPE.pdf.

4. Barthes, "An Introduction"; Seymour Chatman, "What Novels Can Do That Films Can't (and Vice Versa)," in *On Narrative,* ed. W.J.T. Mitchell (Chicago: University of Chicago Press, 1981); Jerome Bruner, "The Narrative Construction of Reality," *Critical Inquiry* 18, no. 1 (Autumn 1991): 1–21.

5. Anthony G. Amsterdam and Jerome Bruner, *Minding the Law* (Cambridge, MA: Harvard University Press, 2000); Roberto Franzosi, "Narrative Analysis—Or Why (and How) Sociologists Should Be Interested in Narrative," *Annual Review of Sociology* 24 (1998): 521.

6. Patricia Ewick and Susan Silbey, "Subversive Stories and Hegemonic Tales: Toward a Sociology of Narrative," *Law & Society Review* 29 (1995): 199; Bruner, "Narrative Construction of Reality," 11n5.

7. Ewick and Silbey, "Subversive Stories and Hegemonic Tales," 207. Some classic examples of legally strategic narratives are aggravating and mitigating narratives in death penalty cases. Benjamin Fleury-Steiner, *Jurors' Stories of Death: How America's Death Penalty Invests in Inequality* (Ann Arbor: University of Michigan Press, 2004); Paul Kaplan, *Murder Stories: Ideological Narratives in Capital Punishment* (Lanham, MD: Lexington Books, 2012).

8. Ewick and Silbey, "Subversive Stories and Hegemonic Tales," 213.

9. Ewick and Silbey, "Subversive Stories and Hegemonic Tales," 215–16.

10. Vincent Bugliosi, with Curt Gentry, *Helter Skelter: The True Story of the Manson Murders* (New York: W. W. Norton, 1974).

11. Bugliosi, *Helter Skelter,* 294.

12. Bugliosi, *Helter Skelter,* 294.

13. Ed Sanders, *The Family: The Story of Charles Manson's Dune Buggy Attack Battalion* (New York: Thunder's Mouth Press, 2002), 45.

14. Sanders, *The Family,* 46.

15. Sanders, *The Family,* 76.

16. Sanders, *The Family,* 79.

17. Sanders, *The Family,* 83.

18. Virginia Graham, *Manson, Sinatra and Me: A Hollywood Party Girl's Memoir and How She Helped Vincent Bugliosi with the Helter Skelter Case,* as told to Hal Jacques (British Columbia: CCB Publishing, 2015), 178.

19. Graham, *Manson, Sinatra and Me,* 181.

20. Graham, *Manson, Sinatra and Me,* 184.

21. Graham, *Manson, Sinatra and Me,* 188.

22. Alisa Statman, with Brie Tate, *Restless Souls: The Sharon Tate Family Account of Stardom, the Manson Murders, and a Crusade for Justice* (New York: HarperCollins, 2013), 123.

23. Statman, *Restless Souls,* 123.

24. Nicholas Schreck, *The Manson File* (New York: Amok Press, 1988); Nicholas Schreck, *The Manson File: Myth and Reality of an Outlaw Shaman,* expanded 2nd ed. (World Operations, 2011), 3.

25. Schreck, *Manson File,* 126.

26. Schreck, *The Manson File,* 141.

27. John McNamara, *Aquarius,* starring David Duchovny, TV series, NBC, 2015.

28. Karlene Faith, *The Long Prison Journey of Leslie Van Houten: Life beyond the Cult,* Northeastern Series on Gender, Crime, and Law (Boston: Northeastern University Press, 2001.

29. Faith, *The Long Prison Journey,* 9.

30. Faith, *The Long Prison Journey,* 79.

31. Faith, *The Long Prison Journey,* 16–17.

32. Peter Chiaramonte, *No Journey's End: My Tragic Romance with Ex-Manson Girl, Leslie Van Houten* (self-published, 2015). Faith, who was close to Van Houten at the time and is mentioned in Chiaramonte's book, mentions that Van Houten had many suitors over the years, but has no recollection of Chiaramonte. Interview with Karlene Faith, February 6, 2016.

33. Chiaramonte, *No Journey's End*, 62.

34. Chiaramonte, *No Journey's End*, 62.

35. Matthew W. Dunne, *A Cold War State of Mind: Brainwashing and Postwar American Society* (Amherst: University of Massachusetts Press, 2013).

36. Edward Hunter, *Brainwashing in Red China: The Calculated Destruction of Men's Minds* (New York: Vanguard Press, 1951).

37. *The Manchurian Candidate,* dir. John Frankenheimer, MGM, October 24, 1962; Richard Condon, *The Manchurian Candidate* (New York: Four Walls Eight Windows, 1959).

38. Michael Watts, *West of Eden: Communes and Utopia in Northern California* (Oakland, CA: PM Press, 2012).

39. Mendocino County Museum, Mendocino, California, https://www.mendocinocounty.org/ government/museum/.

40. Harrison Pope, *Voices from the Drug Culture* (Boston: Beacon Press, 1971).

41. John Harrigan, "Brainwashing in Small Groups, China or America: A Counselor's View," *Journal of Counseling and Development* 58, no. 1 (1979): 16–19.

42. State of California Senate Select Committee on Children and Youth, Hearing on the Impact of Cults on Today's Youth, California State University, Northridge, CA, August 24, 1974, California State Legislature Archives.

43. Dymally, California's first black assemblyman and then senator, went on to become California's lieutenant governor and then to represent Compton and other heavily black, low-income areas in Los Angeles in Congress. William Yardley, "Mervyn M. Dymally, Who Broke Racial Barriers in California, Dies at 86," *New York Times,* October 9, 2012, http://www.nytimes.com/2012/10/09/us/mervyn-dymally-who-broke-racial-barriers-in-california-dies-at-86.html.

44. Mervyn Dymally, California Senate Committee Hearing on Impact of Cults, introduction. The dilemmas Dymally presents here are not unique to the American context; for example, in 1981 the Italian Constitutional Court struck down the legal provision on brainwashing, which dated back to the fascist regime. The provision was deemed incompatible with a democratic constitution in light of the "imprecision and vagueness of the law provision" leading to "an impossibility to assign to it an objective content, that is consistent and rational; . . . show[ing] therefore an absolute arbitrariness of its practical application." The idea was that it was impossible to prove brainwashing as there was no shared and accepted definition of such practice. "Brainwashing Controversies: Full Text of the Italian Constitutional Court Decision of 1981 in English," http://www.cesnur.org/2005/brainwashing81.htm.

45. California Senate Committee Hearing on Impact of Cults, 5.

46. California Senate Committee Hearing on Impact of Cults, 14–15.

47. California Senate Committee Hearing on Impact of Cults, 20–21.

48. California Senate Committee Hearing on Impact of Cults, 25.

49. California Senate Committee Hearing on Impact of Cults, 53–54.

50. California Senate Committee Hearing on Impact of Cults, 55.

51. California Senate Committee Hearing on Impact of Cults, 61.

52. California Senate Committee Hearing on Impact of Cults, 134.

53. California Senate Committee Hearing on Impact of Cults, 134.

54. David G. Bromley and Anson D. Shupe, *Strange Gods: The Great American Cult Scare* (Boston: Beacon Press, 1981).

55. Joseph R. Gusfield, *Symbolic Crusade: Status Politics and the American Temperance Movement* (Champaign: University of Illinois Press, 1986).

56. Nachman Ben-Yehuda, "The European Witch Craze of the 14th to 17th Centuries: A Sociologist's Perspective," *American Journal of Sociology* 86, no. 1 (1980): 1–31.

57. Joseph R. Gusfield, *The Culture of Public Problems: Drinking-Driving and the Social Order* (Chicago: University of Chicago Press, Chicago, 1981).

58. Stanley Cohen, *Folk Devils and Moral Panics: The Creation of the Mods and the Rockers* (New York: Routledge, 2002).

59. Erich Goode and Nachman Ben-Yehuda, "Moral Panics: Culture, Politics, and Social Construction," *Annual Review of Sociology* 20 (1994); Ronald Burns and Charles Crawford, "School Shootings, the Media, and Public Fear: Ingredients for a Moral Panic," *Crime, Law and Social Change* 32, no. 2 (October 1999,):147–68.

60. Bromley and Shupe, *Strange Gods,* 92.

61. Anson D. Shupe and David G. Bromley, *The New Vigilantes: Deprogrammers, Anti-Cultists, and the New Religions* (New York: Sage Library of Social Research, 1980).

62. Bromley and Shupe, *Strange Gods,* 92.

63. Bromley and Shupe, *Strange Gods,* 65.

64. Shupe and Bromley, *New Vigilantes,* 30.

65. Shupe and Bromley, *New Vigilantes,* 246.

66. Shupe and Bromley, *New Vigilantes,* 30.

67. Bromley and Shupe, *Strange Gods,* 92.

68. "Religion in the Age of Aquarius: A Conversation with Harvey Cox and T. George Harris," in *Mystery, Magic and Miracle: Religion in a Post-Aquarian Age,* ed. Edward Heenan (Upper Saddle River, NJ: Prentice Hall, 1973), 15–29.

69. "Religion in the Age of Aquarius," 22.

70. Jacob Needleman, "Winds from the East: Youth and Counterculture," in Heenan, *Mystery, Magic and Miracle,* 78, citing Marcia Cavell, "Visions of a New Religion," *Saturday Review of Literature,* December 19, 1970, 13.

71. Edward Heenan, "Religion and the Occult: The Resurgence of Magic," in Heenan, *Mystery, Magic and Miracle,* 85.

72. Patrick Morrow, "*Sgt. Pepper, Hair,* and *Tommy:* Forerunners of the Jesus-Rock Movement," in Heenan, *Mystery, Magic and Miracle,* 155–67.

73. Ronald Enroth, *The Lure of Cults* (New York: Christian Herald Books, 1979), 14.

74. Emma Cline, *The Girls* (New York: Random House, 2016), 36.

75. Cline, *The Girls,* 120–21.

76. Cline, *The Girls,* 204.

77. Cline, *The Girls,* 277.

78. Jeffrey Melnick, *Creepy Crawling: Charles Manson and the Many Lives of America's Most Infamous Family* (New York: Arcade, 2018).

79. Runaway and Homeless Youth Act of 1974 (Title III of the Juvenile Justice and Delinquency Prevention Act, P.L. 93–415).

80. Melnick, *Creepy Crawling,* 88.

81. Jeff Guinn, *Manson: The Life and Times of Charles Manson* (New York: Simon & Schuster Paperbacks, 2012).

82. Charles Manson, *Manson in His Own Words,* as told to Nuel Emmons (New York: Grove Press, 1986).

83. Patt Morrison, "Remembering the Revolutionary, Hedonistic and Sexist 'Summer of Love,'" *Los Angeles Times,* June 14, 2017, http://www.latimes.com /opinion/op-ed/la-ol-patt-morrison-william-schnabel-1967-revolution-20170613- htmlstory.html.

84. Frederick H. Meyers, Alan J. Rose, and David E. Smith, "Incidents Involving the Haight-Ashbury Population and Some Uncommonly Used Drugs," *Journal of Psychedelic Drugs* 1, no. 2 (1968), http://www.tandfonline.com/doi/abs/10.1080/0279 1072.1968.10524531?journalCode=ujpd19; Roger C. Smith, "The World of the Haight- Ashbury Speed Freak," *Journal of Psychedelic Drugs* 2, no. 2 (1969), http://www .tandfonline.com/doi/abs/ 10.1080/02791072.1969.10524418?journalCode=ujpd19.

85. Nina Bai, "Born in the Summer of Love: The Haight-Ashbury Free Clinic Transformed Drug Addiction Treatment," Campus News, University of California San Francisco, June 7, 2017, https://www.ucsf.edu/news/2017/06/407286 /born-summer-love-haight-ashbury-free-clinic-transformed-drug-addiction- treatment.

86. Sanders, *The Family.*

87. Guinn, *Manson,* 95.

88. Guinn, *Manson,* 100.

89. Guinn, *Manson,* 80.

90. Guinn, *Manson,* 80.

91. Guinn, *Manson,* 221, 223.

92. The Manson-Melcher connection later served as a cautionary tale for the Los Angeles musicians and artists elevated to capitalist knighthood to stop associating with the countercultural "freaks." Melnick, *Creepy Crawling.*

93. Guinn, *Manson,* 227.

94. Guinn, *Manson,* 227.

95. Charles Watson, *Will You Die For Me? The Man Who Killed for Charles Manson Tells His Own Story,* as told to Chaplain Ray (New York: Fleming H. Rev- ell, 1978); Tex Watson, *Manson's Right-Hand Man Speaks Out* (Jackson, CA:

Abounding Love Ministries, 2003); Susan Atkins, *Child of Satan, Child of God: Her Own Story* (San Juan Capistrano, CA: Menelorelin Dorenay's Publishing, 2011); Susan Atkins-Whitehouse, *The Myth of Helter Skelter* (San Juan Capistrano, CA: Menelorelin Dorenay's Publishing, 2012).

96. Watson, *Manson's Right-Hand Man*, 205.

97. Watson, *Manson's Right-Hand Man*, 223.

98. Watson, *Manson's Right-Hand Man*, 275.

99. Atkins, *Child of Satan*, 116.

100. Atkins-Whitehouse, *The Myth of Helter Skelter*, xi, xiii.

101. Atkins-Whitehouse, *The Myth of Helter Skelter*, 57–59.

102. *Once Upon a Time in Hollywood*, dir. Quentin Tarantino, Columbia Pictures and Heyday Films, 2019.

103. Melnick, *Creepy Crawling*, 12–13.

4. REVISITING THE PAST

Notes on hearings transcripts. Pursuant to Penal Code 3042(b), the Board of Parole Hearings is required to record and transcribe parole hearings for inmates serving life sentences. The hearing transcripts are available to the public upon request from the California Department of Corrections and Rehabilitation (CDCR). Electronic versions of the newer, digitized transcripts are available free of charge; printed copies of the earlier transcripts are available for a fee, as detailed on the CDCR website: www.cdcr.ca.gov/bph/psh-transcript/. Some transcripts are available online from other sources, such as www.cielodrive.com.

The hearings transcripts do not include the first names of Board members, and a search has not uncovered historical records with their first names, so Board members are identified only by last name.

Epigraph: *The Tibetan Book of the Dead*, 3rd ed., ed. W.Y. Evans-Wentz, trans. Lama Kazi Dawa-Sawdup (New York: Oxford University Press, 2000), 242.

1. UnCommon Law, http://www.uncommonlaw.org.

2. Austin Sarat and William F. Felstiner, *Divorce Lawyers and Their Clients: Power and Meaning in the Legal Process* (New York: Oxford University Press, 1995).

3. Hadar Aviram, "How Law Thinks of Disobedience: Perceiving and Addressing Desertion and Conscientious Objection in Israeli Military Courts," *Law and Policy* 30 (2008): 277–301.

4. Malcolm Feeley, *The Process Is the Punishment: Handling Cases in a Lower Criminal Court* (New York: Russell Sage Foundation, 1979); Abraham Blumberg, "The Practice of Law as Confidence Game: Organization Cooptation of a Profession," *Law and Society Review* 1, no. 2 (June 1967).

5. Victor L. Shammas, "The Pains of Parole Hearings: California Lifers, Performative Disadvantage, and the Ideology of Insight," *Political and Legal Anthropology Review* 42, no. 2 (2019), 142–60, 152.

6. Shammas, "The Pains of Parole Hearings," 152.

7. Alessandro de Giorgi, "Back to Nothing: Prisoner Reentry and Neoliberal Neglect," *Social Justice* 44, no. 1 (2017): 83–120.

8. de Giorgi, "Back to Nothing," 88–89.

9. de Giorgi, "Back to Nothing," 94.

10. de Giorgi, "Back to Nothing," 107.

11. Charles Carbone, *Parole Matters,* Summer 2009, 2, https://www.charlescarbone.com/parole-matters-summer-2009.

12. Nick Smith, *I Was Wrong: The Meanings of Apologies* (New York: Cambridge University Press, 2008.

13. Richard Weisman, *Showing Remorse: Law and the Social Control of Emotion* (London and New York: Routledge, 2014).

14. Albeit insufficient in itself for parole denial: *In re Lawrence,* 44 Cal. 4th 1181 (2008).

15. The lack of reasoning for a conviction verdict is, of course, an issue in post-conviction judicial review as well. When criminal defendants appeal their conviction, they cannot point directly to an error in jury decision-making, as the deliberations are a "black box." Instead, they typically point to constitutional violations in the investigation or to problems in the jury instructions given by the judge and invite the appellate court to deduce from the magnitude of the error that, but for the error, no rational jury would have convicted them.

16. Initial Parole Consideration Hearing, Patricia Krenwinkel, State of California Community Release Board, 1978, 46.

17. Parole Board Hearing, Charles Manson, State of California Community Release Board, 1980, 6.

18. Initial Parole Consideration Hearing, Susan Atkins, State of California Community Release Board, 1978, 12.

19. Initial Parole Consideration Hearing, Atkins, 1978, 31.

20. Initial Parole Consideration Hearing, Atkins, 1978, 14.

21. Initial Parole Consideration Hearing, Atkins, 1978, 19.

22. Initial Parole Consideration Hearing, Atkins, 1978, 60–61.

23. Initial Parole Consideration Hearing, Atkins, 1978, 64.

24. Initial Parole Consideration Hearing, Atkins, 1978, 66.

25. Parole Board Hearing, Susan Atkins, State of California Community Release Board, 1979, 33.

26. Parole Board Hearing, Atkins, 1979, 33.

27. Parole Board Hearing, Susan Atkins, State of California Community Release Board, 2005, 15.

28. Parole Board Hearing, Atkins, 2005, 79.

29. Life Term Parole Consideration Hearing, Robert Kenneth Beausoleil, State of California Community Release Board, August 15, 1978, 5.

30. Life Term Parole Consideration Hearing, Beausoleil, 1978, 6.

31. Life Term Parole Consideration Hearing, Beausoleil, 1978, 7.

32. Life Term Parole Consideration Hearing, Beausoleil, 1978, 8.

33. Life Term Parole Consideration Hearing, Beausoleil, 1978, 8–9.

34. Life Term Parole Consideration Hearing, Beausoleil, 1978, 10–15.

35. Life Term Parole Consideration Hearing, Beausoleil, 1978, 19.

36. Life Term Parole Consideration Hearing, Beausoleil, 1978, 17.

37. Life Term Parole Consideration Hearing, Robert Kenneth Beausoleil, State of California Community Release Board, 1979, 16.

38. Life Term Parole Consideration Hearing, Beausoleil, 1979, 23.

39. Life Term Parole Consideration Hearing, Robert Kenneth Beausoleil, State of California Community Release Board, 1980, 58.

40. Life Term Parole Consideration Hearing, Beausoleil, 1980, 12–13, 18.

41. Life Term Parole Consideration Hearing, Robert Kenneth Beausoleil, State of California Community Release Board, 1981, 12.

42. Life Term Parole Consideration Hearing, Beausoleil, 1981, 18.

43. Life Term Parole Consideration Hearing, Beausoleil, 1981, 20.

44. Life Term Parole Consideration Hearing, Beausoleil, 1981, 23.

45. Life Term Parole Consideration Hearing, Robert Kenneth Beausoleil, State of California Community Release Board, 1983, 4.

46. Life Term Parole Consideration Hearing, Robert Kenneth Beausoleil, State of California Community Release Board, 1984, 30–31.

47. Life Term Parole Consideration Hearing, Beausoleil, 1984, 32.

48. Life Term Parole Consideration Hearing, Robert Kenneth Beausoleil, State of California Community Release Board, 1985, 19.

49. Life Term Parole Consideration Hearing, Robert Kenneth Beausoleil, State of California Community Release Board, 1992, 6.

50. Life Term Parole Consideration Hearing, Beausoleil, 1992, 16–17.

51. Life Term Parole Consideration Hearing, Beausoleil, 1992, 55.

52. Life Term Parole Consideration Hearing, Beausoleil, 1992, 68.

53. Life Term Parole Consideration Hearing, Robert Kenneth Beausoleil, State of California Community Release Board, 2005, 30.

54. Parole Board Hearing, Bruce Davis, State of California Community Release Board, 1982, 24.

55. Parole Board Hearing, Bruce Davis, State of California Community Release Board, 1984, 20.

56. Parole Board Hearing, Bruce Davis, State of California Community Release Board, 1985, 8–9.

57. Parole Board Hearing, Davis, 1985, 80.

58. Parole Board Hearing, Patricia Krenwinkel, State of California Community Release Board, 2011, 144.

59. *In re* Rico, 171 Cal. App. 4th 659 (2009).

60. Parole Board Hearing, Bruce Davis, State of California Community Release Board, 1978, 40.

61. Parole Board Hearing, Davis, 1978, 62.

62. Parole Board Hearing, Davis, 1982, 54–55.

63. Parole Board Hearing, Bruce Davis, State of California Community Release Board, 1986, 26–27.

64. Initial Parole Consideration Hearing, Krenwinkel, 1978, 59.

65. Life Term Parole Consideration Hearing, Beausoleil, 1980, 40.

66. Life Term Parole Consideration Hearing, Beausoleil, 1978, 26–27.

67. Life Term Parole Consideration Hearing, Beausoleil, 1980, 42–43.

68. Life Term Parole Consideration Hearing, Beausoleil, 1978, 27.

69. Life Term Parole Consideration Hearing, Beausoleil, 1983, 22–25.

70. Parole Board Hearing, Bruce Davis, State of California Community Release Board, 1981, 7.

71. Parole Board Hearing, Davis, 1981, 39–40.

72. Parole Board Hearing, Susan Atkins, State of California Community Release Board, 1985, 206.

73. Parole Board Hearing, Susan Atkins, State of California Community Release Board, 1988, 122.

74. Life Term Parole Consideration Hearing, Beausoleil, 1984, 72.

75. Parole Board Hearing, Davis, 1984, 52–53.

76. Life Term Parole Consideration Hearing, Beausoleil, 1992, 91.

77. Life Term Parole Consideration Hearing, Beausoleil, 1992, 103.

78. Parole Board Hearing, Patricia Krenwinkel, State of California Board of Parole Hearings, 1980, 27.

79. Parole Board Hearing, Krenwinkel, 1980, 42.

80. Parole Board Hearing, Patricia Krenwinkel, State of California Board of Parole Hearings, 1988, 28.

81. Life Term Parole Consideration Hearing, Robert Kenneth Beausoleil, State of California Community Release Board, 1997, 9.

82. Subsequent Parole Consideration Hearing, Robert Kenneth Beausoleil, State of California Board of Parole Hearings, 2005, 40.

83. Subsequent Parole Consideration Hearing, Beausoleil, 2005, 42.

84. Subsequent Parole Consideration Hearing, Robert Kenneth Beausoleil, State of California Board of Parole Hearings, 2008, 21.

85. Subsequent Parole Consideration Hearing, Robert Kenneth Beausoleil, State of California Board of Parole Hearings, 2010, 164.

86. Shammas, "Pains of Imprisonment," 15.

87. Subsequent Parole Consideration Hearing, Beausoleil, 2010, 168.

88. *In re* Wen Lee, 143 Cal. App.4th 1400 (2006).

89. *In re* Barker, 151 Cal. App.4th 346 (2007).

90. *In re* McDonald, 189 Cal. App.4th 1008 (2010).

91. *In re* Jackson, 193 Cal. App.4th 1376 (2011).

92. *In re* Twinn, 190 Cal. App.4th 447 (2010).

93. *In re* Rodriguez, 193 Cal. App.4th 85 (2011).

94. *In re* Lewis, 172 Cal. App. 4th 13 (2009).

95. *In re* Rozzo, 172 Cal. App. 4th 40 (2009).

96. *In re* Singler, 169 Cal. App. 4th 1227 (2008).

97. Subsequent Parole Consideration Hearing, Leslie Van Houten, State of California Board of Parole Hearings, 2013, 263–64.

98. Martin Kasindorf, "Keeping Manson Behind Bars: Prosecutor Stephen Kay Still Fights to Make Sure the Evil of the Tate-LaBianca Murders Is Never Forgotten," *Los Angeles Times,* May 14, 1989, http://articles.latimes.com/1989-05-14/magazine/tm-13_1_stephen-kay-sharon-tate-parole.

99. Initial Parole Consideration Hearing, Krenwinkel, 1978, 10.

100. Initial Parole Consideration Hearing, Krenwinkel, 1978, 12.

101. Initial Parole Consideration Hearing, Krenwinkel, 1978, 29–30.

102. Parole Board Hearing, Patricia Krenwinkel, State of California Community Release Board, 1979, 45.

103. Parole Board Hearing, Patricia Krenwinkel, State of California Community Release Board, 1981, 32.

104. Parole Board Hearing, Patricia Krenwinkel, 1989, State of California Community Release Board, 76.

105. Initial Parole Consideration Hearing, Krenwinkel, 1978, 31.

106. Initial Parole Consideration Hearing, Charles Manson, State of California Community Release Board, 1978, 9–10.

107. Initial Parole Consideration Hearing, Manson, 1978, 18–19.

108. Parole Board Hearing, Krenwinkel, 1979, 11.

109. Parole Board Hearing, Krenwinkel, 1980, 8.

110. Parole Board Hearing, Krenwinkel, 1989, 7.

111. Life Term Parole Consideration Hearing, Beausoleil, 1979, 5.

112. Life Term Parole Consideration Hearing, Beausoleil, 1984, 47.

113. Life Term Parole Consideration Hearing, Beausoleil, 1985, 16.

114. Parole Board Hearing, Charles Manson, State of California Community Release Board, 1986, 24–25.

115. Life Term Parole Consideration Hearing, Beausoleil, 1983, 72.

116. Life Term Parole Consideration Hearing, Beausoleil, 1985, 26.

117. Life Term Parole Consideration Hearing, Beausoleil, 1983, 69.

118. Life Term Parole Consideration Hearing, Beausoleil, 1982, 74.

119. Parole Board Hearing, Atkins, 2005, 84–85.

120. Parole Board Hearing, Atkins, 2005, 85–86.

121. Parole Board Hearing, Susan Atkins, State of California Board of Parole Hearings, 2009, 4.

122. California Penal Code § 3043, as amended 1982.

123. Life Term Parole Consideration Hearing, Beausoleil, 1981, 26.

124. California Penal Code § 3041, as amended 2008.

125. Parole Board Hearing, Leslie Van Houten, State of California Community Release Board, 2002, 2.

126. Parole Board Hearing, Leslie Van Houten, State of California Board of Parole Hearings, 2006, 2; Parole Board Hearing, Van Houten, 2007, 2.

127. Parole Board Hearing, Leslie Van Houten, State of California Board of Parole Hearings, 2010, 2.

128. Subsequent Parole Consideration Hearing, Van Houten, 2013, 2.

129. Parole Board Hearing, Atkins, 2009, 12.

130. Parole Board Hearing, Bruce Davis, State of California Board of Parole Hearings, 2012, 10–11.

131. Paul Kaplan, *Murder Stories: Ideological Narratives in Capital Punishment,* Issues in Crime and Punishment (New York: Lexington Books, 2012).

132. Parole Board Hearing, Krenwinkel, 2011, 40.

133. Parole Board Hearing, Charles Watson, State of California Board of Parole Hearings, 2011, 121.

134. Parole Board Hearing, Watson, 2011, 118.

135. Parole Board Hearing, Watson, 2011, 129–30.

136. Laura Santhanam, "Does the Death Penalty Bring Closure to a Victim's Family?," *Newshour,* PBS, April 25, 2017, https://www.pbs.org/newshour/nation/death-penalty-bring-closure-victims-family

137. ACLU, "Voices from California Crime Victims for Alternatives to the Death Penalty," January 2008, https://www.aclunc.org/sites/default/files/voices_from_california_crime_victims_for_alternatives_to_the_death_penalty.pdf

138. Parole Board Hearing, Watson, 2011, 131.

139. W. N. Neill, "The Professional Pricker and His Test for Witchcraft," *Scottish Historical Review* 19, no. 75 (April 1922), https://www.jstor.org/stable/25519 4f42?seq=1#page_scan_tab_contents; Russel Zguta, "The Ordeal by Water (Swimming of Witches) in the East Slavic World," *Slavic Review* 36, no. 2 (June 1977), https://www.cambridge.org/core/journals/slavic-review/article/ordeal-by-water-swimming-of-witches-in-the-east-slavic-world/162145AE9F57EC23F3D5E46D8D3A8831.

140. Alisa Statman, *Restless Souls: The Sharon Tate Family Account of Stardom, the Manson Murders, and a Crusade for Justice* (New York: HarperCollins, 2013), 263.

141. Statman, *Restless Souls,* 273.

142. Josh Page, *The Toughest Beat: Politics, Punishment, and the Prison Officer's Union in California,* Studies of Crime and Public Policy (New York: Oxford University Press, 2011).

143. The City of Sacramento is implementing Advance Peace, a program that provides young people at the heart of the gun violence scene with stipends, mentorships, and opportunities; despite the fact that the program ostensibly benefits perpetrators, it enjoys support from victims' families, who believe it will lead to an overall reduction of violence in the city. For more information on Advance Peace, which has also been successfully implemented in the City of Richmond, see https://www.advancepeace.org/.

144. Statman, *Restless Souls,* 232.

145. Statman, *Restless Souls,* 377.

146. California Penal Code § 3014.5 (a)(6), as amended (2008).

147. Parole Board Hearing, Krenwinkel, 2011, 124–25.

148. Parole Board Hearing, Krenwinkel, 2011, 146.

149. Nick Smith, *Justice through Apologies: Remorse, Reform, and Punishment* (Cambridge, UK: Cambridge University Press, 2014).

150. Kathryne M. Young, "Parole Hearings and Victims' Rights: Implementation, Ambiguity, and Reform," *Connecticut Law Review* 49 (2016): 431–98.

151. Young, "Parole Hearings and Victims' Rights," 472.

152. Young, "Parole Hearings and Victims' Rights," 473.

153. Robert Weisberg, Debbie A. Mukamal, and Jordan D. Segall, *Life in Limbo: Parole Release for Prisoners Serving Life Sentences with the Possibility of Parole in California* (Stanford, CA: Stanford Criminal Justice Center, 2011), 12.

154. Young, "Parole Hearings and Victims' Rights," 471.

155. Young, "Parole Hearings and Victims' Rights," 457.

156. Young, "Parole Hearings and Victims' Rights," 459–60.

157. Young, "Parole Hearings and Victims' Rights," 462.

158. Young, "Parole Hearings and Victims' Rights," 476.

159. This number excludes "security" prisoners, such as Palestinians doing time for politically motivated offenses, so the actual parole prospects are worse.

160. W. David Ball, "Heinous, Atrocious, and Cruel: Apprendi, Indeterminate Sentencing, and the Meaning of Punishment," *Columbia Law Review* 109 (June 2009): 893–972, at Santa Clara Digital Commons, https://digitalcommons.law.scu.edu/facpubs/16/.

5. REINVENTING THE PRESENT

Epigraph: *The Tibetan Book of the Dead,* 3rd ed., ed. W.Y. Evans-Wentz, trans. Lama Kazi Dawa-Sawdup (New York: Oxford University Press, 2000), 252.

1. Alessandro de Giorgi, "Reentry to Nothing: Urban Survival after Mass Incarceration," *Social Justice* (blog), May 24, 2014, http://www.socialjusticejournal.org/reentry-to-nothing-urban-survival-after-mass-incarceration/. See chapter 4, under "The Courtroom Transcript Becomes King: The Crystallization of the Factual Past".

2. OPEC Staff, "A Decade Ago, A New Name Affirmed Mission of CDCR," *Inside CDCR*, August 28, 2015, https://www.insidecdcr.ca.gov/2015/08/a-decade-ago-a-new-name-affirmed-mission-of-cdcr/.

3. Robert Martinson, "What Works? Questions and Answers about Prison Reform," *The Public Interest* (Spring 1974).

4. Michelle S. Phelps, "Rehabilitation in the Punitive Era: The Gap between Rhetoric and Reality in U.S. Prison Programs," *Law and Society Review* 45, no. 1 (March 16, 2011), https://onlinelibrary.wiley.com/doi/abs/10.1111/ j.1540–5893.2011.00427.x.

5. Joan Petersilia, "When Prisoners Return to the Community: Political, Economic, and Social Consequences," Papers from the Executive Sessions on Sentencing and Corrections, National Institute of Justice, *Sentencing and Corrections: Issues*

for the 21st Century 9 (November 2000): 1–7, http://www.nationaltasc.org/wp-content/uploads/2012/11/When-Prisoners-Return-to-the-Community-Political-Economic-and-Social-Consequences-NIJ.pdf; Joan Petersilia, "Prisoner Reentry: Public Safety and Reintegration Challenges," *Prison Journal* 81, no. 3 (September 1, 2001): 360–75, Pennsylvania Prison Society, http://journals.sagepub.com/doi/abs/10.1177/0032885501081003004.

6. Jonathan Simon, *Mass Incarceration on Trial: A Remarkable Court Decision and the Future of Prisons in America* (New York: New Press, 2014), 133.

7. Valerie Jenness and Kitty Calavita, *Appealing to Justice: Prisoner Grievances, Rights, and Carceral Logic* (Oakland: University of California Press, 2014).

8. These psychiatric assessments will be discussed in chapter 6, under "Risk Assessment: The Psychiatric Report as a Panacea."

9. Parole Board Hearing, Patricia Krenwinkel, State of California Community Release Board, 1981, 5–6.

10. Jenness and Calavita, *Appealing to Justice*.

11. Erving Goffman, "Characteristics of Total Institutions" in *Crime, Law, and Society,* ed. Abraham S. Goldstein and Joseph Goldstein (New York: Free Press, 1971), 239–73, 245.

12. Victor Shammas, "The Perils of Parole Hearings: California Lifers, Performative Disadvantage, and the Ideology of Insight," *Political and Legal Anthropology Review* 42, no. 1, 142–60 (2019).

13. *In re* Reed, 171 Cal. App. 4th 1071 (2009).

14. Kathryne M. Young, Debbie A. Mukamal, and Thomas Favre-Bulle, "Predicting Parole Grants: An Analysis of Suitability Hearings for California's Lifer Inmates," *Federal Sentencing Reporter* 28, no. 4 (April 2016): 273, http://www.kathrynemyoung.com/uploads/2/4/8/6/2486969/fsr2804_07_young.pdf.

15. Parole Board Hearing, Susan Atkins, State of California Community Release Board, 2005, 57–58.

16. Parole Board Hearing, Leslie Van Houten, State of California Community Release Board, 1979, 48.

17. Parole Board Hearing, Van Houten, 1979, 54.

18. Life Term Parole Consideration Hearing, Robert Kenneth Beausoleil, State of California Community Release Board, August 15, 1978, 32.

19. Life Term Parole Consideration Hearing, Beausoleil, 1978, 3.

20. Life Term Parole Consideration Hearing, Beausoleil, 1978, 55.

21. Life Term Parole Consideration Hearing, Robert Kenneth Beausoleil, State of California Community Release Board, 1979, 80.

22. Life Term Parole Consideration Hearing, Beausoleil, 1979, 39.

23. Life Term Parole Consideration Hearing, Beausoleil, 1979, 43.

24. Life Term Parole Consideration Hearing, Robert Kenneth Beausoleil, State of California Community Release Board, 1980, 26.

25. Life Term Parole Consideration Hearing, Robert Kenneth Beausoleil, State of California Community Release Board, 1982, 41.

26. Brown v. Plata 563 U.S. 493 (2010).

27. Simon, *Mass Incarceration on Trial.*

28. Megan Comfort, *Doing Time Together: Love and Family in the Shadow of the Prison* (Chicago: University of Chicago Press, 2007).

29. Jay Borchert, "Controlling Consensual Sex Among Prisoners," *Law and Social Inquiry,* 41, no. 3 (August 15, 2016): 595–615. When same-sex marriage was legalized in California in 2013, CDCR released guidelines according to which the prison could now authorize and perform same-sex weddings between an inmate and a visitor, but not between inmates. Rina Palta, "California Prisons Extend Same Sex Marriage Rights to Inmates," Southern California Public Radio via KALW News, September 4, 2013, https://www.scpr.org/news/2013/09/04/39059/california-prisons-extend-same-sex-marriage-rights/.

30. Parole Board Hearing, Bruce Davis, State of California Community Release Board, 1980, 51.

31. Life Term Parole Consideration Hearing, Beausoleil, 1979, 66.

32. Life Term Parole Consideration Hearing, Beausoleil, 1980, 27.

33. Life Term Parole Consideration Hearing, Robert Kenneth Beausoleil, State of California Community Release Board, 1985, 30.

34. Life Term Parole Consideration Hearing, Beausoleil, 1985, 41.

35. Life Term Parole Consideration Hearing, Beausoleil, 1985, 34–35.

36. Life Term Parole Consideration Hearing, Beausoleil, 1985, 41.

37. Life Term Parole Consideration Hearing, Robert Kenneth Beausoleil, State of California Community Release Board, 2005, 90–91.

38. Life Term Parole Consideration Hearing, Beausoleil, 2005, 100.

39. Life Term Parole Consideration Hearing, Beausoleil, 2005, 137–38.

40. Initial Parole Consideration Hearing, Patricia Krenwinkel, State of California Community Release Board, 1978, 65.

41. Parole Board Hearing, Patricia Krenwinkel, State of California Board of Parole Hearings, 1980, 18–19.

42. Parole Board Hearing, Susan Atkins, State of California Community Release Board, 1985, 200.

43. Parole Board Hearing, Leslie Van Houten, State of California Community Release Board, 1982, 74–75.

44. Van Houten, 1982, 77.

45. Van Houten, 1982, 78–80.

46. Van Houten, 1982, 99.

47. Ruth Wilson Gilmore, *Golden Gulag: Prisons, Surplus, Crisis, and Opposition in Globalizing California* (Berkeley: University of California Press, 2006.

48. Petersilia, "When Prisoners Return to the Community," 4.

49. Parole Board Hearing, Krenwinkel, 1981, 14.

50. Life Term Parole Consideration Hearing, Robert Kenneth Beausoleil, State of California Community Release Board, 1982, 103–4.

51. Life Term Parole Consideration Hearing, Beausoleil, 1982, 105.

52. Parole Board Hearing, Charles Manson, State of California Community Release Board, 1979, 15.

53. Parole Board Hearing, Manson, 1979, 41.

54. Parole Board Hearing, Patricia Krenwinkel, State of California Community Release Board, 1982, 37.

55. Parole Board Hearing, Patricia Krenwinkel, State of California Community Release Board, 1989, 23.

56. Author conversations with Kimberly Richman, cofounder of Alliance for C.H.A.N.G.E, July 23 and August 4, 2018.

57. Shammas, "The Perils of Parole Hearings," 6.

58. Young, Mukamal, and Favre-Bulle, "Predicting Parole Grants," 272.

59. Jake Flanagin, "The Surprising Failures of 12 Steps: How a Pseudoscientific, Religious Organization Birthed the Most Trusted Method of Addiction Treatment," *Atlantic,* March 25, 2014, https://www.theatlantic.com/health/archive/2014/03/the-surprising-failures-of-12-steps/284616/.

60. Maia Szalavitz, "After 75 Years of Alcoholics Anonymous, It's Time to Admit We Have a Problem: Challenging the 12-Step Hegemony," *Pacific Standard,* February 10, 2014, https://psmag.com/social-justice/75-years-alcoholics-anonymous-time-admit-problem-74268.

61. Maia Szalavitz, *Unbroken Brain: A Revolutionary New Way of Understanding Addiction* (New York: Picador, 2017).

62. For more about the unrealistic expectation that addicts completely cease using the addictive substance, see Andrew Tatarsky, *Harm Reduction Psychotherapy: A New Treatment for Drug and Alcohol Problems* (Plymouth, UK: Jason Aronson, 2007).

63. Francesca Alexander and Michele Rollins, "Alcoholics Anonymous: The Unseen Cult," *California Sociologist* 7, no. 1 (1984): 33–48.

64. Redonna Chandler, Bennett W. Fletcher, and Nora D. Volkow, "Treating Drug Abuse and Addiction in the Criminal Justice System: Improving Public Health and Safety," *PubMed Central* 301, no. 2 (2009): 183–90, https://www.ncbi.nlm.nih.gov/pmc/articles/PMC2681083/.

65. Parole Board Hearing, Krenwinkel, 1980, 23.

66. Parole Board Hearing, Krenwinkel, 1982, 41.

67. Parole Board Hearing, Robert Kenneth Beausoleil, State of California Community Release Board, 1993, 47.

68. Ryan Schroeder and John F. Frana, "Spirituality and Religion, Emotional Coping, and Criminal Desistance: A Qualitative Study of Men Undergoing Change," *Sociological Spectrum* 29, no. 6 (2009): 718–41.

69. Todd Clear, Bruce Stout, Harry Dammer, Linda Kelly, Patricia Hardyman, and Carol Shapiro, "Does Involvement in Religion Help Prisoners Adjust to Prison?," *NCCD Focus,* November 1992, https://www.issuelab.org/resources/3385/3385.pdf; Jason Sexton, "Greystone Chapel: Finding Freedom inside Folsom Prison's Walls," *Boom: A Journal of California* 6, no. 2 (2016): 104–10.

70. Harry R. Dammer, "The Reasons for Religious Involvement in the Correctional Environment," *Journal of Offender Rehabilitation* 35, no. 3–4 (2002): 35–58.

71. Jason Sexton, "Toward a Prison Theology of California's *Ecclesia* Incarcerate," *Theology* 118, no. 2 (2015): 83–9.

72. Eric Cummins, *The Rise and Fall of California's Radical Prison Movement* (Stanford, CA: Stanford University Press, 1994); Dan Berger, *Captive Nation: Black Prison Organizing in the Civil Rights Era* (Chapel Hill: University of North Carolina Press, 2014).

73. James Queally, "Manson Family Member Bruce Davis Found Eligible for Parole," *Los Angeles Times,* August 27, 2015, http://www.latimes.com/local/lanow/la-me-ln-manson-bruce-davis-20150827-story.html.

74. Susan Atkins, *Child of Satan, Child of God: Her Own Story* (Logos International, 1978); Charles "Tex" Watson, *Manson's Right-Hand Man Speaks Out* (Jackson, CA: Abounding Love Ministries, 2003).

75. James M. Ault, *Spirit and Flesh: Life in a Fundamentalist Baptist Church* (New York: Vintage Books, 2004).

76. Michael Simons, "Born Again on Death Row: Retribution, Remorse, and Religion," *Catholic Lawyer* 43 (2005): 311–38; Steven Tipton, *Getting Saved from the Sixties: Moral Meaning in Conversion and Cultural Chance* (Berkeley: University of California Press, 1982).

77. Tanya Erzen, "Testimonial Politics: The Christian Right's Faith-Based Approach to Marriage and Imprisonment," *American Quarterly* 59, no. 3 (2007): 991–1015.

78. Parole Board Hearing, Bruce Davis, State of California Community Release Board, 1978, 45–46.

79. Parole Board Hearing, Bruce Davis, State of California Community Release Board, 1981, 22.

80. Parole Board Hearing, Davis, 1981, 23.

81. Parole Board Hearing, Davis, 1981, 28.

82. Parole Board Hearing, Davis, 1981, 28–29.

83. Parole Board Hearing, Davis, 1981, 42–43.

84. Parole Board Hearing, Davis, 1981, 43–44.

85. Parole Board Hearing, Davis, 1981, 44–45.

86. Parole Board Hearing, Bruce Davis, State of California Community Release Board, 1982, 35–36.

87. Parole Board Hearing, Charles Watson, State of California Community Release Board, 1978, 25–26.

88. Parole Board Hearing, Watson, 1978, 59–60.

89. Parole Board Hearing, Watson, 1978, 61–62.

90. Parole Board Hearing, Susan Atkins, State of California Community Release Board, 1978, 88.

91. Parole Board Hearing, Atkins, 1978, 84.

92. Parole Board Hearing, Atkins, 1978, 99.

93. Parole Board Hearing, Atkins, 1978, 103.

94. Parole Board Hearing, Atkins, 1978, 104.

95. "Go therefore and make disciples of all the nations, baptizing them in the name of the Father and of the Son and of the Holy Spirit, teaching them to observe all things that I have commanded you; and lo, I am with you always, even to the end of the age," Matthew 28:19–20.

96. This is arguably not unique to Evangelicals. In *Confessions,* St. Augustine catalogues a list of his bad deeds prior to salvation: "And thus, with the flash of a trembling glance, it [my mind] arrived at that which is. And then I saw Thy invisible things understood by the things that are made. But I was not able to fix my gaze thereon; and my infirmity being beaten back, I was thrown again on my accustomed habits, carrying along with me naught but a loving memory thereof, and an appetite for what I had, as it were, smelt the odour of, but was not yet able to eat." *Confessions of St. Augustine,* VII, 17, trans. Joseph Green Pilkington (Altenmünster: Jazzybee Verlag, 2012) 88.

97. David Wilkerson, *The Cross and the Switchblade* (New York: Jove Books, 1977).

98. Shammas, "The Perils of Parole Hearings," 12.

99. Parole Board Hearing, Krenwinkel, 1989, 22.

100. Parole Board Hearing, Van Houten, 1979, 57.

101. Life Term Parole Consideration Hearing, Beausoleil, 1978, 38–39.

102. *Lucifer Rising,* dir. Kenneth Anger, Puck Film Productions, 1972, https://youtu.be/aKHWrwi6YaI. Beausoleil stars in the movie and in a shorter predecessor, *Invocation of My Demon Brother* (the footage was filmed before his arrest), and he composed the music behind bars after a fallout between Anger and Led Zeppelin's Jimmy Page, who had originally been announced as the film's composer.

103. Life Term Parole Consideration Hearing, Beausoleil, 1978, 40.

104. Life Term Parole Consideration Hearing, Beausoleil, 1978, 57.

105. Life Term Parole Consideration Hearing, Beausoleil, 1979, 68.

106. Life Term Parole Consideration Hearing, Beausoleil, 1979, 69.

107. Life Term Parole Consideration Hearing, Beausoleil, 1980, 21.

108. Life Term Parole Consideration Hearing, Beausoleil, 1980, 47.

109. Life Term Parole Consideration Hearing, Beausoleil, 1980, 51–52.

110. Life Term Parole Consideration Hearing, Beausoleil, 1980, 69.

111. Life Term Parole Consideration Hearing, Robert Kenneth Beausoleil, State of California Community Release Board, 1983, 30.

112. Life Term Parole Consideration Hearing, Beausoleil, 1985, 52.

113. Subsequent Parole Consideration Hearing, Robert Kenneth Beausoleil, State of California Board of Parole Hearings, 2008, 30.

114. Parole Board Hearing, Van Houten, 1979, 6.

115. Parole Board Hearing, Patricia Krenwinkel, State of California Community Release Board, 1985, 9–10.

116. Shammas, "The Perils of Parole," 12.

117. Parole Consideration Hearing, Charles Watson, State of California Parole Board, 2006, 51.

118. Parole Consideration Hearing, Charles Watson, State of California Parole Board, 2011, 20.

119. Parole Board Hearing, Patricia Krenwinkel, State of California Community Release Board, 2011, 102–3.

120. Meredith Rountree, "'I'll Make Them Shoot Me': Accounts of Death Row Prisoners Advocating for Execution," *Law & Society Review* 46, no. 3 (2012): 589–622.

121. Parole Board Hearing, Charles Manson, State of California Community Release Board, 1978, 35–36.

122. Parole Board Hearing, Manson, 1978, 109.

123. Parole Board Hearing, Charles Manson, State of California Community Release Board, 1979, 6.

124. Parole Board Hearing, Charles Manson, State of California Community Release Board, 1980, 76.

125. Parole Board Hearing, Charles Manson, State of California Community Release Board, 1981, 4.

126. Parole Board Hearing, Charles Manson, State of California Community Release Board, 1986, 12.

127. Parole Board Hearing, Manson, 1986, 80.

128. Parole Board Hearing, Charles Manson, State of California Community Release Board, 2002, 1.

129. Parole Board Hearing, Manson, 2002, 2.

130. Parole Board Hearing, Manson, 2002, 7.

131. Parole Board Hearing, Manson, 2002, 14–15.

132. Parole Board Hearing, Manson, 2002, 19.

133. Parole Board Hearing, Manson, 2002, 20.

134. Parole Board Hearing, Manson, 2002, 30.

135. Parole Board Hearing, Manson, 2002, 30.

136. Parole Board Hearing, Manson, 2002, 36.

137. Parole Board Hearing, Charles Manson, State of California Board of Parole Hearings, 2007, 6.

138. Parole Board Hearing, Manson, 2007, 17–18.

139. Parole Board Hearing, Manson, 2007, 20–21.

140. Parole Board Hearing, Manson, 2007, 29.

141. Parole Board Hearing, Manson, 2007, 34–35.

142. Lewis explains that Manson had refused to come out of the cell and discuss the case with him at his visit, thirty days prior to the hearing. Parole Board Hearing, Charles Manson, State of California Board of Parole Hearings, 2012, 8–9.

143. Parole Board Hearing, Manson, 2012, 7.

144. Parole Board Hearing, Manson, 2012, 11.

145. Gilman v. Davis, Case No. CIV. S-05–830 LKK/GGH (E.D. Cal. March 2, 2010).

146. Parole Board Hearing, Manson, 2012, 17.

147. Parole Board Hearing, Manson, 2012, 18.

148. Parole Board Hearing, Manson, 2012, 21.

149. Parole Board Hearing, Manson, 2012, 21–22.

150. Parole Board Hearing, Manson, 2012, 34.

151. Parole Board Hearing, Manson, 2012, 35–36.

152. Parole Board Hearing, Manson, 2012, 42.

6. REIMAGINING THE FUTURE

Epigraph: *The Tibetan Book of the Dead,* 3rd ed., ed. W. Y. Evans-Wentz, trans. Lama Kazi Dawa-Sawdup (New York: Oxford University Press, 2000), 254.

1. Samuel Bercholz, *A Guided Tour of Hell: A Graphic Memoir,* ill. Pema Namdol Thaye (Boulder, CO: Shambhala, 2016); Pema Namdol Thaye, *A Guided Tour of Hell,* Asian Art Museum, San Francisco, California, April 20–September 16, 2018, http://www.asianart.org/exhibitions/guided-tour-of-hell.

2. See, generally, Ronald W. Neufeldt, ed., *Karma and Rebirth: Post Classical Developments* (New York: SUNY Press, 1986), chaps. 1 and 2, https://books.google.com/books?id=iaRWtgXjplQC&dq=concept+of+karma+past+rebirth&lr=&source=gbs_navlinks_s.

3. Neufeldt, *Karma and Rebirth,* 2.

4. Kathryne M. Young, Debbie A. Mukamal, and Thomas Favre-Bulle, "Predicting Parole Grants: An Analysis of Suitability Hearings for California's Lifer Inmates," *Federal Sentencing Reporter* 28, no. 4 (April 2016): 276, http://www.kathrynemyoung.com/uploads/2/4/8/6/2486969/fsr2804_07_young.pdf.

5. Parole Board Hearing, Bruce Davis, State of California Community Release Board, 1978, 60–61.

6. Parole Board Hearing, Bruce Davis, State of California Community Release Board, 1985, 75–76.

7. Initial Parole Consideration Hearing, Patricia Krenwinkel, State of California Community Release Board, 72.

8. Charles Carbone, "Parole Matters: How to Prepare for the Psychological Evaluation," *Parole Matters,* Spring 2014, https://www.charlescarbone.com/parole-matters-spring-2014.

9. Life Term Parole Consideration Hearing, Robert Kenneth Beausoleil, State of California Community Release Board, 1980, 34.

10. Life Term Parole Consideration Hearing, Beausoleil, 1980, 36.

11. Life Term Parole Consideration Hearing, Beausoleil, 1980, 39.

12. Life Term Parole Consideration Hearing, Robert Kenneth Beausoleil, State of California Community Release Board, 1982, 50.

13. Life Term Parole Consideration Hearing, Beausoleil, 1982, 52.

14. Life Term Parole Consideration Hearing, Beausoleil, 1982, 60.

15. Life Term Parole Consideration Hearing, Robert Kenneth Beausoleil, State of California Community Release Board, 1983, 44.

16. Life Term Parole Consideration Hearing, Beausoleil, 1983, 47.

17. Life Term Parole Consideration Hearing, Beausoleil, 1983, 49.

18. Life Term Parole Consideration Hearing, Robert Kenneth Beausoleil, State of California Community Release Board, 1984, 69.

19. Life Term Parole Consideration Hearing, Beausoleil, 1984, 109.

20. Life Term Parole Consideration Hearing, Robert Kenneth Beausoleil, State of California Community Release Board, 1985, 63.

21. Parole Board Hearing, Bruce Davis, State of California Community Release Board, 1982, 41.

22. Parole Board Hearing, Davis, 1982, 42.

23. Parole Board Hearing, Susan Atkins, State of California Community Release Board, 2005, 79.

24. Parole Board Hearing, Atkins, 2005, 82.

25. Parole Board Hearing, Patricia Krenwinkel, State of California Community Release Board, 1982, 44.

26. Parole Board Hearing, Patricia Krenwinkel, State of California Community Release Board, 1981, 29.

27. Jeffrey Melnick, *Creepy Crawling: Charles Manson and the Many Lives of America's Most Infamous Family* (New York: Arcade Publishing, 2018).

28. Parole Board Hearing, Leslie Van Houten, State of California Community Release Board, 1979, 65.

29. Parole Board Hearing, Van Houten, 1979, 73.

30. Parole Board Hearing, Van Houten, 1979, 123.

31. Parole Board Hearing, Leslie Van Houten, State of California Community Release Board, 1980, 118.

32. *In re* Gaul, 170 Cal. App. 4th 20 (2009).

33. *In re* Criscione, 180 Cal. App. 4th 1446 (2009).

34. Yael Hassin, "Early Release Committee for Prisoners Versus Computer: Which Is Preferable?," *Criminology* 18, no. 3 (1980): 385–97.

35. Daniel P. Mears and Joshua C. Cochran, *Prisoner Reentry in the Era of Mass Incarceration* (Washington, DC: SAGE, 2015).

36. Young, Mukamal, and Favre-Bulle, "Predicting Parole Grants", 276.

37. Parole Board Hearing, Susan Atkins, State of California Community Release Board, 1985, 169.

38. Parole Board Hearing, Atkins, 1985, 170.

39. Parole Board Hearing, Atkins, 1985, 175.

40. Parole Board Hearing, Susan Atkins, State of California Community Release Board, 1988, 115–16.

41. Parole Board Hearing, Atkins, 1988, 119–20.

42. Parole Board Hearing, Atkins, 2005, 50.

43. Parole Board Hearing, Atkins, 1988, 123.

44. Parole Board Hearing, Atkins, 2005, 82–83.

45. Life Term Parole Consideration Hearing, Beausoleil, 1983, 61.

46. Life Term Parole Consideration Hearing, Robert Kenneth Beausoleil, State of California Community Release Board, 1997, 29.

47. Initial Parole Consideration Hearing, Patricia Krenwinkel, State of California Community Release Board, 1978, 69.

48. Parole Board Hearing, Patricia Krenwinkel, State of California Community Release Board, 1979, 25–26.

49. Parole Board Hearing, Patricia Krenwinkel, State of California Board of Parole Hearings, 1980, 32.

50. Eric Cummins, *The Rise and Fall of California's Radical Prison Movement* (Stanford, CA: Stanford University Press, 1994).

51. Michelle S. Phelps, "Rehabilitation in the Punitive Era: The Gap between Rhetoric and Reality in U.S. Prison Programs," *Law and Society Review* 45, no. 1 (March 16, 2011), https://onlinelibrary.wiley.com/doi/abs/10.1111/ j.1540–5893 .2011.00427.x.

52. Robert Martinson, "What Works? Questions and Answers about Prison Reform," *The Public Interest* (Spring 1974).

53. Francis Cullen and Karen Gilbert, *Reaffirming Rehabilitation,* 2nd ed. (Waltham, MA: Anderson Press, 2013).

54. Atkins, 1988, 124.

55. Atkins, 1988, 125.

56. Life Term Parole Consideration Hearing, Robert Kenneth Beausoleil, State of California Community Release Board, August 15, 1978, 48.

57. Life Term Parole Consideration Hearing, Beausoleil, 1980, 46.

58. Life Term Parole Consideration Hearing, Beausoleil, 1982, 84.

59. Life Term Parole Consideration Hearing, Beausoleil, 1982, 90.

60. Life Term Parole Consideration Hearing, Beausoleil, 1983, 63.

61. Life Term Parole Consideration Hearing, Beausoleil, 1985, 85–86.

62. Life Term Parole Consideration Hearing, Beausoleil, 1985, 47.

63. Karlene Faith, *The Long Prison Journey of Leslie Van Houten: Life beyond the Cult* (Boston: Northeastern University Press, 2001); Parole Board Hearing, Leslie Van Houten, State of California Community Release Board, 2003, 73.

64. Parole Board Hearing, Atkins, 2005, 14.

65. Subsequent Parole Consideration Hearing, Robert Kenneth Beausoleil, State of California Board of Parole Hearings, 2005, 55.

66. Subsequent Parole Consideration Hearing, Beausoleil, 2005, 67–68.

67. Krenwinkel, 1979, 4.

68. Parole Board Hearing, Bruce Davis, State of California Community Release Board, 1984, 9–10.

69. Parole Board Hearing, Leslie Van Houten, State of California Community Release Board, 1981, 84.

70. Parole Board Hearing, Van Houten, 1981, 85.

71. Parole Board Hearing, Leslie Van Houten, State of California Community Release Board, 1985, 54.

72. Parole Board Hearing, Leslie Van Houten, State of California Community Release Board, 1993, 60.

73. Parole Board Hearing, Van Houten, 1979, 81–82.

74. Parole Board Hearing, Krenwinkel, 1980, 25–26.

75. Young, Mukamal, and Favre-Bulle, "Predicting Parole Grants."

76. Parole Board Hearing, Susan Atkins, State of California Board of Parole Hearings, 2009, 6–7.

77. Parole Board Hearing, Atkins, 2009, 19.

78. Parole Board Hearing, Atkins, 2009, 33.

79. Parole Board Hearing, Atkins, 2009, 37.

80. Parole Board Hearing, Atkins, 2009, 38.

81. Parole Board Hearing, Atkins, 2009, 44–45.

82. Parole Board Hearing, Atkins, 2009, 45.

83. Parole Board Hearing, Atkins, 2009, 47.

84. Parole Board Hearing, Atkins, 2009, 52.

85. Parole Board Hearing, Atkins, 2009, 74–75.

86. Parole Board Hearing, Atkins, 2009, 77.

87. Parole Board Hearing, Atkins, 2009, 73.

88. Parole Board Hearing, Atkins, 2009, 107–8.

89. Parole Board Hearing, Atkins, 2009, 124–25.

90. Parole Board Hearing, Atkins, 2009, 128–31.

91. Parole Board Hearing, Atkins, 2009, 132–33.

92. Parole Board Hearing, Atkins, 2009, 167–68.

93. Parole Board Hearing, Atkins, 2009, 169.

7. IN BARDO

Epigraph: *The Tibetan Book of the Dead,* 3rd ed., ed. W.Y. Evans-Wentz, trans. Lama Kazi Dawa-Sawdup (New York: Oxford University Press, 2000), 269.

1. Bobby Beausoleil, *The Ride Out of Bardo,* 2017, Prismacolor and oil on Bristol board, https://fineartamerica.com/featured/the-ride-out-of-bardo-bobby-beausoleil.html.

2. Donald Lopez, "Introduction," Evans-Wentz, *The Tibetan Book of the Dead,* 19.

3. W.Y. Evans-Wentz, "Preface to the Second Edition," Evans-Wentz, *The Tibetan Book of the Dead,* 35–36.

4. Institute for Living and Dying, Bardo-Meditation, http://www.bardo-meditation.com.

5. Sogyal Rinpoche, *The Tibetan Book of Living and Dying* (New York: Harper-Collins, 2002), 10.

6. Kathryn Abrams and Hila Keren, "Law in the Cultivation of Hope," *California Law Review* 95, no. 2 (2007), https://scholarship.law.berkeley.edu/californialaw review/vol95/iss2/1/.

7. Alessandro de Giorgi, "Back to Nothing: Prisoner Reentry and Neoliberal Neglect," *Social Justice* 44, no. 1 (2017): 83–120.

8. Donald Clemmer, "Observations on Imprisonment as a Source of Criminality," *Journal of Criminal Law and Criminology* 41, no. 3, art. 6 (1940).

9. Tomer Einat and Haim Einat, "Inmate Argot as an Expression of Prison Subculture: The Israeli Case," *The Prison Journal* (Pennsylvania Prison Society) 80, no. 3 (September 2000), https://www.researchgate.net/publication/249707535_Inmate_Argot_as_an_Expression_of_Prison_Subculture_The_Israeli_Case.

10. Joshua Page, Michelle Phelps, and Philip Goodman, *Breaking the Pendulum: The Long Struggle over Criminal Justice* (New York: Oxford University Press, 2017). This book identifies such overgeneralizations in the accounts leading to mass incarceration, including David Garland, *Culture of Control: Crime and Social Order in Contemporary Society* (Chicago: University of Chicago Press, 2001); Jonathan Simon, *Governing through Crime: How the War on Crime Transformed American Democracy and Created a Cult of Fear* ((New York: Oxford University Press, 2007); Loïc Wacquant, *Prisons of Poverty* (Minneapolis: University of Minnesota Press, 2009); Katherine Beckett, *Making Crime Pay: Law and Order in Contemporary American Politics* (New York: Oxford University Press, 1997); John Pfaff, *Locked In: The True Causes of Mass Incarceration* (New York: Basic Books, 2017); Michelle Alexander, *The New Jim Crow: Mass Incarceration in the Age of Colorblindness* (New York: New Press, 2010); and in the accounts of the shift away from mass incarceration, such as Hadar Aviram, *Cheap on Crime: Recession-Era Politics and the Transformation of American Punishment* (Oakland: University of California Press, 2015); Natasha Frost and Todd Clear, *The Punishment Imperative: The Rise and Failure of Mass Incarceration in America* (New York: New York University Press, 2015); David Dagan and Steven Teles, *Prison Break: Why Conservatives Turned Against Mass Incarceration* (New York: Oxford University Press, 2016).

11. Aviram, *Cheap on Crime;* Frost and Clear, *The Punishment Imperative;* Dagan and Teles, *Prison Break.*

12. Rita Shah, *The Meaning of Rehabilitation and Its Impact on Parole* (New York: Routledge, 2017).

13. Malcolm Feeley and Jonathan Simon, "The New Penology: Notes on the Emerging Strategy of Corrections and Its Implications," *Criminology* 30, no. 4 (1992), https://scholarship.law.berkeley.edu/cgi/viewcontent.cgi?article=1717&context=facpubs.

14. Mona Lynch, "Waste Managers? The New Penology, Crime Fighting, and Parole Agent Identity," *Law and Society Review* 32, no. 4 (1998).

15. Gunther Teubner, "How The Law Thinks: Toward a Constructivist Epistemology of Law," *Law and Society Review* 23, no. 5 (1989).

16. Gilman v. Brown, et al., D.C. No. 1:05-CV-00830-LKK-CKD, 9th Cir., https://cdn.ca9.uscourts.gov/datastore/opinions/2016/02/22/14–15613.pdf.

17. Johnson v. Shaffer, No. 2:12-CV-01059-KLM (E.D. Cal.), Civil Complaint for Declaratory and Injunctive Relief, https://www.clearinghouse.net/chDocs/public/CJ-CA-0017–0002.pdf.

18. Johnson v. Shaffer, No. 2:12-CV-01059-KLM (E.D. Cal.), Order Granting Preliminary Approval of Class Action Settlement, https://scholar.google.co.il /scholar_case?case=18062658320489883143&hl=en&as_sdt=6&as_vis=1&oi= scholarr.

19. Civil Rights Litigation Clearinghouse, Johnson v. Shaffer, https://www .clearinghouse.net/detail.php?id=15394.

20. Daniel Medwed, *Prosecution Complex: America's Race to Convict and Its Impact on the Innocent* (New York: New York University Press, 2012); Hadar Aviram, "Legally Blind: Hyperadversarialism, Brady Violations, and the Prosecutorial Organizational Culture," *St. John's Law Review* 87, no. 1, 2014; Carole Hill, Amina Memon, and Peter McGeorge, "The Role of Confirmation Bias in Suspect Interviews: A Systematic Evaluation," *Legal and Criminological Psychology* 13, no. 2 (September 2008), https://onlinelibrary.wiley.com/doi/10.1348/135532507X238682.

21. UPI, "Houten May Be Set Free," *Lodi News-Sentinel-California,* August 8, 1977; Tim Walker, "Leslie Van Houten, Youngest Member of Charles Manson's 'Family', Has Parole Denied for 20th Time," *The Independent,* June 6, 2013, https:// www.independent.co.uk/news/world/americas/leslie-van-houten-youngest-member-of-charles-mansons-family-has-parole-denied-for-20th-time-8646473.html.

22. State v. Jeffs, 243 P.3d 1250 (2010); Jed Gottlieb, "The Amazing World of Sri Chinmoy and His Devoted Disciples," *San Diego City Beat,* August 10, 2005, http:// sdcitybeat.com/culture/film/amazing-world/; Samantha Schmidt, "Arrest Warrant Issued for Bikram Choudhury, the Hot-Yoga Guru Accused of Sexual Harassment," *Washington Post,* May 26, 2017, https://www.washingtonpost.com/news/morning-mix/wp/2017/05/26/arrest-warrant-issued-for-bikram-choudhury-the-hot-yoga-guru-accused-of-sexual-harassment/.

23. Seth Augenstein, "Manson Family Member Seeks Parole—and Access to Infamous Tex Watson Tapes," *Forensic Magazine,* June 7, 2017, https://www .forensicmag.com/news/2017/07/manson-family-member-seeks-parole-and-access-infamous-tex-watson-tapes.

24. *The Central Park Five,* dir. Ken Burns, David McMahon, and Sarah Burns, co-production of WETA and Florentine Films, 2012.

25. Craig Reinarman and Harry Levine, *Crack in America: Demon Drugs and Social Justice* (Berkeley: University of California Press, September 1997).

26. Khalil Gibran Muhammad, *The Condemnation of Blackness: Race, Crime, and the Making of Modern Urban America* (Cambridge, MA: Harvard University Press, 2011).

27. Jay D. Aronson, "Brain Imaging, Culpability and the Juvenile Death Penalty," *Psychology, Public Policy, and Law* 13, no. 2 (2007): 115–42; Laurence Steinberg, "Cognitive and Affective Development in Adolescence," *Trends in Cognitive Sciences* 9, no. 2 (2006): 69–74; Thomas Grisso and Robert G. Schwartz, eds., *Youth on Trial: A Developmental Perspective on Juvenile Justice* (Chicago: University of Chicago Press, 2000).

28. Roper v. Simmons, 543 U.S. 551 (2005).

29. Graham v. Florida, 560 U.S. 48 (2010).

30. Miller v. Alabama, 132 S.Ct. 2455 (2012).

31. Montgomery v. Louisiana, 136 S.Ct. 718 (2016).

32. Griffith v. Kentucky, 479 U.S. 314 (1986); Teague v. Lane, 489 U.S. 288 (1989).

33. S.B. 9 (Cal., 2016).

34. S.B. 260 (Cal., 2013).

35. Prison Law Office, "SB 260 and 261—Youthful Offender Parole Hearings," (letter incl. Human Rights Watch, *Youth Offender Parole: A Guide for People in Prison and Their Families,* updated May 2016), http://prisonlaw.com/wp-content /uploads/2016/05/SB-260-261-Youth-Offender-Parole-Guide-w-ltr.pdf.

36. S.B. 394 (Cal., 2017), https://leginfo.legislature.ca.gov/faces/billNavClient .xhtml?bill_id=201720180SB394.

37. Parole Board Hearing, Leslie Van Houten, State of California Board of Parole Hearings, 2016, 185.

38. Beth Schwartzapfel, "When Parole Boards Trump the Supreme Court," News, Marshall Project, May 2016, https://www.themarshallproject.org/2016/05/19 /when-parole-boards-trump-the-supreme-court.

39. Associated Press, "Gov. Brown Denies Parole for Manson Follower Leslie Van Houten," *CBS Bay Area,* January 20, 2018, https://sanfrancisco.cbslocal .com/2018/01/20/gov-brown-denies-parole-manson-follower-leslie-van-houten/; Associated Press, "Newsom Denies Parole to Charles Manson Follower Leslie Van Houten, Overruling Parole Board," *Los Angeles Times,* June 3, 2019, https://www .latimes.com/local/lanow/la-me-ln-newsom-leslie-van-houten-20190603-story.html.

40. Author's telephone conversation with Mr. Beausoleil, March 5, 2017.

41. Parole Board Hearing, Van Houten, 2016.

42. Christine Pelisek, "L.A. Cops Search for Two in 1969 Unsolved Murder of Reet Jurvetson, Say No Charles Manson Connection," *People,* September 8, 2016. https://people.com/crime/lapd-seeks-to-identify-two-men-in-connection-with-murder-of-reet-jurvetson/.

43. Tom O'Neill, "The Tale of the Manson Tapes," Law of the Land, *Medium,* September 16, 2014, https://medium.com/law-of-the-land/the-tale-of-the-manson-tapes-324b4a6138d9.

44. Vincent Bugliosi and Curt Gentry, *Helter Skelter: The True Story of the Manson Murders* (New York: W.W. Norton, 1974), 538.

45. Aviram, *Cheap on Crime,* ch. 3.

46. The Sentencing Project, "Fact Sheet: Trends in U.S. Corrections," 2016, https:// sentencingproject.org/wp-content/uploads/2016/01/Trends-in-US-Corrections.pdf.

47. Katherine Beckett, "Mass Incarceration and Its Discontents," Review Essays, *Contemporary Sociology: A Journal of Reviews* 47, no. 1 (December 21, 2017): 11–22, http://journals.sagepub.com/doi/abs/10.1177/0094306117744801.

48. Aviram, *Cheap on Crime.*

49. Christopher Seeds, "Bifurcation Nation: American Penal Policy in Late Mass Incarceration," *Punishment and Society* 19, no. 5 (October 19, 2016): 590–610, http://journals.sagepub.com/doi/abs/10.1177/1462474516673822.

50. Pfaff, *Locked In;* James Forman, *Locking Up Our Own: Crime and Punishment in Black America* (New York: Farrar, Straus and Giroux, 2017).

51. Seeds, "Bifurcation Nation."

52. Senate Committee on Public Safety, Hearing, Cal. S.B. 1242, April 24, 2018, https://spsf.senate.ca.gov/sites/spsf.senate.ca.gov/files/sb_1242_analysis.pdf.

53. Senate Committee on Public Safety, Hearing, S.B. 1242, 3–4.

54. Senate Committee on Public Safety, Hearing, S.B. 1242, 6–7.

55. Sophia Bollag, "'Ineffective, Irreversible and Immoral:' Gavin Newsom Halts Death Penalty for 737 Inmates," *Sacramento Bee,* March 12, 2019, https://www.sacbee.com/news/politics-government/capitol-alert/article227489844.html.

56. Jazmine Ulloa and Anita Chabria, "What Families of Murder Victims Have to Say about Gavin Newsom's Death Penalty Ban," *Los Angeles Times,* March 15, 2019, https://www.latimes.com/politics/la-pol-ca-death-penalty-victims-families-newsom-20190314-story.html.

57. Hadar Aviram, "Death Penalty Moratorium in California—What It Means for the State and for the Nation," *The Conversation,* March 20, 2019, https://theconversation.com/death-penalty-moratorium-in-california-what-it-means-for-the-state-and-for-the-nation-113634.

58. Among many examples, see "Patricia Krenwinkel 1993 Parole Hearing," YouTube, https://youtu.be/e-kZ40T7EUA; "Krenwinkel 1985 Parole Hearing," https://youtu.be/pqbzfkQQm3E; "Leslie Van Houten '99 Parole Hearing (Leslie Walks Out!)," https://youtu.be/9CQVuKyqJiU.

59. Saul Kassin, Christian A. Meissner, and Rebecca J. Norwick, "'I'd Know a False Confession If I Saw One,' A Comparative Study of College Students and Police Investigators," *Law and Human Behavior* 29, no. 2 (2005): 211–27.

60. Lilliana Paratore, "'Insight' into Life Crimes: The Rhetoric of Remorse and Rehabilitation in California Parole Precedent and Practice," *Berkeley Journal of Criminal Law* 21, no. 1 (Spring 2016), http://www.bjcl.org/articles/21.1%20Paratore.pdf.

61. June Price Tangney, Jeff Stuewig, and Logaina Hafez, "Shame, Guilt and Remorse: Implications for Offender Populations," *Journal of Forensic Psychiatry* 706 (September 2011).

62. Paratore, "'Insight' into Life Crimes," 118.

63. Paratore, "'Insight' into Life Crimes," 120.

64. Robert Weisberg, Debbie A. Mukamal, and Jordan D. Segall, *Life in Limbo: An Examination of Parole Release for Prisoners Serving Life Sentences with the Possibility of Parole in California* (Stanford, CA: Stanford Criminal Justice Center, 2011), https://law.stanford.edu/publications/life-in-limbo-an-examination-of-parole-release-for-prisoners-serving-life-sentences-with-the-possibility-of-parole-in-california/.

65. Edward E. Rhine, Joan Petersilia, and Kevin R. Reitz, "Improving Parole Release in America," *Federal Sentencing Reporter* 28, no. 2 (2015): 96–104.

66. Kathryne M. Young, "Parole Hearings and Victims' Rights: Implementation, Ambiguity, and Reform," *Connecticut Law Review* 49 (2016): 494–95.

67. Young, "Parole Hearings and Victims' Rights," 497.

68. Rhine, Petersilia, and Reitz, "Improving Parole Release in America," 100.

69. Weisberg, Mukamal and Segall, *Life in Limbo,* appended to Fran Ternus, *Strange Vicissitudes of Lifer Parole Victories and Defeats,* First District Appellate Project Training Seminar, January 20, 2012, 25, http://www.fdap.org/downloads /articles_and_outlines/Seminar2012-LiferParole.pdf.

70. R. J. Sampson and J. H. Laub, "Life Course Desisters? Trajectories of Crime among Delinquent Boys Followed to Age 70," *Criminology* 41, no. 3 (August 2003): 555–92.

71. Weisberg, Mukamal, and Segall, *Life in Limbo,* 9.

72. Rhine, Petersilia and Reitz, "Improving Parole Release in America," 98.

73. W. David Ball, "Heinous, Atrocious, and Cruel: Apprendi, Indeterminate Sentencing, and the Meaning of Punishment," *Columbia Law Review* 109 (June 2009): 893–972, at Santa Clara Digital Commons, https://digitalcommons.law.scu .edu/facpubs/16/.

INDEX

acceptance: and approval of peers, 102, 103; of responsibility, 85, 93, 95, 106, 184

ACLU, 46, 217

Adam Walsh Act, 2

addiction, 154. *See also* substance abuse

admission criteria for rehabilitative programs, 137

adversarialism, 221

advocacy groups, 126, 132

advocates, 3, 38–39, 53, 83, 120, 198

African Americans, 34, 58, 80, 126, 212

age, 4, 8, 178, 199, 212–15, 221; aging, 14, 38, 124, 181, 191, 198

aggravating circumstances, 20–21, 44, 90

agnosticism, 90

Alabama, 129

Alamo Christian Foundation, 66

alcohol: and moral panic, 68; in prison, 139, 155, 191

Alcoholics Anonymous, 155, 167

anger, 82, 100, 127, 130, 151

Antioch College, 164

antisocial personality disorder: Manson and, 175, 185–86; Beausoleil and, 188

apology: and acceptance of blame, 18; to victim, 127–28

Aquarius (TV series), 63, 77

arbitrariness, 19, 22, 137, 241

Aryan Brotherhood, 142–43, 152, 186

Atkins, Susan: behavior at trial, 40; brain tumor of, 54, 199–204; changed circumstances of, 191–93; *Child of Satan, Child of God,* 75; and common-crimi-

nals narrative, 76–77; commutation of death sentence, 37, 40; confessions of, 60–61, 62; and crime of commitment, 199; on gurney, 54, 199, 202, 204; and Helter Skelter narrative, 59, 76–77; insight of, 156; and judicial dilemma, 88; letters in support and opposition to, 195, 197; manicure business, 193–94; on motive for Tate murders, 59; and Museum of Death, 56; *Myth of Helter Skelter,* 52; news coverage of, 48; parole plans of, 191; plea for release, 55; and religion, 157, 162–63; and remorse, 99, 113; revisiting the past, 86–89, 113–15, 127; spouse, 148

attorney in absentia, 175, 179

Baranes, Amos, 132

Bardo, 180, 205–6, 222

Beatles, 58, 70, 73

Beausoleil, Bobby: and bad drug deal, 115; and common-criminals narrative, 87; and commutation of death sentence, 37; evaluations of, 151, 185–87, 92; and GED certificate, 164; and Hinman murder, 65, 66, 78; and inmate-related changes, 215; and insight, 99–100, 113; and intimacy, 146; Marsy's Law, 124; musical career of, 60, 164–67, 194; narratives about, 65, 78; objection to prosecutor's presence, 112; paintings of, 147, 164, 165; parole plans of, 192; revisiting the past, 89–92, 96–97,

poor performance and parole denial, 169
positive programming, 151
postrelease plans, 13, 181, 190–95, 217
Prisoners' Rights Union, 51
prison guards, 4, 51, 135
prisonization, 207
prisons: conditions in, 4; high security, 25; overcrowding, 3, 48, 137, 208
PRNN. *See* Peer Reentry Navigation Network
probation officer's report (POR), 91, 104
professionalism, 51, 55, 182, 211
programming: Beausoleil and, 151, 166, 168; and concept of parole, 16; contradictions in, 153; and Criscione, 189; and insight, 94; in Israel, 132; Krenwinkel and, 155; positive, 151; scarcity of, 150; substance abuse treatment, 137, 154
programs: bibliotherapy, 193; and PPRN, 207; rehabilitative, 81, 136–38, 142, 150–53, 163, 193, 220, 222; religious, 159; self-help, 166; twelve-step, 137, 151, 154–56, 167
Proposition 7, 44–45, 48
Proposition 8, 49–53
Proposition 9. *See* Marsy's Law
Proposition 17, 5, 43–44
Proposition 89, 50–52
prosecutor, role of, 83, 108–14. *See also* moral memory; *names of individual prosecutors*
protective custody, 143–44, 151, 186
Protective Custody subject, 144
psychiatric treatment, 30, 163
psychiatrists, 69, 141, 155, 174, 181–82, 185, 188, 220
psychic excavation, 102, 104
psychological evaluations, 27, 35, 158, 182, 189, 211
psychologists, 4, 69, 155, 178, 182, 185
psychotherapy, 186, 191
public safety: and California parole process, 26–27, 31–32, 35; and CDCR mission, 136; and determinate sentencing, 47; Manson and, 176; and Marsy's Law, 55; and psychiatric reports, 190; reforms, 217; and risk assessment, 181, 222

punishment: Atkins and illness, 203; capital, 5, 39, 43, 218; cruel or unusual, 41; extreme-punishment trifecta, 38, 44, 55, 58, 109, 208; for juveniles, 213; retroactive application, 209
punitivism, 207–8

race war, 12, 58–59, 77, 86
Reagan, Ronald, 2, 42, 49
recidivism, 22, 98, 132, 193, 200, 221
recommendations, 46–47, 164, 184, 214–15, 220
Red (movie character), 17–18
redball crimes, 2, 45–47, 51, 55, 217
redemption, 4, 127, 136
reentry programs, 84
reforms: bibliotherapy, 193; and California's Criminal Justice Realignment, 216; death penalty and life without parole, 38–39; and inmates, 16, 82; and institutional structure of parole boards, 220; and Proposition 7, 45, 48; of psychological evaluations, 211; Victims' Bill of Rights, 49
rehabilitation: authenticity, 168–69; and California parole hearings, 11, 14, 16, 18–19, 222; CDRC mission, 136–37; determinate sentencing, 47; eligibility, 25; inmate-related changes, 215; insight, 32, 94, 101, 107; judicial review, 209, 211; juveniles, 213; Katsav, 132; moral memory, 108; overcrowding, 208; parole granting rates, 21; programming, 13, 81, 150, 193; programs, 83, 136–37, 178, 207; recency of, 106; religion, 163; shame and remorse, 220
rehabilitation centers, 84
religion: and cult narrative, 67–70; and sexual exploitation, 212; and sincerity, 156–64
remorse: Atkins and, 99, 113; authentic, 206, 219; and California parole hearings, 10–12; Davis and, 95–97, 100; and demeanor, 168–70, 184; and insight, 33, 81, 83, 85, 89, 106, 156; in Israel, 131–32; Krenwinkel and, 101, 109, 128; Manson and, 178; and reforms, 217; and rehabilitation, 220; and risk assessment,

virtual life, 24

vocational training and interests, 126, 132, 138, 148, 152, 158; Davis and, 158, 161; and gun violence, 126; Manson and, 152, 178; suspicion of, 138, 148, 164, 166–68, 190–94

Vogelin, Harold, 46

Walleman, T.J., 74

Warren, Earl, 42

War on Drugs, 2, 216

Wattley, Keith, 8, 29, 34, 80–81, 83–84, 150–51

Watergate, 43

Watkins, Paul, 60

Watson, Charles "Tex": absence at hearing, 169–70; Atkins and, 86–88; commutation of death sentence, 37; and Helter Skelter narrative, 59, 75–76; and Kay, 111; and lack of remorse, 123; letters of support and opposition, 122, 197; and Mason Family murders, 1, 5, 51; narratives about, 52, 60, 74–75, 77; news coverage of, 48; and religion, 157, 161–62; taped confession, 8, 212, 216; and victims' families, 48, 115, 124

Whitehouse, James: at 2005 hearing, 141; at 2009 hearing, 199–203; complaints to Board, 113–14; marriage to Atkins, 191–92; Marsy's Law, 120; *The Myth of Helter Skelter,* 52

Will You Die for Me? (Watson), 52, 75

Wright, Donald, 42

write-ups, 107–8, 136, 137, 139–42, 146; Atkins and, 162, 199; for personality flaws, 150

youth offender parole, 21. *See also* age

Zimmerman, George, 178

Founded in 1893,
UNIVERSITY OF CALIFORNIA PRESS
publishes bold, progressive books and journals
on topics in the arts, humanities, social sciences,
and natural sciences—with a focus on social
justice issues—that inspire thought and action
among readers worldwide.

The UC PRESS FOUNDATION
raises funds to uphold the press's vital role
as an independent, nonprofit publisher, and
receives philanthropic support from a wide
range of individuals and institutions—and from
committed readers like you. To learn more, visit
ucpress.edu/supportus.